ANROTH THE DRUID

A Mythological Tale of the Last Celtic Kingdom of Northumbria

MICHAEL BURKE

DEDICATION

This novel is dedicated to the dispossessed, the innocents caught up and killed in brutal battle. Their lands and livelihoods reduced to rubble, leaving behind, all the lost love they shared. Slaughtered by those who reject the assumption, that these blameless lives are precious to be cherished and protected. Misguided mass executioners, driven on by a poisonous cocktail of greed, arrogance, and perverted political belief.

Deluded by the assumption that their lives, and the lives of those they claim to represent, have an intrinsically greater value and virtue, than the lives they so indiscriminately extinguish.

Throughout history, society regularly falls victim to the predation of such evil tyrants. This novel reminds us there were also noble tyrants like Midar, the last great warlord of Celtic Northumbria.

However, it is a depressing truth, that even today, it remains pure chance whether we are born into a peaceful society or one plagued by warfare. There is nothing to suggest that state of affairs will ever change.

ACKNOWLEDGEMENTS

Writing and recording 'Anroth the Druid' was most enjoyable and stimulating. However, I did not look forward to the process of self- publishing. In the event it turned out to be a family affair.

My daughter Lucy a Social Media Marketer launched us on Instagram, my son in law Stephen, a film editor, handled all the audio material, and my son Michael dealt with the map, formatting the novel and business requirements. It was marvelous working as a team, many thanks and a big thank you to my dear friends who checked the final draft.

Someone once told me I was very good at delegating. I hope I can delegate the general public to do the rest, listen to, or read 'Anroth the Druid'!

ANROTH THE DRUID

Published by Mindglow Memories

Paperback edition ISBN: 978-1-7385432-0-5

E-Book edition ISBN: 978-1-7385432-1-2

www.michaelburkeauthor.com
instagram.com/mfburkeauthor

Table of Contents

Gododdin
Balor's Stronghold
Mouth of the River of the High Waters
Valley Of The High Waters
Lindisfarne
The Dark Waters
WatchTower
Midar's Stronghold
Rheged
Auroth's Cave
Midar's Kingdom
AD 543
Deira

Those Who Walked Into The Fire Light

1. Anroth, the Druid, nickname 'Snout'
2. Danu, the Goddess
3. Dancer, 'the Woodwose'
4. Snibo, his Raven
5. Midar, High Chieftain of the Brigantes
6. Cliona, his Queen
7. Goibniu, their eldest son
8. Nuada, their second son
9. Dian, their youngest son
10. Sirona, a Novice Druidess
11. Luchtain, a Novice Druid
12. Keeva, a Novice Druid
13. Aine, the Head Cook
14. Ollathir, the Swineherd
15. Crimthain, the Marshal
16. Lugh, Midar's Champion
17. Balor, the High Chieftain of the Picts
18. Birog, his sister, a Black Druidess
19. Cu roi, her son, who Birog shape shifts into the monstrous hound, Ominnios
20. Frii, the Wave Wanderer
21. Ida, a Saxon Prince

Prologue

Greyeyes looked across the lake, remembering those violent, magical times, from long ago. It was a lifetime away, when he was still young, that fateful year of the Christian, AD 543. His mind turned to the gathering of Celts, soon to join him. They had become outcasts, strangers in a foreign land that had once been their own. He remembered Danu. Together, they found the Mindglow, only to part by those mysterious dark waters. He had carried her body there, watching her fade into the mists, never to return. He remembered the day when together, they went to war, she had shown all the courage of a warrior.

He gazed at the trees, swaying in the summer breeze. Hazel, alder, willow and oak, hid his secrets beneath their cloak. How many times had he whispered?

'Danu, where are you?' As he'd stood there, all alone, beseeching the moon, life's brief summer gone too soon.

The lake sparkled; its shallow shoreline glowed golden-brown. A finger of sunlight pushed through the clouds and spread from the lake to embrace the trees. He watched entranced, in some strange state of grace. Then, unannounced, she showed her face, framed by those swaying trees, raven hair still dancing in the breeze. She was happy and smiling. It was a brief moment of rapture more beautiful than anything he'd experienced since her death.

Clouds drifted over the sun and he watched, as her face faded back into the swaying branches. Her love was all around him and lived on in everything bountiful. Now the renowned seer, and storyteller knew which tale to tell at the gathering, a story only he remembered, of what befell the house of Midar in the ancient Celtic Kingdom of Northumbria. He told his tales the traditional way, in prose and rhyme, and sometimes they would intertwine.

Outside his cave was a crumbling circle of stone and, at its centre, a fire burned. He gazed at the carcass suspended above it, its skin bronzed, golden and glistening. He smelt the scents of wood smoke and roasting wild boar. The smells intermingled and wafted around the clearing then, borne on the wind, swirled down to the valley below, his invitation to the feast.

His guests arrived and the clearing filled with a mighty gathering. The Celts had come to celebrate the festival of Lunasa, but everything they believed in, the traditions they lived by, were by degrees dying. Bound together by their tribal identity, the world they'd once understood was slipping away. They came to listen to Greyeyes, the magical storyteller.

As he moved among them, they eagerly suggested stories they wanted him to tell.

'Tell us about the goddess Boann, she of the white cattle.'

'We have Chillingo, and our own wild white cattle,' he reminded them.

'Then tell us tales from Wales,' they said. 'Of the beautiful Blodeuedd, a maiden fashioned from the flowers of the meadowsweet, broom and oak.'

Two young girls sat together, giggling. One summoned up the courage to speak.

'Greyeyes tell us a love story,' she said. 'Tell us of the Lydian queen Omphale and how she made Hercules prove his love.'

'How many ways of loving are there, Greyeyes?' asked the other.

Greyeyes smiled. 'Listen to my tale and you may find the answer,' he said.

'Tell us now, we might fall asleep!' they insisted.

He laughed. 'You probably will, girls.'

An old lady, worn out by life's journey, sat alone, wailing into her shawl. Greyeyes sat down beside her. A skinny arm snaked out from under her shawl, and he felt her cold, deformed hand. She turned towards him; her furtive eyes studied his face.

'Tears that flow and never dry, the innocents are first to die,' she said, pulling him closer. 'Let me look at you again, you never said you were going. Why did you leave me?'

'Have you a tale you wish to tell me?' he asked. He leant forward, plucked seven small, long-stemmed red flowers of the bird's eye primrose and laid them carefully on the log beside him. Then, finding three long blades of dried grass, he knotted them at one end and plaited the strands together. As he listened to her tale, one by one, he worked in the seven ruby-red flowers.

'The mouth of the river is well hidden from the sea,' she said. 'They came, you know? They broke my pots. Come closer.'

It was the same tale she always told. Reassured by his company, she retold the story as if it had happened only yesterday. Some tales never go away, it's always only yesterday. Greyeyes studied her strangely familiar face, her high cheekbones, hollow cheeks, sallow skin and familiar, toothless, nervous grin.

'It was late afternoon. There were children laughing and playing. The men returned from fishing. The Saxons followed them up the estuary. They broke my pots.'

Greyeyes looked around the crowded clearing. A little girl, so full of life, squabbled with her brother. He gazed at her rosy cheeks, her flashing smile and disheveled hair.

'Ilona, stop scrapping with your brother, your clothes will get dirty,' called out her mother. 'Come here now!'

The little girl ignored her and continued to tussle beside the campfire.

In the clearing, there were women of all ages, all of whom were beautiful in different ways. Pure chance dictated how their ages fell that summer's evening. The young may well have been old; the old might have been children tumbling in the dust.

For those who have eyes to see, a face grown old is ageless, just one of the many changing faces within. And with the precious gift of the Seer, Greyeyes was able to imagine the weary old woman when she was young enough to still believe in the happiness her life would bring. He ran his fingers slowly through his hair, feeling for a lump that wasn't there. The old woman started to cry as she began going around in circles with her garbled tale.

'Did I tell you about my…?'

He interrupted. 'You mentioned your pots.'

'Where are you?' she said. 'I can't see you. I thought you died that day.'

Greyeyes put down the blades of grass and bent closer. 'I'm here,' he said. 'Sitting beside you, holding your hand.'

'We had nothing to give,' she said. 'So, they took our lives and laughed. What brave, brave warriors they were! Not one of them will rest beside the river or drink a cup in paradise. They slaughtered those they didn't take as slaves, even the children and those who'd grown old.'

'The children?'

'Yes, Greyeyes, the children,' she said. 'They were contemptuous of the beautiful and the innocent. They burnt our roundhouses to the ground. Then they tossed the dead and dying in. Did I mention my pots?'

He nodded.

'They feasted on our slaughtered beasts,' she said. 'Then, one day, they sailed away, leaving only grief and woe, and a place where lonely briars grow.'

Greyeyes finished plaiting the flowers into the dried grass and knotted the end. 'I've made you something,' he said, stroking her hand.

Wrapping the bracelet around her wrist, he threaded the knot of one end through a gap in the plait at the other. She gasped with delight as he bent forward and kissed the flowers one by one. They sparkled in the firelight like garnets set in gold. Greyeyes looked lovingly into her eyes, then he kissed her softly on the cheek.

'One day, my love, the memories of those of us who've grown old will be young again, and none shall weep.' He paused, then added.

'You look so beautiful tonight.'

'Would that the world had your grey eyes to see with,' she whispered with a smile.

Greyeyes, the weaver of words, stepped inside the stone circle.

'You've asked me to tell you many stories,' he said, as he began to walk round it. 'There's one tale you've never heard before. It happened long before your days of recollection. It played out its dying moments by these dark waters in the Christian's year 543.'

Such was the magic in his voice that the people were spirited away into their tribal past. The old man's tale did not dwell in the memory of his mind, but in his eyes. He saw everybody he introduced standing before him. Though they were sleeping, that night Greyeyes woke them all.

One by one, they walked out of the shadows into the firelight: Anroth the Druid; Midar the Warlord; his queen Cliona; Danu; Dancer and his raven; Birog, the evil Black Druidess and daughter of the Unforgiven Dead; her brother Balor, the Pictish high chieftain; the hound Ominnios; the three princes; Ollathir the swineherd; Sirona; Ida the Saxon prince; and the childless Aine, who mothered warrior and young druid alike. All came to join the gathering.

Greyeyes had shared so much happiness with those who had once loved him. Their love had seeped deep into the stones of the circle wall. Sensing his presence, the stones radiated out all that love from long ago. Casting dark shadows, Greyeyes, the renowned weaver of words, raised his arms. The gathering fell silent.

The First Day Of Lunasa

1 The Heroes Return

It was that unsettled time of the changing seasons, when our world and the Otherworld intermingled. It was that restless place, where the sea and sky waited in the half-light for the sun's rising. It was that uncertain time before the dawn, when the watchers in the watchtower first saw, out on the horizon, white, foaming waters catch the last of the moonlight. It was late summer and the start of the six-day festival of Lunasa.

A steady westerly gusted off the headland and flattened the waves of the outgoing tide. As the lustrous whiteness moved slowly towards them, the watchers made out a boat, buoyed up, by a mantle of foam. There were no oarsmen and no sail, yet against wind and wave it would prevail. They knew, that only the great sea god Manannan's ship, could cut through wind and wave that way. Fearful of what the ghostly craft might bring, they sent for Crimthain the Marshal.

The sun crested the horizon and rose from the sea. One of the watchers cried out, 'Riders from the north!'

Two horsemen rounded the rocky northern promontory. The Marshal arrived and saw them, then looked out to sea, before sending for Midar, the high chieftain.

Three large hounds with coarse, thick coats and massive shoulders that rose to a warrior's waist, ran out from the great hall. Their huge heads hung low as they sniffed the ground and circled around. One hound hung back. Larger than the others, Oengus stood alone and waited, head held high. Then came his master, the high chieftain of the Brigantes, the legendary Midar of the Thirty Battles. Like his hunting hounds, he was grey-haired, strong, tall and lean. Beside him stood his queen and Anroth the druid, the warrior of the mind.

Midar and Anroth left to meet the Marshal. Queen Cliona hesitated, remaining beside the doors of the great hall. She was of royal blood, the daughter of the high chieftain of the western Kingdom of Rheged, tall and assured, with pale-blue eyes set wide below a high and noble brow. Her long hair, the colour of fading gold, fell about her shoulders. She was the very noblest of queens, with skin as soft and blushed as the petals of the wild rose, hiding the passing of the years with grace, still holding her beauty in her face.

The riders drew closer. She recognised them as outriders from the cattle raid and looked beyond them, over the Longsands to the northern promontory of the bay. Her sons had been on many raids, but this was the first time Midar, hadn't personally led them into battle. It had been a reprisal raid against Balor, the powerful leader of the southern Picts. The brutal ruler of the Kingdom of Gododdin, who constantly harassed their northern borders. Balor was foul of mind and countenance, and was toothless save for one blackened fang that projected down from his upper jaw.

Cliona had tried to persuade Midar to lead the raid, for Balor was a ruthless, cunning enemy. But Midar, had refused, and pointed out the Picts' defeat would be all the more humiliating if it were inflicted by their sons. Cliona had been fearful, imagining at least one of them would take wounds or worse. But then, three riders emerged from the shadows and into the sun. They rounded the point and broke into a canter. Recognising her sons she breathed a sigh of relief, shed the mantle of the worried mother and rediscovered the confident queen within.

The three princes rode boldly towards her, their spear points flashing and the bosses of their shields sparkling in the sunshine. She noticed that from each of the princes' belts dangled large, leather bags, bouncing on their naked thighs. Goibniu, Nuada and Dian, their heads held high, rode in a line along the shore where dying waves caressed the sand. They rode together, three as one. Their ponies' hooves splashed in the surf. The harnesses of the heroes' mounts hung loosely as they picked up speed, knowing they were nearly home.

Unobserved, below the sand dunes, a motionless man stood in the shadow of the rocks. On his shoulder perched a raven as black as the night, its cruel beak gently pulling at his ear. The sun shone brightly on the wet sand, making a mirror of the sky, and – for a moment, as those riders rode on by – three ghostly riders rode beneath them, Otherworld riders from far below the sand and sea.

The watcher waited till they'd gone on their way, then gazed along the sands with their changing shades of yellow, gold and grey, and felt the restless breeze as it blew towards him then sucked away. He watched the waves, the heartbeat of the living sea, as they caressed the sands and rejoiced in their uncertainty. One wave swirled inwards, probing and gushing into the rock pools. In that small and narrow space, it found new meaning, pulsating, with strength and grace.

He looked into a rock pool and saw the bleached and empty shells of those who had once clung so close. He watched the tentacles of the sea anemones with their sensitive fingers wafting to and fro, imagining they were his fingers, remembering a summer's day, from long ago. His body began to turn and sway, then sad at heart, Dancer slowly walked away.

The outriders drew closer.

'How went the raid?' Midar called out, to them.

'Your sons fought as heroes, my lord,' said one. 'They bring you honour and fine beasts.'

Cliona shielded her eyes, as she watched the little boat move towards her, swirling and bobbing in the surf. A cloud brushed over the sun. She gasped and turned to Midar.

'It's a girl, alone in that coracle, borne on the sea from who knows where,' she said.

Midar, with eyes only for the three princes, said nothing. He was stern of countenance, careworn with his concerns for the kingdom. Cliona turned to the Druid.

'It's a girl, Anroth,' she said. 'She's all alone in the coracle. I don't understand.'

Anroth reached out to her, taking her hand.

Slipping from their saddles, the three proud princes bowed low in respectful homage to their warrior father. Though the battle had long since been won, they remained in the grip of the fever pitch of combat. The journey home had done nothing to calm their excitement.

They turned towards their mother to seek her approval. Goibniu, Nuada and Dian, bright-eyed, bragging and boastful, pushed, argued and bellowed with laughter as they fought to hug and kiss her. They were as wild as the wind and as changeable as the tide, and their greatest strength was the harmony of their differences.

This was the part of their homecoming Cliona had been waiting for. She took a deep breath, closed her eyes in mock resignation and made a half-hearted attempt to push them away. She could smell Goibniu's beer-sozzled breath and Dian's overripe body odour, she could feel Nuada as he forced his way up between his much larger brothers. She waited in eager anticipation for his gentle kisses on her cheek. She sighed, comforting herself with the thought that adoration took many forms.

She heard a scraping sound on the pebbles and turned around to see the coracle had landed close by. The queen, looked at the girl. She was about the same age Cliona had been when she first came to Northumbria as Midar's young bride; barely sixteen, but trying to look older. After the three princes, Cliona had given birth to two daughters. Both died in childhood. Their lives so brief, only a mother really remembers they had ever been. Those precious memories still slept in shallow graves, an enduring, veiled emptiness living on in her heart.

The girl's eyes reached out to the queen and, for the briefest of moments, an enquiring, hesitant smile played upon her lips before her feelings retreated back into her dark-brown eyes. The girl stood up, tall, slim and dignified. In her hand she held a long spear, tipped with a shining spearhead, curving round the shaft, covered with strange symbols and beasts. Its edges undulated like the waves of the sea.

From her narrow shoulders fell a crimson cloak of shimmering sheen and glowing heat, flowed like a river to her milk-white feet. None had seen one so fair, with golden torque and raven hair.

She stood quite still, uncertain of all she saw around her, until her eyes rested once more upon the queen. The girl felt the warmth, saw the suppressed longing and love in Cliona's eyes, and stretched out her arms. Stepping neatly from the coracle, she handed Anroth her spear. He examined it and felt the groove across its base.

He remembered a warning from long ago.

'Make welcome strangers from the sea, but have a care, evil miasmas may hover in the air.'

Cliona felt herself drawn towards the girl, wondering what to do. She looked at Anroth, who nodded.

'Bid her welcome,' he said. 'We need each other.'

Cliona didn't hesitate, stepping forward, embracing the girl as her own, a sister to those she had lost. So much unfocused love, so many tears she'd never cried, flowed like a river deep inside. The girl stood still, confused, beguiled, never before had she been loved as a child.

And so it was that Danu first stepped ashore on the sands of the beaches of Bamburgh, below the stronghold of the high chieftain of the Brigantes, his great hall, his barns, stables, kennels and courtyards. And, with the queen beside her, she walked towards these, through the sand dunes, past sturdy seagoing boats, safe from the summer storms and beached well above the tide-line. Midar and the princes went to meet the rest of the raiding party, which they could see in the distance coming down the drover's trail.

Cliona took Danu into the great hall, where weapons and trophies from previous battles hung on the walls. Around the fireplace were some of their own weapons and carnyxes, of many different shapes and sizes, the Celts' fearsome battle horns. At the far end, a long table was positioned in front of the fireplace, two other tables ran down towards the doors. Beside the doors, in one corner, was an alcove in which shelves displayed some fine helmets and the venerated heads of enemy warriors from past conflicts.

The most recent trophies hung by their hair from the rafters above the fire, swinging slowly in the smoke. In the other corner there was a well and a small shrine. The pure, clear waters gurgled and gushed up from the base of a deep stone font. Behind the font, set in the angle of the two walls, was an impassive statue of a goddess with a hare sat on her lap. It had been carved from sandstone and much of the finer detail had weathered away with age.

Danu dipped her fingers into the waters and wet the statue's lips to slake her thirst. She saw herself in another life, far away in another place, a world away from where she was that summer's day.

'Who is she?' she asked innocently.

'We don't know for certain,' said Cliona. 'She was brought here from a shrine in the forest. We think she's a powerful earth and river goddess, the waters from her spring always flow crystal clear. We call it the Druid's Well. Anroth uses the water for his purification ceremonies.'

Above the main table, a large golden cauldron hung from its handle, and, higher in the rafters, a mighty bow fashioned from a lustrous wood glowed like red gold in the firelight.

Danu walked across to the alcove and picked up a helmet. Mounted on top of it was a wild boar, the thick long hairs running along its spine, fashioned into a series of sharp metal points. As she held the helmet, a severed head fell out. She picked it up and studied the face. It still smelt of the cedar wood oil it had been preserved in.

'Did you know him?' she asked, handing the head to Cliona.

They walked over to the open doors and the queen looked carefully at the wizen features. His eyelids covered sunken sockets, and an old scar ran across the bridge of the nose and down over the right cheek.

'Yes,' she said. 'He was a noble warrior, the champion of the high chieftain of Deira.'

She carried the head back to the alcove and respectfully set it down on a shelf. 'We don't usually have them all out,' she explained, as they walked towards the kitchen. 'But we're celebrating Lunasa, and Midar's chieftains, their families and champions are all coming. It's important to have the banqueting hall looking at its best.'

The queen sat Danu down at the kitchen table. A large, coarse-featured woman came over. Her unkempt, blonde hair hung down to what had once been her waist.

'This is Aine,' said the queen, smiling.

Aine set down goblets of milk, honey cakes and bowls of curds, some of which she spilt on the table. As she left, she patted Danu roughly on the back and told her she was most welcome. The simplicity and warmth of the woman, was the nicest welcome Danu could remember. With the queen beside her, her simple meal became a feast. Aine returned with a towel, pointing out that Danu's hair was wet. She casually pushed Danu's head forward, then from one side to the other, as she rubbed it dry. Danu relished the attention as the big woman fussed over her. It was as if Aine had always been drying her hair.

From time to time, Cliona unthinkingly stroked an intricate, gold-and-green necklace that hung down from her throat.

'That's such a lovely necklace you're wearing,' said Danu.

'Oh,' smiled Cliona, stroking it again. 'Fond remembrances.'

The necklace consisted of eight dark green pieces, each partly covered in shiny facets of different shapes and sizes. They were set in two rows, strung in a loose latticework of golden chains. The combination of green and the gold and the manner of their setting, highlighted the beauty of Cliona's face.

'I've never seen anything like it,' said Danu. 'It's really clever how so many different shapes and sizes have been combined in such harmony. Where was it made? Are the stones jade?'

'It was a birthday present,' said Cliona. 'My youngest son Dian made it for me. He loves doing things with gold. It's the most precious thing I own.'

'And are the stones jade?' repeated Danu.

'Well, no actually, but lots of people think that. I'll let you into a family secret, if you promise not to tell. They're my elder brother Segomo's wrist bones. Dian stained them green with ivy leaves. Segomo was my favourite brother, it feels so good to always have him close to me.'

Danu smiled.

'He was a great hero, the champion of Rheged, my father's kingdom,' Cliona continued. 'After he was slain in battle, his right arm was taken to the high mountains and given a sky burial. The golden eagles picked his bones clean. His strength became their strength and, in return, the power in their wings took him to the

Otherworld. Knowing how much I adored him, my father kindly sent me his arm bones to remember him by.'

'Your father must have been a very kind and thoughtful man,' said Danu.

'Oh indeed,' said Cliona. 'In old age, he became a Christian and he handed over the high chieftainship so he could join a monastic community on one of the western isles. They put him in charge of relics.'

Cliona stood up and took the towel from Aine. The servant returned to the kitchen and the queen continued drying Danu's hair, her touch gentle, maternal.

'I like Aine. Is she your slave?' asked Danu.

'No, she's my dearest friend and maid,' said Cliona. 'I was about your age when I first came to Northumbria as Midar's bride. Aine came with me. She was born in the land of the Kerrymen in Ireland, but was stolen by pirates. Later, she was given to my father as a slave, as part of a truce settlement. Some years after we arrived in Northumbria, Aine gave birth to a baby girl. She never revealed the father. The other servants said it was Dancer and she never denied it.'

'Were you annoyed with her?'

'Not at all,' said Cliona. 'I was delighted for her. A child is always a blessing.'

'Who's Dancer?'

'Some say he's a woodwose,' said Cliona.

'A woodwose?'

'Yes, a self-appointed guardian and wild man of the woods,' said Cliona. 'But he's much more interesting than that. Woe betides the Picts when he finds them intruding on our lands to the north, or anyone who kills an animal without need for that matter. He is a self-appointed protector of the wild woods. Husbands warn their wives to beware of his charms, but I sometimes wonder if they pay much heed!'

Danu grinned.

'Dancer comes and goes as he pleases, like a will-o'-the-wisp,' said Cliona, smiling knowingly. 'And Snibo, his raven, is never far from his shoulder.'

Danu's eyes widened.

'Shortly after Aine's child was born, I gave birth to my second son, Nuada,' Cliona continued. 'Midar calls him the runt of the litter – though you mustn't repeat that – but, at the time, Nuada frightened both of us. We were fearful we might lose him. Compared to his two lusty brothers, he was a weakling. It was the time of the great famine and my milk dried up. Aine's daughter had just died of the fever, so she wet-nursed Nuada for me. After that, he wouldn't go to anyone else. And, all these years later, there's still a deep bond between them.'

'Is Nuada smaller than the others?' asked Danu.

'Yes, I used to worry he wasn't made of the stuff of warriors,' said Cliona. 'With Midar's encouragement, I tried to persuade him to become a druid, but he refused to consider any life other than that of the warrior. When the princes take up arms, they fight as one, with Nuada in the middle. He fights the Roman way, with a short sword. He may lack strength, but he has a fast, accurate thrust, so maybe he's not such a bad fighter. Well, there's me, the proud mother, boring you with stories about my children.'

Cliona found she was enjoying this sharing of confidences and having the opportunity to chat about the boys and domestic goings-on in the great hall. She felt so good with Danu beside her. It made a wonderful change from listening to boring hunting tales or conversations about how the barleycorn was ripening in the field.

And, for the first time in her life, Danu felt as though she belonged. That the queen so obviously cared about her and had chosen to share family secrets with her made her feel very special. She was relaxed, contented and warm. In due course, sleepiness assailed her.

The queen took Danu to her bed, and sat beside her, holding her hand. Danu had never known such happiness. Why, she wondered, had she been denied the priceless gift of childhood?

'Can I stay here forever?' she asked.

Cliona nodded and smiled. Danu flopped back on the bed, exhausted, but still hungry for the warmth of human kindness.

'Tell me more about your brother Segomo,' she said, trying to deny the dreamtime. And as her eyes closed, she felt as if she were still bobbing around in the coracle. Finally, she drifted into a sea of slumber, falling fast asleep.

Cliona continued to hold her hand and looked down at her in wonder. She decided Danu, was a gift from the goddesses, a daughter born from the waters, who was hers to cherish and love. She had thought herself too old to entertain such emotions. She knew nothing about Danu, but suspected she was just like she had been when she'd first arrived in Northumbria, loath to part with what remained of her childhood, but trusting time would, one day, reveal a greater love. And then she'd met Midar, who had loved and guided her. She thought of her three sons. Why had Danu come?

Cliona's guests looked forward to celebrating the festival of Lunasa. Her warmth and effortless hospitality counterbalanced Midar's often bleak demeanour. She was approachable and seemingly had all the time in the world for everyone. Such was her composure and charm that the chieftains and their wives often betrayed confidences to Cliona they might not have shared with Midar. She was a good listener, there was something in her smile that reassured them, put them at their ease and drew them out. She rarely commented, but her concern and compassion were mirrored in her face.

That summer afternoon, as she sat beside the sleeping Danu, Cliona's mind was far from the subtle interrelationships of the tribal elders. The sudden surge of affection she'd experienced had surprised her. Whatever the reason, and however briefly it might last, it was there to be cherished.

Until Danu had arrived, Cliona had found love in three different ways, all of them enduring and quite natural. There was the certainty of the bonds she shared with Midar, driven by status, duty and admiration; there was the mother's love for her boisterous sons, intermingled with the frustration of trying to retain some sort of authority over them; and then there was her devotion to Anroth, who in the early years had guided her and looked after her like a father or brother.

Anroth's wife had died not long after Cliona had given birth to her eldest child Goibniu. And, in the sombre months that followed, Cliona had realised Anroth was a man who needed to feel loved. She could have chosen to love him like a sister or a mother, but curiosity had got the better of her and she found herself rewarded. Her feelings for Danu were different; they transformed her unfocused grief for her dead daughters into something beautiful.

She reflected that love was never pure, it was always conditional, and it came with its own uncertain assumptions and needs. The circumstances of love, in all its many forms and dreams, were fickle and forever changing. She wondered if the more exquisite and intense her feelings, the more transient and fleeting might be their duration. Cliona's mind wandered in wakeful dreams. Slowly she laid Danu's hand down and left to organise the banquet.

Down on the beach, Anroth the Druid, had stayed behind when the others had left. He stood beside the coracle, as the waves washed around his feet, he studied the sky. He listened to the sound of the breakers and searched for a sign. There was much to ponder.

Once a year, during the six-day festival of Lunasa, was a time when tributes were given, sacrifices were made, the harvest was celebrated and the warrior's ponies raced along golden beaches. The chieftains would feast and, on those long summer evenings, they would listen to the storyteller's mystical tales. It was a busy time for Anroth, who presided over the thanksgiving offerings. Doubtless he would be called upon to reconcile the views of those in dispute and, if it were needed, to pass judgement.

To those who viewed Midar's fertile lands from the outside with envious eyes, Northumbria seemed impregnable. But Midar knew it had one great weakness. Though the size of his kingdom was vast, comparing it with his neighbours, the population of Northern Brigantes he ruled over was small, and thinly spread. They would always be vulnerable to the sustained predations of a determined enemy.

Midar never rested on his reputation. During the summer fighting season, he was often away from his stronghold as he rode the boundaries of the kingdom to reassert his authority and sometimes lay claim to more land. He was an inspiring leader, but he had the sense to recognise that, above all, he was a warrior chieftain. He listened to the advice of Anroth and his champion, Lugh, and took heed of his thoughtful queen's opinions.

Anroth picked up the coracle and swung it over his shoulder, carrying it up to where the rest of the boats lay. Crimthain and his men were checking they were well-secured.

'When they woke me this morning, I thought they'd sighted the sea captain,' said Crimthain, taking Anroth to one side. 'He's overdue. On his last visit, he brought word from Rome. The merchants there, wished us to send them three of the high chieftain's finest hunting hounds in return for their wines.'

Anroth nodded, 'I remember.'

'The hounds we're sending have already been chosen,' said Crimthain. 'The sea captain was expected to return last week and the wines should have been with us in time for the banquet. I fear he's fallen foul of Pictish pirates or run into Saxon raiding parties. We'll have to hold the banquet without the wine.'

'Which captain did you strike the bargain with?' asked Anroth.

'It was the one you call the Wave Wanderer.'

Anroth smiled.

'Fear not, Crimthain, he won't disappoint us,' he said. 'He's far too skilful to get caught by the Saxons. I once sailed with him on a diplomatic mission to Elmet and he's an even better sailor than the Pictish pirates. How do you think he's survived so many hazardous journeys all these years? With such a strong westerly wind, he'll have chosen the shortest crossing south then worked his way north, hugging the coast and trading along the way.'

Crimthain nodded.

'I'll go to the sacred grove,' continued Anroth, 'and make offerings to the sea gods Manannan and Tethra to speed his journey. Tell your lookouts not to strain their eyes scanning the horizon. When he comes, he'll sail inshore and round the southern headland.'

'How many amphorae of wine do you suggest I demand for the hounds?' asked Crimthain.

'Twenty,' suggested Anroth.

'Twenty! For all three?' said Crimthain. 'Anroth, when we trade in slaves, they only give us an amphora for each slave.'

'Our hunting dogs are highly renowned and much sought-after,' said Anroth. 'Demand twenty amphorae for each hound. They never send us their best wines.'

Crimthain shook his head. 'This should prove a memorable day's bargaining.'

'Be sure you don't give them Midar's favourites,' laughed Anroth, pointing to the high chieftain's three hounds up on the plateau. 'If it makes you feel any better, try for twenty and accept eighteen, but don't go any lower than that. Taste the wine, appear disappointed and insist he sweeten the bargain with an amphora of olive oil as a gift for the queen.'

Crimthain nodded again.

Bidding him farewell, Anroth returned to the stronghold and, after gathering together some dried roots, he went to the kitchen and filled a clay pot with burning charcoal, then headed for the sacred grove close by the Dark Waters.

Once there, he walked slowly around the rustling oaks and tapped each tree with his battered, old wand. Aromatic smoke rose from his pot. He beseeched Manannan, the great god of the sea, and the feckless Tethra, he of winds, storms and fog, to protect the sailors and their precious cargo, and to bring them safely to shore, preferably before the banquet.

He looked up high into a sacred oak. Nestling between its branches, mistletoe grew. Anroth frowned and looked around, disturbed by what he'd seen. As he strained his eyes to better see, a raven swooped down low, then perched beside the mistletoe.

Anroth held out his arm. The raven stripped off a bunch of berries and brought them down to him. They were engorged, white and waxy. Anroth's heart was heavy. For a while he stroked the raven behind its eye then, lifting his arm, he encouraged the bird to fly. He watched it rising in the sky.

'Mistletoe ripe before its season, mistletoe ripe so find the reason,' he whispered to himself. It was an old omen, a warning that if a stranger came from the east, Midar's kingdom could fall, however, the stranger might also protect them from impending disaster.

On that late summer's afternoon, there was a chill in the air. For a long time Anroth sat cross-legged with his eyes closed, his back resting against the trunk of the sacred oak. Like the Etruscans of old, Anroth possessed the gifts of the soothsayers, seers and diviners.

He listened to the prophetic rustle of the oak leaves, but failed to find their meaning. He walked to an old hazel tree close by the Dark Waters. As he feared, its spreading branches were heavily laden with nuts, foretelling many freshly dug graves. Much troubled by these omens and warnings, Anroth departed.

Beside the birch trees, holding the mistletoe, Dancer waited and watched Anroth go. Then he saw, beneath the trees, a maiden resting on her knees. He moved towards her without a sound as she lifted mushrooms from the ground. Some grow large and some grow small, and some will hardly grow at all. Her touch was gentle, her manner mild and, seeing Dancer, she stopped and smiled.

Dancer bowed, then swayed, in admiration of the maid, who continued to search the ground, filling her basket with what she found. As she did so, he danced to the touch of the passing breeze, danced to the rhythm of the trembling leaves. He danced in circles like the mystical hare, white, waxy berries in his hand. When she made as if to go, he gave her his gift of mistletoe. The maid hesitated then laughed out loud. And, as she left, politely bowed.

Long ago, a winter storm had blown down a pine tree into the Dark Waters. Like the leg bone of a long-dead giant, one end of its bleached white trunk rested on the bank while the other disappeared beneath the golden, peaty water. Over the years, the ground from which its roots had been torn had filled in and smoothed over, covered with sweet-smelling mosses and grasses. Dancer rested his back against the cushioned remains of the root. It was a beautiful bed, both long and wide, with room for another there beside.

When it came to affairs of the heart, Dancer never forced his attentions on the fairer sex. Some thought him as timid as harvest mice, never ever asking twice, (but gossips sometimes said; he could laugh a maiden into bed). Truth to tell, he was content to pass the time of day, relishing the games they chose to play.

Then out from the trees, just to tease, tucking up her skirt above her knees, wandered the maiden at her ease. Dancer smiled and, just to please, he charmed the birds down from the trees. Enchanted, she ogled him for a while, bidding him welcome with a smile.

Some will reap and some will sow, and some give maidens mistletoe. As polite custom so demands, she rubbed the berries in her hands; waxy, white and all aglow, the lustrous juice of mistletoe. The sacred symbol of the seed, everything a maid might need. Who could say where this might lead? Giving him nectar from her lips, she teased him with her fingertips; the sensual pleasures of the day, to rest awhile and then to play. And so, she moved and so she lay, in silence save for a gentle moan, lifting one last mushroom then walking home.

The queen came down to the kitchen. Reassured by Anroth that the Wave wanderer and his ship would arrive that day, Crimthain was giving orders to the cooks. There were loaves and oatmeal biscuits to be baked, three ducks to be roasted, a side of pork to be salted, and four hides full of fresh water and a hogskin of barley beer to be made ready for his men to collect later in the day. If he was going to have to bargain, as Anroth had suggested, he wanted the sea captain to feel welcome when he arrived.

Cliona heard Goibniu, Nuada and Dian laughing and shouting in the great hall. Occasionally the room filled with a deafening bellow as the eldest, Goibniu, who was built like a bull, blew into a carnyx. She stepped smartly into the great hall.

'Goibniu, how many times do I have to tell you about your coarse behaviour?' she said. 'One day you'll succeed your father and it's unbecoming that those of royal blood should play the carnyx. Stop behaving like a lout come and sit at the table.'

She turned. 'Dian, stop chewing those raw onions. You know how foul your breath smells. We have important guests tonight.'

'I wouldn't worry too much about his breath, mother,' Goibniu commented helpfully.

The queen turned on her regal heel and headed for the kitchen.

Later, as the servants were getting together some cold meats, bread and a hogskin of beer, she asked one of them to bring in a cauldron of soup to warm over the fire. By now Dian, bright red in the face, was unsuccessfully trying to make a battle horn bellow, much to the amusement of his brothers. Worried their high spirits might show them in a poor light at the banquet, Cliona did her best to calm things down.

'Dian, you look very silly,' she scolded. 'Come and eat something, and stop being a lummox!'

Sitting opposite her sons, she dispensed the food as they competed for her attention, guzzling down their soup, their minds still flushed with the excitement of the raid. Dian, the tallest and best-looking, went out of his way to provoke his mother, and alternated between slurping his soup and belching. They could drive her to distraction, but life simply wouldn't be the same without their raucous behaviour. Banging the banqueting table to gain their attention, she laid down the law.

'I won't tolerate any unseemly arguments tonight regarding which of you should be awarded the Hero's Portion,' she said. 'Kindly decide this among yourselves beforehand. If there's one thing I won't put up with, its family arguments breaking out in front of the clan chiefs and our other guests. As your father's sons, you must live by his standards. Remember our family motto,

'When in public, behave with dignity and decorum.'

'Yes, mother, - when in public, behave with dignity and decorum,' they chorused loudly.

'And stop shouting at me!' she said. 'If you don't behave, I'll call Aine in to box your ears.'

All three leant forwards across the table and whispered in unison.

'Sorry, mother, when in public, behave with dignity - and don't fart!'

They banged the table and roared with laughter.

The queen shook her head in exasperation but, unable to help herself, she burst out laughing.

'Utterly deplorable!' she tutted, wondering how she and Midar could be the parents of such wild young men. At least they were, in part, balanced by the recent addition of Danu and her good manners, to the family.

'And another thing,' she said. 'How many times do I have to tell you to stop liming your hair? You have fine heads of hair. Liming is old-fashioned. If you don't stop doing it, your hair will fall out. You can all get yourselves down to the sea and wash it out. Tonight, is an important occasion. I want to your hair to be well-washed and oiled when you present yourselves to your father and his chieftains.'

The three princes looked at her.

'And, Dian, how many times do I have to ask you to cut that ridiculously long moustache?' she continued. 'You know how much it distresses me when it droops in the soup and drips all over my table. You might as well be an uncouth youth from the midden.'

'Do not be disconcerted mother,' said Nuada, 'Goibniu and I will endeavour to make Dian and his moustache presentable for the banquet, so it no longer droops in the soup.'

Satisfied she'd done her best to make them presentable for their big night, she left. Goibniu picked up the carnyx, its head fashioned like that of a ferocious wild boar, and handed it to Dian.

'Well, you certainly can't play it,' he said. 'So, I'm going to fill it to the brim with my Dragon's Blood Barley Beer and, if you can drink it all in one go, Nuada and I will let you claim the Hero's Portion at the banquet.'

Before long, the horn had been filled with beer and Dian had one of his thumbs over the mouthpiece. He grasped the stem with his other hand and slowly raised the Carnyx. Then, in one quick movement, he removed his thumb and stuck the mouthpiece into his mouth. To steady things, he grasped the other side of the instrument, with his free hand.

Nuada and Goibniu stood on either side of him. Nuada took two paces back and indicated Goibniu do the same. Then he drew his dagger, Goibniu did likewise, Nuada motioned for Goibniu to grab one side of Dian's long, droopy moustache. He grabbed the other. As Dian contentedly gulped down the beer, the brothers struck simultaneously. With the blade-wielding accuracy only a warrior can lay claim to, they sliced the hapless excrescence right back to the sides of Dian's nose, leaving him with nothing but a square-shaped tuft of hair above his upper lip.

Horrified, Dian dropped the carnyx. Beer spilt everywhere and a fight ensued in which all three rolled around the floor. Cliona returned, realising what had happened, she called for reinforcements in the substantial shape of Aine, who grabbed Nuada, while the queen battered the other two into submission with a broom. Seeing how crestfallen Dian was, she tried to comfort him. She cupped his face in her hands and studied what was left of his shorn pride and joy.

Finally, she spoke. 'Yes, I like it. It suits you, Dian.'

'Really mother?' Dian perked up.

'Oh indeed,' she said. 'There's little doubt that, by the end of the banquet, many will choose to follow your example. Nuada, could I have the hair you cut off? I want to put it in a locket and treasure it.'

Dian was delighted, mother was going to treasure part of his circumcised moustache. However, he had serious doubts about how his fellow warriors would react to what he had been left with.

'I'm meant to strike fear into the hearts of our enemies,' he said.

'I can't imagine a stubby little moustache like this frightening anyone.'

'Look on the bright side,' said Nuada. 'They might die laughing.'

Still arguing and fighting, the princes went down to the sea to wash away the sins and stains of war. As they walked back to the kitchen, Aine turned to the queen. 'Did you say you liked his new moustache?' she asked.

Cliona shook her head. 'It looks ridiculous.' Aine stirred some broth, tasted it and offered some to Cliona.

'It tastes a little insipid to me,' she said. 'More seasoning?'

'No, it's fine as it is.'

Because it was Lunasa, the feast that night would be particularly well-attended. For the rest of the day, cooks and servants made ready for the banquet. They cleaned the queen's magnificent oak tables and polished them with beeswax, its welcoming scent intermingled with many more. They pushed open the massive doors of the great hall to clear the smoke and stale air, then swept the floors and spread around heather, mountain thyme and rushes. They dampened these with water splashed from pitchers, to keep down the dust and bring out the fragrances underfoot.

The smell of roasting venison mixed with juniper wafted in from the kitchen. In the great hall, above the fire, a huge pig on a long skewer hung from two tall firedogs. From time to time, one of the cooks came in to rotate it and ladle fat along its length. The fat hissed and spat as it ran down onto the smouldering logs and into the ash.

2 The Wrath Of The Gods

Aine had reached that settled stage in the preparation of a banquet when she could relax, wait for the venison and pork to roast through, and leave the less-demanding chores to her helpers.

Cliona turned to her. 'Let's go down to the headland and get some fresh air,' she suggested. 'You need a break before putting your finishing touches to the banquet.'

A broad grin broke out on Aine's flushed face and she followed Cliona through a door at the back of the kitchen.

The companionship between Aine and the queen surprised some people. Others didn't find it so strange, for a mother and the woman who had wet-nursed her child often develop an enduring friendship. The milk of human kindness is a precious thing, but Aine and Cliona's friendship went much deeper. It was written in blood; Cliona's blood.

They stood on the headland below the stronghold, surrounded by sea on three sides. It was a special place, where the wind blew in from any direction, and you could let your mind wander. Aine's took the familiar path back to the remote fishing community in Ireland where she'd been born.

She hadn't shared the usual dream of those afflicted by poverty – to find a better future –she'd expected no more from life than to eke out a precarious existence from the few crops they managed to nurture in the stony fields, and to fish the often stormy and treacherous western sea. She had always been a law unto herself, a rebel from the day she'd been born, and proud of that. If she'd only obeyed her father, she would never have been snatched away as a slave.

He spotted the pirate ship approaching when he was out fishing and hurried back to warn the villagers. This gave the women and children, Aine's little sister among them, just enough time to escape into the woods. Defending the village against the marauders, proved brief and futile; the raiders took what little food they could find and kidnapped anyone they could sell as a slave, including Aine's brother.

When she saw him being dragged off, she followed, fearful but determined. Grabbing a large stone, she swung it at the head of the pirate holding her brother. He jerked sideways, the stone merely grazed his temple, dropping down, point first, on his bare foot. He cursed her and, in the confusion, released her brother.

'Run!' Aine gasped, as the infuriated and humiliated pirate reached for his blade.

Thankfully the boy did, as the pirate seized her. Aine braced herself for the pain but it never came.

'She's a fine-looking one,' one of the other pirates said, staying her captor's hand.

'Think what she'd fetch.'

'More than the prisoner you lost,' another pointed out.

'Keep her, she's valuable and you'll have nothing to show for your pains otherwise.'

Openly hostile, untamed and undernourished she may have been, but Aine's cold, sullen beauty saved her life during the turbulent times that followed. Traded from one place to another, she came eventually to the Kingdom of Rheged, ruled by the father of the woman who was to become her closest friend. The promise of a better life and the grandeur of her surroundings had a calming effect on Aine. She settled well, but that feral nature she could never completely control, lived on.

One day, when the young Cliona and her elder brothers were playing, the boys pushed the little princess. She fell awkwardly, badly twisted her ankle and cried out in pain. It was nothing more than mischief; the young princes had intended Cliona no great harm. But Aine, who was working nearby, didn't see it that way. She laid into one of the boys, knocked him to the ground and then, for good measure, set about his bigger brother.

A slave attacking one of royal blood was an outrage the Queen of Rheged would not normally countenance. She sent Aine back to the kitchen and the princes out of the room.

'Please don't punish Aine, mother,' Cliona had implored. 'She was just trying to be nice, but she doesn't know how. Please don't be unkind to Aine or send her away. I want her to help me until I can walk again.'

The queen was surprised by Cliona's outburst. Then it dawned on her that Aine's behaviour had been driven by affection for Cliona. The slave hadn't thought of the risks she was taking.

At that moment, ignoring the queen's instructions to stay in the kitchen, Aine reappeared with a bowl of cold water and a cloth, and gently bathed Cliona's ankle.

'Aine, you are to help Cliona until she can walk again,' said the queen.

If she'd expected an apology, she was disappointed. Aine had just nodded.

The queen persevered. She was sympathetic to the girl and tried to civilise her, for, with a little effort, Aine could have achieved some advancement in her life. But Aine stubbornly refused. It was not in her nature to accept she belonged to anyone but herself.

But she found it easy to dream, to imagine Cliona as the little sister she'd left behind when she'd been torn from the heart of her family No one could have been more attentive or caring towards Cliona but, once the princess had fully recovered, Aine made it clear she wanted to return to the kitchen.

To one who had lived out her childhood in hunger, working in the royal kitchen more than fulfilled any modest dreams for her life she had entertained. The idea of any further advancement above the life she was born to, frightened her.

When Midar took Cliona in marriage, Aine was the obvious choice to send with her to Northumbria. Aine could not have been happier. She loved Bamburgh. The windswept coastline and ever-changing sea reminded her of her childhood. By now a fine cook, she worked in the kitchen, and later on, she helped Cliona with Goibniu's birth and looking after him.

Her own mysterious pregnancy followed, then tragedy struck. Her daughter died of the fever a matter of weeks after her birth. Losing the most beautiful gift life had given her, was a wicked profanity against all the love she had, hidden deep inside, a body blow she'd scarcely been able to endure.

Cliona was into her second pregnancy and, right from the start, it was different from her first. Even just a few weeks before the baby was born, it was hard to tell she was carrying. Labour came early, just after Aine's daughter had died; and, though the birth was straightforward, Nuada's body was small and wasted, and he struggled to cry.

Then Cliona bled. The blood flowed out of her, as if being poured fast from a jug, soaking the bed in an ever-expanding pool. Aine stared at it, then she screamed. She screamed so loud it woke the sentries sleeping in the distant watchtower. It was a horrific, slicing-down-to-the bone scream, cutting through the darkest night.

Then Anroth, who had been hovering on the other side of the door, burst in. Cliona was deathly white and had lost consciousness. In an instant, he slipped one hand beneath her robe and, the other within her. Feeling her stomach, he discovered her empty womb was soft and floppy. Dragging Aine's hand up beside his own, he showed her how to rub the womb until it contracted into a tight ball. The bleeding stopped. It was a lesson Aine would never forget.

One of the other women took Nuada, who was barely breathing, and held him to Cliona's breast. It was all the distressed woman could think of doing. It was a foolish, futile gesture, for the comatose queen had nothing to give and everything to lose. Aine's courage deserted her. A few minutes earlier, she had been involved in a seemingly normal birth. Now the world was crashing down all around her. It had only been days since she'd watched her beautiful daughter die and now it looked as if Nuada would join her, and probably Cliona, the only person she had left to love. Everything in her life had been snatched away before and now it was happening all over again.

Nuada's pathetic little cries dragged Aine back to reality. Picking him up, she opened her blouse. He hardly moved and his cold, pale skin was a shade of blue. She pressed his little body against the warmth of her soft breast and she pushed her nipple into his mouth. He was too weak to respond to her welcome.

Aine was frantic. If she could just get some milk inside him, to warm and nourish him, he might feel all their love.

She squeezed her nipple and showered his mouth with milk. Some went up his nose and he managed a weak sneeze. It seemed to rouse him. His little tongue came out and tasted the milk.

Warmed by her body, he renewed his feeble efforts. Then, a miracle, - at last, his little lips found her nipple and he started to suck. For Aine, the moment was one of blissful release. Her milk flowed freely and, with it, all her love and the uncertain promise that the new baby might yet survive the night.

Cliona regained consciousness, sustained by the sight of Aine giving succour to her struggling child.

Anroth stood back, surveying the traumatic scene, feeling impotent he realised all he could do now was pray. He headed for the sacred grove of oaks and taking with him a pot of smouldering embers. One mighty oak towered above all the others. Its massive branches stretched out to touch the heavens above and its roots ran so deep they hung like curtains in the echoing caverns of the Otherworld below.

Anroth placed his pot in the centre of the clearing and covered the embers with willow leaves. Kneeling beneath his old friend, he rested his forehead on its trunk and prayed to Sirona, the goddess of healing, and Bridget, the goddess of childbirth. He called upon them to intervene, to save Cliona's life and that of their child. Responding to the passion of his pleadings, the bowl of embers burst into bright-blue flames and illuminated the clearing. Out of the darkness and into that light walked one who loved him. Dancer knelt beside Anroth and added his prayers to the druid's litany of hope and love. Anroth listened. The whispering voices of the oak leaves spread up the ancient tree and waves of sound washed all around them, as the whispering leaves of other trees sang softly in sympathy.

In concert with the swaying branches and sighing leaves, the earth shuddered as massive roots twisted and turned. Then there was peace. Anroth stood up and embraced Dancer before returning to Cliona. Dancer remained the whole night through and whispered.

'Grow strong little brother, grow stronger, grow stronger my little brother.'

Midar was ill-prepared for such an unwelcome turn of events. He spent what time he could by Cliona's bedside, frightened to leave lest he returned to find her dead. Regaining her composure, Aine took charge. She was not above telling Midar to leave if needs be. Midar admired anyone who stood up to him and displayed leadership when others faltered, and he came to love Aine, putting his faith in her devotion, desperate for anything to cling to.

Despite her apparent confidence, in the uncertain weeks that followed, Aine was driven purely by fear. Cliona's recovery proved unpredictable. Her breathing was shallow and the slightest exercise made her breathless.

When the queen grew stronger, Aine started to give Nuada to her, she watched her hold the child, still scarce clinging to life. Aine could feel Cliona willing her son to live, determined she would never, ever give up on him. In doing so, her willpower improved the prospects of her own uncertain recovery.

Nuada struggled. One problem followed another – sometimes his belly would swell, at other times he would suffer from attacks of shivering – but he was a fighter and Aine began to believe she might actually succeed in saving him, which softened the brutality of her daughter's death. Nuada had given Aine back the lost love and dignity of motherhood. When he smiled for the first time, he gave his smile to Aine.

Aine and Cliona grew closer and they would sit on the bed together, sharing casual reassuring kisses, an intimacy conceived out of fear. Aine had become a caring elder sister, someone for Cliona to share her thoughts with. And, as the months passed by and Cliona slowly regained her strength, she would watch Aine feed Nuada. It reminded her of how greedy Goibniu had been when he'd fed from her breasts, how proud she'd been of her first-born and how a mother with a child on the breast is an exceedingly beautiful thing.

When Cliona held Nuada, the baby's eyes would follow Aine as she moved around the room; his contented little gurgles were as much for Aine as they were for his mother. Once they started believing Nuada would live, the effect on Aine was dramatic. Cliona had never seen her so content, so complete. Life for Aine could not have been more fulfilling. Cliona realised Nuada was no longer just her child, he would always be part of both of them.

'Nuada may have started his little life within my womb, but, once he was born, keeping him alive was beyond me,' she said. 'You gave him his life, Aine, when I failed him. Without you, he was destined to die. Against all the odds, you did what no one else could. You are just as much his mother as I am. For the rest of his life, Nuada will always have two mothers.'

Aine held Cliona, but there was fear in her face.

'Don't make promises you can't keep,' she sobbed. 'You may think differently once you've recovered. Don't put another sword through my heart. I've already lost one child. Don't give me another, only to take him away one day.'

'I'll never take him away,' said Cliona. 'He's, our child. We'll both lose him soon enough. Before we know it, Midar will be training our little warrior in the art of war.'

This all took place in spring, at the start of the fighting season when Midar and his warriors rode around Northumbria's boundaries to meet with his tribal chieftains and reassert his authority. But that year, fearful of leaving Cliona, he delayed departure. He'd have preferred to remain at Bamburgh and send his champion, Lugh, in his place, but knew that rumours would spread unless he was seen at the head of his men. Those casting envious eyes on his kingdom would start laying plans for war.

When he left, Anroth began to take Cliona for little walks along the beach, increasing the distance day by day. One day, they reached a driftwood log, thrown high above the tide line. When they'd first gone out walking, it had seemed so very far away, out of reach, unobtainable. Now they sat on it in silence, giving thanks for a precious day neither expected to see. Cliona turned to the druid.

'Why, Anroth?' she asked. 'Having Goibniu was no burden, but giving birth to Nuada almost killed us both. Was making love to you so wrong? We did it for the kingdom, we did it for Midar. He needed your advice, but you had ceased to be of any use to him, for you were too wrapped up in grief, mourning the death of your wife and child. Sharing our love thawed your frozen mind and brought us both happiness, but did we provoke the wrath of the gods?'

'I don't think so Cliona,' said Anroth. 'The gods could give us plenty of lessons in infidelity – it's their way of life. The terrifying experience you endured serves to remind us what I teach my novices, having a baby is always unpredictable and often more dangerous than when a warrior rides out to war. For all their battles and skirmishes, many fighting men live to see old age.'

Cliona sighed. 'I always knew the risks,' she said. 'I just didn't imagine it could happen to me.'

'Let's not look for reasons,' said Anroth. 'But just be grateful you can hold him in your arms. He's a precious miracle, our miracle. Nuada will grow up to be a man with two fathers, but aware of only one.'

'And two mothers. Don't forget Aine's part in all this.'

Anroth paused. His voice was calm, but inside he felt empty and betrayed. He was still shocked at Cliona's revelation as to why she'd made love to him.

'Cliona, you took me to your bed, revived my mind and mended my heart,' he said. 'But, if I understand you rightly, you made love to me for the greater good of the kingdom and Midar. Not because you loved me.' Cliona flushed, more annoyed than embarrassed.

'That's unfair,' she said. 'You're making a difficult decision sound trivial. Yes, if you want to put it that way, but that wasn't how I looked at it. Don't be annoyed. I did what I thought was best for all of us, including you.'

Anroth shook his head.

'Love? Is anything really love?'

Memories of his dead wife answered his question.

Cliona took his hand. 'I didn't mean to upset you,' she said. 'I could never bring your wife or daughter back.

Anroth, don't you understand? There was another reason I made love to you.'

He looked at her.

'You have so much love inside you, trying to get out,' she said. 'What I wanted to give you was a child – yours and ours – and allow you to be a father. Don't ever say I don't love you.' Anroth nodded.

'Day by day he grows stronger,' he said. 'His future seems assured. Unless, one day, our enemies discover the secret of who his real father is. There's only one person who might have the power to discover our secret, Birog the Black Druidess of the North.'

'Can we protect him from her?'

'Yes, I'll seek the help of the gods, there is a right of purification, normally reserved for young druids. When the time is propitious, we'll use it to protect Nuada. Who knows, Cliona? He might grow up to be a druid!'

'I hope he does,' said the queen. 'He's too small to be a warrior. Just think how much joy Nuada will give you one day.'

'He already does,' said Anroth. 'When he's not frightening the life out of me.'

Cliona pressed her fingers to his lips. 'Shush, be quiet now,' she said. 'Let's enjoy each other's silences and secrets.'

Cliona took Anroth's arm, and they walked back to the stronghold. She was still frail but growing stronger by the day.

Anroth persuaded the unpredictable god of lightning, storm and mist, Tethra, to protect Nuada and hide their secrets. Tethra, who was skilled at confusing his enemies, admired Anroth because of his irreverent attitudes to druidism, the request appealed to the grumpy old god's mischievous nature. He promised to create an invisible mist around Nuada to confuse Birog, her assassins and spies. Anroth would have liked to ask for more, but thought better of it. A druid should never expect too much of a god, lest they lose more than they started with.

Anroth waited patiently for the right conditions to perform the ceremony. One night, when thunder rent the air, he took Nuada down to the sacred spring in the corner of the great hall. Witnessed only by Cliona, Aine and the moonlight, he bathed the little boy in the waters and implored Tethra, and other gods and goddesses to protect him. The waters mixed with Nuada's tears, Tethra's rumbling thunder disguised Nuada's cries and lightning lit their way to bed.

When Midar returned from the fighting season, he had a pleasant surprise. He scarcely believed his eyes. Cliona handed over a heavy, plump Nuada. He had chubby cheeks, stout little arms and legs, dimples at the elbows, and wrinkles round his ankles and wrists.

Life returned to normal. Nuada brought with him a more informal approach to the royal court. When he was hungry, Cliona would simply take Nuada down to the kitchen rather than summon Aine. Cliona delighted in busying herself, helping the old head cook to bake or prepare the meal. It was a common enough sight to see Nuada, cradled in Aine's arm, hang from a nipple while she stirred stew with her free hand.

When word spread of Aine's part in saving Nuada and caring for the queen, she became highly regarded as a good woman to have beside you when in labour. With Anroth's advice, she acquired the skills she needed to help at other births. If she was fated not to have children of her own, then helping those who were, gave her life greater meaning.

One day, the old head cook was paring some cold, fatty meat off the bone; when the knife slipped and inflicted a deep wound in her hand. The wound festered and lockjaw followed. It was a death sentence for the poor woman.

Lying in bed one night, not long afterwards, Midar began to talk. Normally his conversations were easy to follow but, that night in the bedchamber, Cliona failed to understand him.

'It's nothing to do with me, of course,' he began.

'What isn't anything to do with you?'

'You're in charge,' he reassured her.

'I'm in charge of what has nothing to do with you?'

'Exactly,' he said. 'I was just wondering if you'd considered making Aine head cook? There are few who can stew an apple as well as she can and what she can do with a wild boar is beyond compare.'

Cliona found these confusing conversations rather endearing. Feeling playful, she poked him in the ribs. 'She's pretty good at keeping you in order, never mind a wild boar,' she said. 'No, it hadn't occurred to me to make Aine head cook. Let me think about it.'

'Exactly my point,' he said.

'Well, if I'm in charge of what has nothing to do with you, what exactly was your point?'

Now Midar was confused. 'I think that's my point,' he said. 'Aine is unquestionably the most exceptional woman in your kitchen. Your kitchen – mark my words – not mine. It doesn't mean she should be head cook. And that reminds me of what I was actually trying to say. Do you think Goibniu and Nuada might like a little baby brother or sister?'

He had speculated as to whether his sons might like an addition to the family on numerous occasions and always received a positive response from Cliona, but he was more scared of the dangers of another pregnancy than she was. As usual, she smiled. 'I don't know,' she said. 'But we could try to find out.'

Midar blew out the candle and took her in his massive arms.

'Midar, I swear there's no man in the kingdom who can hold a woman as gently as you do,' said Cliona.

'How would you know? No other man has ever held you in his arms.'

Later, lying side by side, Cliona kissed him. 'You know, Midar, that was a very good idea,' she said. 'In fact, it was undoubtedly one of your best.'

Midar was proud of himself and pleased she'd found his endeavours fulfilling. 'So, would you like it to be a little boy or a girl?'

Cliona paused.

'Oh, that wasn't the good idea I was thinking about,' she said. 'I'm going to make Aine head cook.'

Some of the best years of their lives followed, the golden years of Midar's Northumbria.

On a number of occasions, Cliona tried to make Aine's demanding life easier, for the wear and tear of her travails were beginning to show. Her once-fine features, sculptured by an upbringing of semi-starvation, had long since disappeared within the plump and confident character she had become.

Cliona would have loved to take Aine out of the kitchen so she could become her companion. There would always be plenty to do. They could ride out together, and visit the sparsely populated small communities on Midar's estates. Cliona could dress Aine in fine garments and let her live out her days in comfort as she deserved. But whenever Cliona raised the matter, their relationship became strained. One day, by way of explanation, Aine said.

'How often have I sat amongst the sand dunes, looking out to sea, and wished those waves would somehow take me home to our mean and damp hovels crouched down low against the fury of the storm? I was torn away from my precious world and family. We will never meet again. What ever became of them?' Cliona sighed, in sympathy.

'Becoming a slave then meeting you, Cliona, turned out to be the best thing that happened to me,' said Aine. 'You gave me a realm and made me the ruler of my own kitchen, there isn't a soul in the kingdom who won't smile and greet me when I pass by. After you, I feel the most loved woman in the land.'

She smoothed out her tattered apron.

'I would love to share your days, dressed in fine clothes,' she said. 'But I wear these stained, old kitchen rags with pride. They keep me close to my lost family. The only clothes they ever wore were the ones they stood up in. Let us rest content, and share our love, living our lives in different ways.'

3 The Novice Master

No one man could presume to fully master the many skills of druidism. But if there had been such a man, it would have been Anroth. He spoke six languages and was well-versed in all three of the druidic disciplines. He was broad-shouldered but short of stature, well past middle age, with a face that was brown and tanned by the elements he sought to understand.

Smile lines played around his grey-blue eyes. He wore a long grey robe and a large leather bag hung from his belt. Around his neck, a bronze raven pendant dangled from a leather thong. With his aquiline nose and assured dignified manner, many took him to be of Roman descent, but he was a high-born Celt.

That afternoon, he sat in the sand dunes with his novices, Sirona, Luchtain and the ghostly pale Keeva. With Anroth's guidance, they searched the shadows to find the light and confronted the mysterious knowledge of the druidic cult and occult. Whenever Anroth could find the time, they ventured into the wildwood, where he would reveal the wisdom of nature's ways. Sometimes Dancer would join them and bring with him the fruits of the forest. They would cook a meal and eat together, then he'd be gone.

Anroth taught the novices to listen to the sounds of the forest, to be one with the ever-changing whispers of the woods, to find the meaning hidden in the rustle of the leaves as they rose and fell in brief echoes of understanding. They looked forward to every moment spent with Anroth, but the times they loved best were those spent exploring the hidden trails, when they lived off the land and used whatever came to hand.

Anroth was widely travelled. As a young man, he'd worked for his father, a prosperous Rheged merchant, who had sent him out to Rome. Trading links with its lost empire remained the lifeblood of the decaying metropolis, and Anroth had delighted in the city's magnificent buildings, mosaics, statues and elegant columns. If anything, as he'd mingled with Rome's colourful, cosmopolitan population, the aura of decay and decadence had enhanced the city's splendour.

Anroth's teachings to his novices, were broadly based. He loved to recount the classical stories, he had heard in Rome. The lessons he gave, were often embellished with reminiscences of his experiences, and of what he had learnt on his numerous journeys.

Anroth's early reaction to Christianity, which he encountered in Rome, had been one of enthusiasm. It was unlike druidism, in which many of the four hundred gods and goddesses seemed to be motivated by jealousy, mischief-making and vengeance. Christianity was informed by love. The idea a god might love you amazed him.

In Anroth's personal pantheon of favourite Celtic gods and goddesses, there were many, he could just imagine sharing a smile or laughing out loud with. Before he visited Rome, he imagined Jesus must have been a happy god and he'd thought of him as someone with a twinkle in his eye. Indeed, he'd already added Jesus to his list of favoured gods he would occasionally pray to.

Jesus's love of nature and mankind seemed to animate him.

Anroth's favourite story was the one about the wedding. Who but a mischief-maker would sit back, watch the wine run out then conjure up quality wine? When the guests realised how good it was, everyone must have got roaring drunk and fallen about laughing. But, much to his surprise, the Christians Anroth met in Rome didn't describe Jesus as a happy person. The pictures they painted suggested he'd been a humourless man who'd never laughed. This didn't commend him to the young Anroth, who believed humourless men weren't to be trusted.

Although disappointed by this portrayal, Anroth had never lost his enthusiasm for Jesus. He remained one of the many gods who inspired him and he refused to believe the Jesus beloved by storytellers had changed. He assumed the Christian bishops had moulded Jesus into their own miserable image and likeness. What a shame, he reflected, that in its long life of five hundred years, Christianity had already grown old, its happy, joyful side suppressed by those who had risen to the top, like fat in a slowly-cooking stew.

Anroth had concluded that religious leaders had quickly become obsessed with pleading their own twisted version of truth and had prostituted Christianity's essential beauty, losing the love along the way. They had subverted the message into only two things: what you were forbidden to do and what you were forced to do. He was not persuaded this was how Jesus intended his message of joy and love to resonate around the world.

Anroth's interest waned. Losing his enthusiasm for the sombre world of the Christian, he returned home, but not before he had married the daughter of a Galatian merchant. Something had drawn him back to even older beliefs, those of his childhood. He'd retreated into feelings of love, and relied on what nature revealed and how druidism animated the world around him. It did not seek to confine Anroth's fertile mind the way Christianity did.

Druidism was far too close to the unpredictability of nature to do so. Whilst willingly conceding his beliefs could well be in error, it was important for Anroth to indulge them. So much to his father's annoyance, he abandoned his promising future as a merchant. Accepting the virtue of conceding to uncertainty, and that much of life's meaning would never be revealed, he decided to train as a druid in Rheged. All those years of dedicated study would be sorely tested this coming Lunasa.

When Cliona became Midar's young bride, Cliona's father – the high chieftain of Rheged – sent Anroth with her to Northumbria. Acting as her spiritual and temporal advisor, he taught her many things. He emphasised that, while her first duty was to Midar and his kingdom, her second was to herself. And he stressed the need for a queen to be independent and in charge of her life. She proved an attentive pupil. Anroth undoubtedly had the gift of second sight, but he did not foresee where his advice would one day take both of them.

When the three princes were old enough, Anroth became their tutor, teaching them alongside his novice druids. Now the princes had grown into men, those days were long gone.

Luchtain, one of the novices, looked around their diminished circle, just himself, Keeva and Sirona. He had always admired Sirona's intelligence and the lucid way in which she expressed herself but, as they all lived such a close-knit life, he failed to recognise the feelings of love for her dawning within him.

Anroth turned to Sirona. 'Take your time,' he said. 'Tell me what you find in the sky.'

Luchtain followed her gaze as she studied the flight of the birds above. The clouds were mottled, broken into bars and ripples of dark and silver, as if ghostly fish swam there. He looked at the seagulls that hugged the shoreline, circled and skimmed the waves, then banked and turned into the wind before they headed back to shore to join those settled on the sand, their heads tucked under their wings.

Sirona's voice was soft, musing. 'I find brooding uncertainty,' she said. 'Restlessness. Foreboding even. Those that swim in the sea are not welcome in the sky.'

'But you have seen that ghostly fish above many times?'

She nodded. 'And it foretells change. But when it aligns with the festival of Lunasa, it's a bad omen.'

'Explain,' said Anroth.

'I watch the way the gulls fly, listen to their plaintive cry,' she said. 'I watch their close-held wings, then rapid wing-beats. Why? Why not choose to stretch those wings and sail the mackerel sky?' Anroth nodded in approval.

'Perceptive.'

He turned to Keeva. 'If I were to ask you to tell a tale at tonight's banquet, which story would you choose?'

Luchtain listened with interest. Keeva was the most outspoken of their little group and often provoked heated discussion.

'I'd tell the tale of she whose eyes were as pale-blue as the flower of the linseed,' he said. 'I'd tell of the beautiful Blodeuedd, created and born out of flowers. Of the prince she married and how she betrayed him.'

'Intriguing,' said Anroth. 'Why?'

Keeva smiled faintly. 'It's a tale of treachery. She tricks her husband and persuades her lover to murder him.'

'Is death and murder in the air?' asked Anroth.

'The success and fame of one is the jealousy and treachery of another,' said Keeva. 'The best man at the wedding is the last man the bridegroom should trust.'

'Do you agree, Luchtain?' Luchtain had almost forgotten he was part of the discussion and not just a casual observer. He thought for a moment.

'Blodeuedd's love was like… like a badly lit fire,' he said. 'It burnt itself out long before the flames of love could fill her heart.'

Anroth nodded. Luchtain grew bolder.

'Beware the woman who blows too hot when first you meet, for sooner still she will grow cold.' Anroth turned to Sirona again.

'Is he correct? Should a woman be impetuous, or hesitant?'

Sirona's lips twitched. Luchtain was certain her eyes had flickered towards him, but they moved on in an instant.

'A young woman often observes and understands a man better than the man appreciates,' she said softly. 'She can be as forward or distant as she pleases.'

'Enlightening,' murmured Anroth.

He raised an eyebrow, waiting for her to clarify what she'd meant. Luchtain too, was curious. Recently, he'd noticed, Sirona often gave him the impression she was looking at him. He didn't mind. He had the body of a warrior, but the gentle mind of a mystic, and he'd have liked it very much if she were looking at him. But every time he thought she was and he looked at her, she wasn't. Her behaviour confused him.

'Blodeuedd had been created out of flowers,' Sirona ventured. 'Her behaviour was understandable. She…'

'Since she was created out of flowers,' Keeva rudely interrupted, 'she had a poor start in life. The flower people are always airy-fairy. Even worse, she was Welsh and not to be trusted.'

'Have a care Keeva,' said Anroth. 'Yet again, you're finding fault with those you know nothing about. You're becoming far too certain in your opinions and you're far too quick to dismiss the virtue of doubt.'

He reached behind him and brought out a spear, which he handed to Luchtain. 'You've made many fine spears,' he said. 'Tell me about this one. Where does it come from?'

Luchtain examined it. The two sides of the broad spearhead curved and scrolled around the sides of the shaft, as the sharp, serrated blade extended backwards. The spearhead and shaft were carved with complex symbols and images of gods he did not recognise. The end was grooved, cut in at an angle.

'At first, I thought it was the work of the master craftsmen of the lower Danube,' he said, turning it this way and that. 'But it's not. Apart from the images of the gods, I don't recognise any of the symbolism. I've only seen this wood once before. I've no idea where it comes from.'

'What more can you tell me?' Anroth pressed. Luchtain smiled.

'It isn't a spear.'

'Then what is it?'

'It's an arrow, and made from the same lustrous wood as the bow that hangs in the great hall.'

'Then where are the feathered flights to ensure it shoots true?'

'It doesn't need them,' said Luchtain. 'If it's properly set and loosed, the angled groove at its base will ensure it leaves the bowstring spinning. However far you shoot it, it'll continue to rotate because of the twist in the blades of the arrowhead. It should always shoot true.' Anroth turned to Sirona.

'What does this teach us?'

'It teaches us that, just as an arrow without a bow can be used like a dagger or spear in the hands of an assassin, then so can a spear become an arrow when it's paired with the right bow.'

Keeva frowned. 'I say it is a spear,' he said. 'But it's not of this world. It's the sacred spear of Assal, which always flies true.'

'You're all right,' said Anroth. 'Study it well, for you'll never see it's like again. Just as an arrow and a spear may sometimes be interchangeable, so may a warrior and a druid. Warriors should act wisely; druids sometimes need to think and fight like warriors. Let me set you a problem.'

Anroth led them up to the drover's trail north of the settlement. 'If the stronghold was overwhelmed by our enemies and we were forced to retreat north,' he asked, 'how might we slow our enemy down and make good our escape?'

'If we had fair warning, then ponies under those trees would help,' said Keeva.

'We could make a run for it into the forest,' said Luchtain. 'But attack should be our first line of defence. From this distance, we could knock a few out or at least slow them down with our slingshots. Some of us would get away.'

'If we're going to rely on our slingshots,' added Sirona, 'then we'd need a good supply of stones from the beach hidden somewhere near here. Otherwise, we'd waste too much time looking for stones.'

'And where would you hide the stones?' asked Anroth.

As they discussed the matter, Ollathir the swineherd came wandering through the trees with his mighty club slung across his back. In one hand he held the freshly roasted leg of a suckling pig.

His pigsties and his 'precious children', as he referred to his herd, were situated some distance from the main settlement. There, he could let his pigs loose in the woodlands, so they could forage for food. He was devoted to his extended noisy family and even slept in the piggery.

On cold winter nights, he would cuddle up to his favourite rusty-red sow, the magnificent Bebhionn, patron of pleasure. She reminded him of his childhood, when he sometimes slept with his mother. When he saw Anroth, his face broke out in a broad grin.

'My lord Anroth,' he said. 'I thought I heard voices and came to investigate. What an honour it is to see you. You may be wondering why I'm eating the high chieftain's piglet. You'll know that, tonight, we have a banquet with important guests. I bear the heavy responsibility of providing the pork for my lord Midar. It must be at its finest for our honoured guests. Pork, my lord, is the veritable prince of all meats. Even the reprehensible Romans considered it beyond compare.'

Pulling a strip off the leg, he handed it to Anroth, who put it into his mouth and savoured the flavour.

'Olly, this is quite excellent.'

Catching sight of his favourite novice, Ollathir waved the leg in the air.

'Well, here's the lovely young lady Sirona,' he said. 'Do you want a nibble on my piglet, pet?'

'Olly, you always know how to inflame a lady's sensibilities,' she said, maintaining her poise and cool demeanour as she took the leg. She opened her mouth wide, sank her teeth deep into the meat and tore off a strip before handing it on to Luchtain.

Luchtain had been studying harmoniously with Sirona for many years but, only recently, had he realised just how agreeable and desirable she had become. He was aware of a yearning, a hunger, previously unknown to him. He was only happy and the world was only well when Sirona was there beside him.

In the past, one of his great strengths had been to perform the druidic philosophical exercise of 'thinking pure thoughts'. Of late, though, he'd found this increasingly difficult, and carnal thoughts had begun to intrude into his otherwise unsullied mind. What troubled him even more was he had no idea what one was meant to do when carnal thoughts started to gain the upper hand. How might they be honourably transformed into the virtuous affection of love?

Other than the occasional hug or a kiss, he was totally ignorant of physical intimacy. He felt guilty of his innocent desires and had taken to going off on his own and rolling around naked in the nettles to chastise himself. Having reflected on the matter, he had come to the conclusion he should share his feelings with Sirona. But when he saw how she sank her fangs into the suckling pig, those noble intentions suffered a severe setback. Henceforth, he determined to keep his private thoughts and parts to himself.

4 The Golden Child

Ollathir stood there in the sunshine, hands on hips, delighted his distinguished friends had thought so highly of his piglet. He was an unusual young man. Though he had barely turned twenty, his chestnut curly hair had already retreated back from his forehead to the top of his skull. He was short of stature, almost as broad as he was tall, but his size was by no means his most unusual feature. Some said it was his bright-red floppy ears, but most agreed it was his nose – or rather the absence of it.

Those that made Ollathir's acquaintance after he'd become an adult assumed he'd suffered some terrible affliction as a child; an injury, perhaps, or possibly a strange contagion of the skin that had consumed it? Leprosy had even been mentioned. But Ollathir had been born with large nostrils that opened straight outwards. The real miracle, was that Ollathir had even been born in the first place.

Ollathir's mother had laboured for seven days and nights. She'd been expected to die, but had successfully delivered and, against the odds, Ollathir survived. Even as a new-born baby, it had been immediately obvious he was either directly related to Moccus the pig god or closely resembled a pig, a cause for great rejoicing.

He was a golden child, a gift bestowed by the gods. Some even suggested he might be the son of the Dagda. His status as a swineherd was assured. Ollathir was a man filled with self-confidence, who was forever laughing – although his laughter sounded more like happy little squeals and grunts.

'If I might be so bold to enquire, my lord,' he asked. 'What brings you to this place?'

Anroth explained he had just set his novices the problem of where best to place a supply of stones when retreating from an enemy. Ollathir pointed out they would have to cover each other as they retreated, so they would need at least three piles of stones, not just one. And these would need to be suitably spaced out along the trail with the ponies hidden near the last pile. All agreed this was a prudent solution to the problem and Anroth complimented him.

'You have a fine tactical mind, Olly.'

'Did you know, I owe my life to my lord Anroth?' said Ollathir to the novices. 'My mother had laboured overlong, with great fortitude, and he cut her stomach to bring me into this world.'

Anroth smiled.

'Indeed, had I not been squashed for so long inside my mother's womb, I would have been tall and thin,' laughed Ollathir. 'But I'm happy enough to be small and round because, after all, without the magical skills of my lord Anroth, I'd have been nothing at all.'

'Oh, Olly, that's so sad,' said Sirona. 'I knew your warrior father died in battle, but I never knew your mother died in childbirth. So, you were an orphan child?'

'No, Sirona, that was what was so magical,' said Ollathir. 'Lord Anroth saved my mother's life as well. She lived to a goodly age.'

'Anroth,' said Sirona. 'I insist you tell us the tale of how you cut Olly's mother. Teach us how to cut a baby out without killing the mother.'

'Yes,' they pleaded.

Anroth agreed, provided they did not share the dangerous secret, with another soul. Ollathir asked if he might listen too.

'Certainly, I welcome the chance to tell you of that fateful day and how brave your mother was,' said Anroth. 'First, though, we have preparations to make. We need to collect stones and organise them in three piles as Olly advised. Then you must practice with your slingshots.'

Ollathir nodded, but his normally happy demeanour had changed. He took the club off his back and made a few half-hearted swings. 'You know, my lord Anroth,' he said. 'I've never used my club in anger, only in sadness when I've had to dispatch my children. Now, my children are restless, a disturbing vapour pervades the air.'

Anroth nodded.

Seeing the little fellow downhearted, Sirona asked, 'Can Olly spend the rest of the day with us?'

'Certainly,' said Anroth. 'If he wishes to join us.'

'I'd love to,' said Ollathir. 'My children will be happy enough without me for a while.'

'First, Olly,' said Anroth. 'Go down to the sea and scrub yourself with seaweed. The smells of the pigsty precede you and lingers long after you've gone.'

'Really, my lord, I can't smell anything,' said Ollathir.

This may well have been true, since he was possessed of very little to smell with.

'Keeva, go and find Olly some clean clothes,' said Anroth. 'Then go to my room and find me my mother's pelvis. Her bones were her dying gift to me. Bring them back with you. They'll help me explain how I saved Olly and his mother.'

He paused. 'Before you all go about your business, let me set you a riddle. How can it be that those who travel the furthest must first complete the shortest journey?'

Then, leaving them, Anroth went for a walk along the beach.

Down on the sand, Luchtain found a log washed up by the tide. With a thin, broad stone he scooped out a deep hole in the sand, then upended the log and held it vertically. Sirona packed the bottom with sand so the log stood tall and they finished the job with a couple of heavy stones around the base. Then they practiced with their slingshots, gradually moving further and further away from the target.

Keeva returned with the pelvis, which he left where they had been sitting. Walking down to the water, he gave the shivering, suitably scrubbed Ollathir a grey, hooded woollen shirt. Ollathir pulled it on, delighted to have acquired such a fine garment. It was designed to go down below a man's waist and, as a gown it fitted him perfectly; it extended right down to his chubby little ankles.

Ollathir was more than content to live the life of a swineherd, but now he was suitably robed, he wondered what it might be like to have trained as a druid. He decided to stretch his legs, not too great a challenge, then he wandered up and down the sand dunes, hoping he looked vaguely mystical and otherworldly.

To enhance his image, he thought he might make a wreath of oak leaves to wear on his head. But, finding no oak trees close by, he wondered if something fashioned from seaweed might prove a suitable alternative.

Then he noticed Anroth's mother's pelvis lying in the sand. Delighted with the discovery, he placed it on his head, wearing it like a crown, confident the bones conveyed a sense of dignitas and might even prove to be a portal to the Otherworld.

He continued on his mystical wanderings among the dunes and bestowed a blessing on a solitary seagull. Strictly speaking, the prayer was dedicated to the pig god Moccus and included pleadings such as,

'May your tail be forever curly.'

As he raised his hand in blessing, the confused bird flew off, doubtless perturbed at the prospect of going into a tailspin.

Returning from his walk, Anroth caught sight of Ollathir parading around with his mother's venerable bones perched jauntily on his head. Troubled by the swineherd's unintended irreverence he shouted.

'Olly, what do you think you're doing? Be careful with that, it used to belong to my mother!'

Peace was restored when Aine arrived with beer and freshly baked oatcakes.

After she left, Anroth turned to Ollathir and the novices.

'Answer me this,' he said. 'In all the many worlds of the Celts, how many goddesses do men say there are?'

Ollathir, eager to get involved, jumped in.

'Yosums,' he said, adding, 'nobody knows because there are too many to count. There are more than all my pigs and piglets, and I have problems counting them sometimes.'

'Perceptive" said Anroth.

'Yosums?' Said Keeva, 'I have never heard that word before.'

'No, you wouldn't,' Olly replied. You often hear pigs grunt it, when one wanders off, deep in the wild wood and finds a good foraging area.

Hearing the pig grunt, 'Yosums,' all the other pigs follow. It means plenty, or a lot.' Sensing there was fun to be had, Sirona asked.

'How do you pronounce it?'

Olly and Sirona repeated the word, until both were happy, however this also succeeded in misleading Olly's pigs. Without warning one of them, suddenly stuck its snout through the undergrowth, sniffing the air, closely followed by many more. A little piglet started running towards Keeva, slowly followed by a hostile, large sow, snorting and giving Keeva the eye.

'Do they bite?' he asked.

'The mother might, if you pick her little piglet up.' Sirona said, straight faced. Keeva decided to stand behind her, and whispered.

'They are very noisy.'

'That is why their language is called Pig-din.' She explained. Anroth looked at them, deciding things were getting out of hand. In a loud, guttural, and surprisingly authentic Pig-din voice, he responded.

'Guronk, Guronk, Yosums.' Disappointed, and grunting amongst themselves, the pigs departed searching for somewhere more fruitful to excavate.

'Amazing, Anroth' said a very relieved Keeva, 'you seem to be able to communicate with them very fluently.'

'Oh, I can understand Pigdin, much better than I can speak it.' Anroth said modestly, having just invented, 'Guronk, Guronk, Yosums'.

'It means there is no food here.' Confided Sirona to Keeva, having suddenly decided she was fluent in Pig-din.

Wishing to change the subject, Keeva, returned to Anroth's original question, about how many goddesses there were.

'It depends on how much of the world we see,' he said. 'Those like me with highly developed mystical awareness, will find goddesses in abundance.' Luchtain interrupted.

'You don't seem to have a very highly developed sense of mystical awareness, when it comes to pigs'.

He looked at Sirona, and continued, speaking.

'Every woman is in part a goddess.' Then came that magical moment he had been waiting for. Sirona looked at him and smiled

'Not all the time, Luchtain,' she corrected him. 'It depends on what she's doing. However, when a man makes love to woman Luchtain, then every woman should feel he has transformed her into a goddess.'

'Stimulating,' said Anroth.

Luchtain excused himself, and disappeared into the woods for a furtive but all-too-brief, naked roll around in the nettles, a commendable but doomed attempt to suppress his burgeoning desire. Sirona's mind was already elsewhere, wondering how Anroth had saved not just Ollathir's life, but also his mother's.

'Olly, when Anroth brought you out,' she asked, 'did he bring your head out first or by your bottom?'

Anroth laughed. 'I think we can assume he doesn't remember,' he said. 'Olly came out head first.'

'Anroth, Anroth, I think I've just worked out your riddle,' said Sirona excitedly. 'You asked how could it be that those who travel the furthest must first complete the shortest journey?'

Anroth nodded.

She leant forward and picked up a grey, rounded stone, about the size of a new-born baby's head. Anroth handed her his mother's pelvis. Taking it in her other hand, she held the stone above the upper rim of the pelvis.

'Olly's head must have got stuck up here somewhere,' she said. 'Because, below this bit, the passageway widens as the bones open up. So, if his head had just been able to move half the width of my hand through the rim of his mother's pelvis, Olly would have been able to escape his mother's womb.'

She turned to Luchtain. 'Do you see what I mean, Lucky?'

Luchtain nodded. He had never seen Sirona so animated and excited.

'This explains your riddle, Anroth,' she continued. 'The shortest journey we ever make in our lives is through the rim of our mother's pelvis, which is no more than half the width of my hand. It's the most important journey we'll ever make. Only those who make that journey will take the road to the rest of their lives and travel the furthest. Sadly, all the others will die with their mothers in childbirth.'

Anroth smiled with delight, his star pupil was excelling herself.

Luchtain looked puzzled. 'But, Anroth, that doesn't help us with Olly's mother,' he said. 'We've all seen warriors with their stomachs cut open and their bowels spilled out. None have lived to tell the tale. When Caesar was cut from his mother's womb, she died. How did Olly's mother survive?'

'Before we talk about how Olly was born, there are other important matters to consider,' said Anroth. 'Cure or comfort for those afflicted with sickness starts with your three most important gifts: the warmth of your smile when you first meet; the kindness and confidence in your voice; and your reassuring gentle touch. Sometimes these are enough to provide a complete cure.

'But, at other times, more drastic measures are required. Death in childbirth is a common tragedy. Many deaths happen because the baby, like Olly, is held fast inside. There are those who've resorted to desperate measures to save the mother. Some have tried chopping out bits of the dead baby from below, until what remains can fall or be pulled out. But this well-meaning brutality is a cause of great injury to the unfortunate lady, who often bleeds or festers, until death.'

Anroth picked up the pelvis. 'Olly's mother was of no great height,' he said. 'She laboured off and on for seven days and seven nights. She was dying in front of my eyes. None of us could be certain if the little body inside her still moved. For no particularly good reason, I believed Olly was still alive, so I decided to gamble everything on trying to save him. I went to my room and saw my mother's pelvis. There must have been some reason why she insisted I was given her pelvic bones. Could this have been the reason?'

Holding up the pelvis in front of him, Anroth continued. 'I studied the bones,' he said. 'As you can see, on either side of the curved bone at the back are two bones that complete the circle in front. They curve around, almost meeting in the middle. For a baby to pass into the circle of life, they must first pass through this circle of the mother's bones. It's a circle divided by the mystical number three. What more do we see?'

'It's hard to say now,' said Sirona. 'But it looks as though the side bones don't join up at the front. In the living, there may be a gap between them.'

'Because Olly said you'd cut his mother's stomach,' said Luchtain, 'we've been assuming you must have pulled him out from there. You didn't, though, did you? Somehow, after you cut through her stomach wall, you were able to free Olly so he could be born from below. Was your cut just at the bottom end of her stomach?'

Anroth clapped his hands in delight. 'Yes, Luchtain, well done,' he said. 'You're getting very close now!'

'This gap can't be a gap in real life,' said Sirona. 'Otherwise, we'd all wobble when we walked. In the living, there must be strong sinews binding the two side bones together.'

'Well, if that's true, then dividing the sinews might have allowed the bones to open up and my head to pass through the rim of the pelvis,' said Ollathir. 'You'd have avoided cutting into the guts because you'd have been below them. But there's another big problem…'

'Yes, very perceptive,' said Anroth.

' I often cut into pigs,' said Ollathir, 'and in the pig, just behind where those bones meet at the front of the pelvis, lies the bladder. I don't know much about anything other than pigs but I'm pretty sure my mother's bladder would have been in roughly in the same place as a pig's.'

'I don't think anyone would disagree with your impressive logic, Olly,' said Anroth, wondering where the discussion would go next.

'If you cut between those bones at the front,' said Ollathir, poking his little finger in the air, 'and divide the ligaments that hold them together, I fail to see how you could avoid cutting the bladder that sits just behind those bones. If the woman survived, she'd end up with the curse of the wet women, constantly dribbling urine and never able to rid herself of the smell of it. My mother was never a wet woman. Afterwards, when she walked, she rolled a bit from side, but had an active life, living full thirty years and more.'

'What do you mean when you say you have to cut pigs, Olly?' asked Luchtain. 'I didn't know they had problems birthing piglets.'

'No, they don't very often,' said Ollathir. 'The pigs I cut are already dead, their skulls smashed in with my mighty club when the kitchen needs pork. The bladder comes out when I clean the carcass.'

'Obviously, before I kill the pig, I express my regret and tell it how much I've enjoyed its company and that I hope it's enjoyed its stay in my pigsty. I express my gratitude to the pig for giving its life on behalf of all those who'll feast upon it.'

Anroth nodded his head. 'Inspiring and most comforting for the pig,' he said.

Ollathir bowed.

'Everything you've worked out so far is true, including what Olly's told us about the bladder,' said Anroth. 'With his mother, I'd come to the conclusion that our only hope was to somehow divide the ligaments that held the front of the pelvis together.'

'I did have one big advantage I've so far omitted to mention; this wasn't the first time I'd been faced with this tragic problem. On the previous occasion, when I cut between the bones, I badly damaged the bladder, which was full of urine. I'd left it too late. The baby was already dead and the mother followed shortly afterwards.'

Sirona closed her eyes.

'But I learnt a valuable lesson,' continued Anroth. 'As you've concluded, there are strong ligaments that hold the two bones together at the front, but these aren't connected to the bladder. To my surprise, I was able to push the bladder backwards. I realised it might be possible to use a red-hot blade to cut the sinews holding the bones together, without damaging the bladder behind them.

'I went to see the master blacksmith, who fashioned a short, wide, blunt blade with edges that curved backwards, so I could insert it between the bones in front, and the bladder behind them, thus protecting the bladder. And then, when I cut through the ligaments, my fingers and the bladder were out of harm's way.'

Sirona stood up, inspired by Anroth's teaching. She was wide-eyed, her cheeks all aglow, confident that one day, she'd be able to do what he described. She lay down before the druid.

'Anroth, imagine I'm Olly's mother,' she said, pulling up her robe so he could demonstrate on her bare stomach, above her undergarment.

'Take us through what you did from beginning to end.'

Luchtain grabbed Anroth's mother's pelvis and put it firmly down in his lap, hoping to disguise the fact that his modest little warrior was growing larger.

Anroth looked at Luchtain. Then he looked at the pelvis and, rolling his eyes skywards, recalled that his dearly departed mother always did like to be at the centre of things. He took his battered old wand from his belt and held it up in front of him.

'I plunged my knife blade into a fire,' he said, thrusting his wand deep into the sand. 'And, as I waited for it to heat up, I prayed to Bridget, the goddess of childbirth, and invoked her power to save the child.'

Anroth closed his eyes, deep in prayer. The listeners did likewise. The druid's fantastical tale had passed from the realms of storytelling to a reality they were all living through.

Ollathir was terrified and gripped Keeva's arm as he screwed his little piggy eyes tightly closed. It was as if his own life had never existed and, all these years later, he still had a vested interest in the outcome of Anroth's enthralling tale.

'When the blade glowed red,' said Anroth. 'I lifted it from the fire.'

It was a trick of the light but, as Anroth pulled his wand from the sand, it seemed to glow red-hot. He placed the tip low down, above Sirona's stomach, and made as if to cut deep into her skin.

Like the master storyteller he was, the sound of his voice and the power of his words were mesmerising. What the listeners saw in front of them changed from just a simple description to the reality of the event as it happened. Smelling Sirona's burning flesh, Luchtain grabbed Anroth's hand and shouted loudly at him.

'No, Anroth, no. Stop! You're burning Sirona. Anroth, you mustn't hurt her!' Tears ran down his distraught face.

Sirona stretched out her hand and squeezed Luchtain's. 'It's alright, Lucky, you were only dreaming,' she said. 'I'm fine. Hold my hand and let me dream with you.'

Anroth smiled, delighted the suppressed affection they'd shared for so long was at last asserting itself.

'The red-hot blade cut through the skin and down to the bone without much loss of blood,' he continued. 'I was able to move my fingers down behind the bones and push the bladder backwards. I'd carefully washed the blacksmith's blade in the waters from my well to purity it. I slipped it behind the bones to hold the bladder back. With the blade of my dagger reheated, I carefully sliced through the sinews that held the bones together until I saw them separate. The gap between them grew wider and allowed Olly's head to drop down into the pelvis.'

Ollathir opened his eyes. 'What happened to little me?'

Keeva rubbed his bruised arm.

'Well, Olly, we had to be patient,' said Anroth. 'Nothing much happened straight away. But eventually, your heroic mother got what had been denied her, the urge to push. Where she found the reserves of strength from, I'll never know. As if by magic, you came out naturally from below!'

Anroth held out his hands in front of him, as if cradling a new-born baby, and everyone clapped. Ollathir began to cry with joy and, soon, everyone was weeping. Sirona stretched her arms up, put them around Anroth's neck and dragged him down towards her until she could give him a smacking kiss.

'Oh, Anroth, I truly believed I was dying until you brought me back to life,' she said. 'No one can teach the way you do.'

'Thank you, Sirona,' replied Anroth. 'And no one knows how to show their appreciation the way you do!'

'It's quite all right for me to kiss you, Anroth,' Sirona reassured him. 'You're an old druid. Respectable, refined young ladies like me are allowed to kiss lovely old men.'

'Hmm, debatable but delightful, and less of the old please.' said Anroth. 'Thank you for sharing that with me.'

Sirona got up, dusted herself down and wiped her eyes. Her usual cool demeanour had melted. Holding her welcoming arms out wide, she skipped across to Luchtain and gave him an enormous hug, squeezing the breath out of him.

'I just love babies, Lucky,' she said. 'Come and give me hugs or something when you're so inclined, and stop all this rolling around in the nettles.'

Inviting, thought Anroth.

'My lord Anroth, my mother was a warrior, wasn't she?' asked Ollathir.

'She certainly was, Olly, a heroic lady,' said Anroth. 'And, much to our delight, you started giving out your squeals and grunts in no time at all. So, we welcomed the golden child into this world of ours.'

Sirona turned to Ollathir. 'That was wonderful, unbelievable,' she said. 'And all these years later, here we are on this beach, remembering that magical time. Anroth, can we make Olly an honorary little druid for the day?'

Anroth laughed. 'Olly, you're unanimously elected to the status of a novice druid!' he said.

Ollathir was overcome with emotion. 'I just don't have the words to thank you for what you did for my mother and me, my lord,' he said. 'Today has been the best day of my life.'

'It was a privilege to be allowed to do it,' said Anroth. 'One of my life's greatest joys has been to watch you grow up.' Luchtain and Sirona decided to resume practicing with their slingshots or, at least, find an excuse to be alone.

'I've never seen you cry before, Sirona,' said Luchtain.

'Nor I you,' she said. 'I never realised how protective and caring you are, Lucky. I find it hard to believe anyone feels that way about me. When I lived at home, not once did my father praise me. It didn't matter what I did to try to please him, he never loved or respected me. When you become a druid, people show you respect and love.' Luchtain nodded.

'Anroth is my pretend father,' she continued. 'He's always showing how proud he is of me, making me feel good about myself. He lets me love him as a father. You make me feel good about myself, too, Lucky. I hope you always will. It'd mean so much to me to imagine someone special like you cared for me.'

'You may never know how much I care, Sirona,' stammered Luchtain.

Sirona laughed, then picked up some seaweed and threw it at him. As she ran off, she shouted, 'But I might want to find out!'

Luchtain chased after her as she ran towards the dunes. He had never seen her in such high spirits before, nor felt so happy himself.

5 Pig-Headed

A ship rounded the southern headland and landed further down the beach. Crimthain and his men walked towards it, carrying the provisions he had ordered earlier. The gift of freshly cooked food would be well-received by the crew.

The captain welcomed the marshal aboard. They sat in the bow, and ate and drank, deep in conversation. A flock of gulls settled on the sand beside the ship. Some chased the retreating waves back to sea, but mostly they clustered by the tide line and made a few deliberate steps, hesitated then moved on. Occasionally, one landed on the ship until a sailor shooed it away.

'Why do the sailors do that, Anroth?' asked Keeva.

'Sailors live uncertain lives,' said Anroth. 'They're superstitious. It's a bad omen when a seabird lands on your ship, even worse than a bird flying into a house. They believe the sound of gulls crying is the voices of lost souls searching for a home. A captain won't willingly sail with ghostly passengers, seabirds on a ship bring bad luck and foul weather.'

'Is there anything good about gulls?'

'We can learn from the gull, for it tries to see things from different points of view,' said Anroth. 'Watch the way it observes everything around it, then walks away and studies it all over again. Once it's made its mind up, it moves fast and takes what it can.' Keeva's brow furrowed.

'Be like the gull, Keeva,' said Anroth. 'Hesitate and don't assume your first thought is necessarily the answer to a problem. Consider alternatives. It's better to be a gull than someone set in their ways with a rigid mind.'

'But, Anroth, we Celts are never narrow-minded,' Keeva protested. 'We see things from many points of view. We respect even the simple opinions of the ill-educated, such as Olly, and we don't expect everyone to believe what we know is true.'

Anroth smiled. To him, it seemed as though Keeva was the ill-informed one and Ollathir might be just the man to re-educate him.

Sirona and Luchtain approached. Breathless, Sirona flopped down on the sand.

'Sorry we were away so long,' she explained breezily. 'We were looking in some rock pools. Luchtain showed me a sweet little winkle I'd never seen before. We went further than we expected.'

'Gratifying,' said Anroth. 'Did you discover anything else of interest?' Keeva was looking suspicious.

'Yosums,' added Sirona brightly.

Luchtain put his hand on Keeva's shoulder, looked him in the eye, and nodded.

'Lucky Yosums.' Feeling he was in danger of being made a fool of, Keeva fell silent.

'What have you been talking about?' Sirona asked.

'Well, Keeva was implying – if I understood him correctly – that Celts are tolerant and broad-minded,' said Anroth. 'And I was about to explain to him that none of us are as tolerant as we think. We rarely use our intellect or powers of reason when we give an opinion.'

'But surely,' said Luchtain. 'The whole point of your teaching is that we should use our minds in many different ways?'

'True,' said Anroth. 'What I'm suggesting is that, when we express an opinion, we're often using our powers of reason to hide our inbuilt tribal prejudices. There are three words used interchangeably: "believing", "feeling" and "knowing". But they have three entirely different meanings. From this mixture and confusion of thought, we form our imperfect opinions. When we discuss the secrets of Druidism, I notice the three of you react to the same information in different ways.'

'But, Anroth,' said Luchtain. 'How we think can't be that complicated. When you give us a problem, we consider it and, depending on how we feel, we come to a conclusion.'

'Indeed, you do, and most of the time I feel the same way as you do,' said the druid. 'The important word you used there was "feel". To feel something is a very sloppy way to come to a conclusion, but it's also the commonest. Thought processes are by no means as simple as you suggest.'

'How should we think?' asked Sirona. 'My mind doesn't work like Luchtain's. I prefer to work things out based on what we know. I'm just interested in the facts.'

'Sirona has introduced another variable, which she believes she can be certain of,' said Luchtain. 'This might be entirely different from what Keeva thinks he can be certain of. How can either know what they're certain of is true? I'd like to rely on facts, but there's so little in life we know with any certainty. I fall back on my feelings.'

'Well, that surprises me,' interrupted Keeva. 'I'd assumed we all approached things in roughly the same way, but we don't. I believe everything you teach us,

Anroth. I know what you tell me is true. I dislike doubt. I need the certainty that belief brings.

Recently, I've found the gods have blessed me with visions, and now, when I make my mind up, I trust my visions. In fact, Anroth, I think I find deeper meaning in druidism's ancient ways than you do.'

'Think very carefully about your convictions, Keeva,' said Anroth. 'Sometimes minds like yours can split in two. The deranged imaginings of a demented mind and mystical, religious experiences are hard to tell apart.'

'You haven't told us how you come to your conclusions, Anroth,' Luchtain pointed out.

'Well, like you, I respond mostly to my feelings,' said the druid. 'The big difference is that, as you get older, the more self-doubt creeps in. When time allows, I prefer to let my opinions mature slowly.'

'What's your point, Anroth?' asked Sirona. 'More often than not, we agree. What difference does it make how we make our minds up?'

'As far as we're concerned, none,' said Anroth. 'The way I teach wouldn't work if it weren't based on freedom of thought. But, just for a moment, imagine you were compelled to believe what I teach you. I say that because most religions are taught that way.'

He took a deep breath. 'I, for one, would be living a lie. You can be certain of one thing – mark my words well, Keeva – and that's some of the things I believe to be true will one day be proved to be in error. Don't be too dogmatic about belief.'

'You are inspired by the gods,' said Keeva calmly. 'Therefore, you should insist we believe all your teaching.'

Anroth was stunned. Keeva had brushed aside the pointed remarks he'd aimed at him. This was new and unsettling but, given the freedom of thought he encouraged in his novices, it should not have been a surprise. As if to rub salt in the wound, Keeva concluded, 'When I become a renowned teacher like you, my novices will have to believe everything I teach.'

'What a shame you can't confess doubt and uncertainty will always go hand in hand with religious teaching,' said Anroth. 'Every credo, every statement of religious belief should start with a confession. I confess I can never know the truth or otherwise of any of my beliefs with certainty. Take Christianity, I admire Jesus, but the Christian bishops who follow him are guilty of misleading their flock.

Jesus made no mention of most of what they teach – claiming we're guilty of sin before we're born, angels, the creation of saints, the veneration of relics and many other practices. Why do the church elders leave no room for debate or doubt? Intolerance of any point of view but their own has replaced love as the touchstone and driving force of that repressive religion.'

The three novices looked at him.

'Until they adopted Christianity, not even the Romans tried to enforce their beliefs,' continued Anroth. 'Far from it. They welcomed gods from many altars. When I look into the future, I'm gloomy.'

'In the centuries to follow, religion will be responsible for more bloodshed and evil than any of its dubious virtues. I remind you, Keeva, to have a care. Don't be seduced by reassuring certainty; embrace the humility of uncertainty.'

Sirona tried to lift his mood. 'Well, Anroth,' she said. 'I think, feel or believe – whichever one you prefer – that tolerance and common sense will prevail.'

'I hope you're right,' said the druid. ''The difficulty is that all societies depend on a degree of conformity to maintain their tribal identity. Life's outsiders, like Dancer, who live by their own rules in the shadowlands, rarely see old age.'

'Religion is one of the many banners of tribal identity, but it has little to do with religious belief, its strength is based on its ability to denigrate the beliefs of others, creating a sense of superiority.'

Keeva protested loudly.

'But, Anroth, you must accept tribal and racial prejudice is an essential part of our identity. Where would society be without the mistrust and suspicion of everyone other than our own? Society would break down. Trust has to be earned and always doubted.' .

'If you had to settle a dispute between two farmers on the common boundaries of their land,' said Anroth. 'Would you try to clear your mind of any preconceived prejudices?'

They nodded.

'Why then, when looking at the wider world, are you incapable of detaching yourself in the same manner before passing judgement on a society?'

''That wouldn't make sense, Anroth,' insisted Keeva. 'What some call prejudice is the truth based on our experience of the world. Like you, Jesus the person and his life speak to me, but I know that only druidism holds the secrets of religious truth. Why then would I accept his inferior views?'

'It isn't a question of being narrow-minded, Anroth, it's a question of survival,' said Sirona. 'We know the Picts are scheming and treacherous, and to regard them any other way would be naive. They'd rape me as soon as look at me.'

'Do you think Keeva could rape you?' Anroth enquired.

'Of course not, he's a virtuous man.'

'But doesn't it occur to you, Sirona, there are Picts like Keeva who'd never rape a woman?' asked Anroth.

Keeva was incensed at the thought he could be Pictish-born. 'That's a cruel insult, Anroth,' he said. 'I'm a true Celt, proud to be born into the tribe of the Brigantes. I believe the Picts are nothing more than Celts, in their most primitive, degenerate beginnings. Show me a Pict who can claim to be as virtuous as we are. '

There was an awkward pause, then Anroth spoke to Keeva sharply. 'You believe - you believe. How many times must I tell you? This is not the same as knowing something with certainty. Are you incapable of accepting that, among the Picts and the Saxons, there are good, virtuous women and men?'

Luchtain, tried to take the edge off the argument, but only made matters worse.

'Take your sea captain friend, who has just landed. Everyone knows he's devious and untrustworthy. Give him half a chance and he'd fleece you like a lamb.'

'Have a care, Luchtain,' warned Anroth, spitting out the words. 'I first met Frii long before you were born. More than once, I've trusted him with my life. Bite your tongue when you're as bigoted and ignorant as you are. Never repeat malicious gossip, lest one day you become the victim of it.'

He paused and composed himself.

'I was trying to discover if you're capable of detaching yourself from your prejudices,' the druid said. 'Can you look at life from the sea captain's, or a Christian's or a Pictish point of view?'

'No,' the novices chorused. 'That would never do.'

There was an awkward silence.

'How would it be if I were to walk down there and take over the bargaining with the sea captain?' asked Anroth. 'I might fleece him. Would that be right?'

'Of course,' said Keeva.

'Why?'

'Because you'd be looking after our interests and taking advantage of him in a fair manner,' replied Keeva. ''That's different from him taking advantage of you. And what about a simple little man, like Olly here? He isn't intelligent enough to look after himself. He doesn't have our skills of bargaining, argument and debate.'

'Well spoken for the common people,' said Ollathir, who was getting increasingly infuriated by Keeva's assumption he wasn't very bright. He was a man of status, a swineherd. Seething, he decided to bide his time.

'Is it so important to go against our instincts, Anroth?' asked Luchtain.

'Yes, because your present attitude means you can't see outside your own small world,' said the druid. 'You have no vision, no interest in even trying to find a balance or to discover the truth about the world outside.'

Very deliberately, Anroth had provided Ollathir with the perfect opportunity to attack Keeva.

'Well,' said Ollathir. 'I think you're all being very silly. I can argue things any way I choose, depending on my mood, and I'm in the mood to beat any of you in an argument.'

'Are you sure?' asked Sirona. 'After all, you've spent your whole life communing with swine, not novices with well-educated minds.'

'Patronising,' said Anroth.

'Now then, little sister,' said Ollathir. 'We'll have none of your nonsense. I'd like to see you getting into an argument with a pig, for I fancy you'd come off second-best. At least I do a proper job. All you do is sit around feeling self-important. When have you ever butchered a pig?'

He wagged a stubby little finger at her reproachfully. 'And don't you go insulting my little children or the goddess Bebhionn will surely turn you into a pig for your pains.'

Sirona put her hands to her face and opened her eyes wide, feigning fear and alarm. 'Oh, Olly, forgive me,' she said. 'I've no wish to become one of your pigs. To make amends, will you send for me the next time you slaughter a pig and teach me how to butcher it?'

'You have my word upon it, little sister,' said Ollathir. 'Just as with a pig, nothing in life should be wasted. Whatever we're taught usually comes in useful one day. So, Keeva, in the spirit of goodwill and understanding, I'm going to give you the honour of looking after my pigs while I spend a day with Sirona and Luchtain, being taught by my lord Anroth.'

'Me and Luchtain agree,' said Sirona.

Luchtain laughed, delighted he'd been promoted, and was now part of 'me and Luchtain'. Keeva looked decidedly uncomfortable.

Anroth nodded in agreement, he was enjoying himself. There was nothing he liked more than to stir up an argument between them all, and he was well aware that, in spite of the impression Ollathir gave of being ignorant, this was far from the truth.

Early in the morning, Anroth would often walk along the beach. And, if Ollathir saw him, he would come too. The druid and the boisterous dwarf made an unlikely couple, but they regularly went for long walks together.

The swineherd had a lively, enquiring mind, which often provided a stimulating start to Anroth's day.

Keeva adopted a sympathetic but patronising tone. 'Olly, I respect you,' he said. 'But you must concede you don't have our knowledge or understanding. It's not your fault, you're ignorant. To prove this, I'll set you a challenge.'

Anroth looked at him, knowing Keeva was heading for a fall.

'What happened five hundred years ago, Olly?'

'Wasn't that when the noble Celtic heroine Queen Boudicca attacked and destroyed three Roman cities,' said Ollathir. 'And gave orders that her warriors should hack all the women's breasts off and worse, then burnt everybody to death?'

'No, that's not important now,' snapped Keeva. 'The Romans exaggerated what happened. You can't trust anything they said.'

'Well, I'm just a simple swineherd,' said Ollathir. 'But that sounds like a bit of an atrocity to me.'

'Under the circumstances it was entirely understandable,' said Keeva. 'She was provoked. Don't you know anything? It was the Romans, on the island of Anglesey that committed the atrocity. An atrocity that'll live on in all our minds till the end of time, I'm sure you'll agree?'

Feigning ignorance, Ollathir shook his head. 'No. Not unless you tell me what happened.'

Keeva glared at Ollathir; his normally pale face flushed. Why didn't Olly know? His sense of self-righteous indignation at what the Roman army had done to the Celts hundreds of years before was an important part of Keeva's highly selective cultural identity. It gave him a feeling of moral superiority whenever he talked about it.

'Five hundred years ago, the Romans cornered the Celts on the island of Anglesey,' he said. 'The armies were evenly matched and, on an open plain beside the sea, they joined in battle. One thousand virtuous and holy druids, and their wives and children, looked down from the surrounding sacred mountains, beating their breasts. They howled incantations and cursed the cruel and ruthless Roman army.'

Ollathir raised his stubby little hand. 'Sorry to interrupt, Keeva,' he said. 'But, just to be certain, would you say my lord Anroth does a jolly good job as a druid?'

The apparently irrelevant interruption infuriated Keeva. 'Yes, yes, Ollathir, of course Anroth does an outstanding job as a druid. May I continue?'

'And, sorry Keeva, there's just one other little point I'd like to get straight in my mind,' said Ollathir. 'Do you think the one thousand druids, or their wives or their children, might have been throwing stones at the Romans? Just to distract them a bit? Or even using slingshots like we do?'

'No, that's nonsense, Ollathir,' said Keeva angrily. 'Can I please get on with my story?'

'Yes, of course, sorry Keeva, it was rude of me to interrupt. But, on the other hand, how can we be certain? As you know, there's a lot of shale and loose stones on the sides of mountains. It'd be tempting to throw some, wouldn't it? I know I'd have thrown some stones at them. I'm just a simple swineherd, not a virtuous, holy, young druid like you, but I don't suppose anyone really knows five hundred years later. But please do carry on, it's a jolly interesting little story. Thank you very much for telling it to me.'

Sirona couldn't resist adding to the argument. 'I think Olly has a point,' she says. 'Anglesey is in Wales. Only this morning you were telling us you don't trust the Welsh.'

'Yes, but I would have done five hundred years ago, Sirona,' retorted Keeva testily. 'Will you be quiet? I'm trying to broaden Ollathir's mind.'

'Or narrow it,' said Luchtain.

Keeva turned on Sirona and Luchtain, his voice trembling. 'Sometimes, I really do wonder why Anroth bothers trying to train you as druids,' he said. 'Where's your sense of reverence for our past and all the injustices we've suffered? Show me respect when I'm teaching.'

Ollathir's face was a picture of innocence, save for the mischievous glint in his piggy eyes. He turned to Sirona and said in a loud whisper.

'Oh, he's teaching now, I am lucky. May I say, little sister, how honoured I am to be part of your sophisticated teaching. What was it you accused me of earlier, Sirona? Oh yes, I remember. You said I spent my life communing with swine, not novices with educated minds. You'll be delighted to know I feel completely at home with yours and Keeva's educated minds.'

Keeva, visibly shaking, shouted at Olly. 'The Romans were victorious, but then came utter sacrilege!' he said. 'They slaughtered every druid, woman and child. How can you defend the Romans' behaviour, Olly?' There was silence until Ollathir's little voice piped up.

'I'm still a bit bothered about what the druids were actually doing during the battle,' he said. 'With all their leaping up and down and shouting at the Romans, rather like you shouting at me, they might have dislodged some rocks and started a great, big landslide. They might have killed lots of Romans.'

'Rubbish, of course they didn't cause a landslide,' said Keeva. 'Don't you know anything? It's against our druidic beliefs to start landslides.'

This was news to Anroth, who raised his eyebrows and shook his head in disbelief. Ignoring him, Keeva continued. 'I've spent many years training to be a druid. I know what I'm talking about. Admit it, the Romans' behaviour was indefensible. You should show me respect!'

'Ah, respect,' said Ollathir. 'Why is it that those who are so quick to demand respect, never show it when discussing other people's points of view? Earlier in the day, you asked me the best way to retreat from our enemies. We even collected three large piles of stones for you to use in your slingshots. Are you now suggesting that, if someone attacked us tomorrow, you would just leap up and down in the woods, shouting out incantations?

You're gullible, Keeva. You only believe what suits you. The druids don't deserve any sympathy. They only have themselves to blame for what happened.'

Keeva was furious at this insult. A swineherd should know his place in society. Anroth insisted that he continue.

'It was the druids' fault we lost the battle,' said Ollathir. 'The Romans did us a favour when they killed them.'

'How dare you insult the memory of so many good men!?' shouted Keeva. 'Idiot Ollathir, you're a pig-headed oaf!'

There was a hushed silence. Keeva had gone too far.

'Your powers of observation as regards to what I look like never cease to amaze me,' said Ollathir. 'I'll take that as a compliment.'

Anroth smiled.

'In the whole of the Kingdom of Northumbria, we have fewer than ten druids,' continued Ollathir. 'You've already told me you think Anroth does a good job. Then there are you three novices. Some of the other tribal leaders have their own druids and some claim Dancer is one. I've never heard anyone complain we have too few.

'You told us the battle was a close-run thing, but it never seems to have occurred to you to ask what on earth one thousand druids were doing on Anglesey? I say there were too many of them, they had too much influence and not enough to do. In the end, their wailing and incantations counted for nothing. Not one Celtic life did they save – not even their children's, their wives' or their own.

'Anroth once told me that, in the land of the pharaohs, the high priests enjoyed even greater status than druids. They became more powerful than the pharaohs themselves. Vast cities and temples were built in honour of their gods and the wealth of the kingdom was drained away on futile enterprises. As the high priests rose in power, the strength of the army declined. Their enemies fell upon them. Cities, temples, golden statues, pharaohs and high priests were all swept away.'

Ollathir looked to Anroth. 'Do I have that right, my lord? It's not my intention to mislead Keeva.'

Anroth nodded.

Ollathir turned back to Keeva. 'Imagine Keeva,' he said. 'Instead of one thousand druids wailing from the mountains, there had been only ten, but another nine hundred or more fighting men: those with slingshots, archers, spearmen, horsemen and well trained warriors. Tell me Keeva, who would have won then?'

Keeva sighed.

'Too many high priests with too much influence drain a society of its strength and purpose,' said Ollathir. 'Yes, Keeva, I say the Romans did us a favour. Since those days, we have enhanced the status of our warriors while continuing to respect the wisdom and skills of the druids.'

'You forget that my father was a warrior and taller than you. He died defending Northumbria. It was not my good fortune to know him, nor him me, but don't look down on me because my body is small. I have feelings, Keeva. My heart is as big as yours.'

Sensing the little man was starting to get upset, Anroth stepped in.

'Quite right, Olly,' he said. 'You're as fine a man as any of us. One day you'll meet a good woman and have many children.'

Ollathir wagged his finger at Keeva. 'Fools delude themselves that religion is the solution to every problem,' he said, repeating what Anroth had frequently told him on their morning walks.

There were things Anroth had told Ollathir when they were out walking that he would never dream of teaching his novices. They were the things Anroth only wished he could tell his two sons. He regularly passed the time of day with both of them but, for very different reasons, he was unable to express his inner thoughts to either.

Anroth was immensely proud of Ollathir, and loved him as his dead father would. The miracle of his birth, his life and the bold way he took on the world inspired Anroth to always strive his utmost to save the sick and dying. He loved Keeva, but feared the young man's mind was splitting into two.

Keeva's views merely strengthened Anroth's opinion there were no circumstances in which the religious classes were fit and proper people to govern. Given their rigid and dogmatic minds, they were incapable of listening to or acting in the wider interest of the populace. Even worse, if they were given the chance, they would force their views on everyone and stifle all other opinions.

Anroth counted himself fortunate to have found a religion that informed and inspired him. He did not assume druidism was any better or worse than other beliefs. It was in his nature to question everything. Truth was in the eye of the believer, not in the nature of belief. The common people were best protected and ruled by noble overlords –strong men, like Midar.

Realising Keeva was intent on prolonging the argument, Anroth stepped in. 'Sirona what four great talismans did the tribe of Danu take to Ireland?'

'They took the Spear of Lug, the Shrieking Stone, the Cauldron of the Dagda and the Sword of Nuada,' she said.

'Excellent. By way of a reward, let me set you all a riddle to solve before next we meet,' said Anroth. 'If perfect truth is perfect knowledge and perfect wisdom is believing you will never completely know or understand anything, what can you ever be certain of?'

Looking across to the Wave Wanderer's vessel, he saw the negotiations had concluded and the marshal was leaving. Anroth strolled down the beach to renew an old friendship.

6 The Wave Wanderer

Frii was a tall, powerfully built man, bronzed and weathered by wind and sea. In his cap, he wore a twig of hazel as proof against the storm, jumping down from the deck, he called out to Anroth.

'I've brought presents for you, fish oil from North Africa and a sack of wheat. We will leave them on the deck for now. I could do with stretching my legs. Fancy a walk?'

The two set out, enjoying one of life's simplest pleasures – a long walk on a beach with an old friend. Behind them, a strengthening south westerly flicked up the white tails of invisible cloud horses, cantering across the sky.

'Leaving tonight, my old friend?' asked Anroth.

'Tomorrow will be soon enough,' said Frii. 'It was a long, backbreaking voyage. Thanks to you, my men are all well-fed. Resting up somewhere safe will do them the world of good.'

'Good,' said Anroth. 'Because, tonight, you're going to have a nice, relaxing Celtic evening. You're coming to a banquet as my guest.'

As they rounded the northern promontory, they saw, shimmering in the distance, Lindisfarne in all its captivating beauty. Frii stopped to admire it.

'That magical island is the first thing I look for, when out at sea, Anroth,' he said. 'I spend my days sailing the restless waves. Seeing something so tranquil and timeless, brings peace to my restless mind. How fortunate you are to have a time and a place like this to call your own. Is this why you always seem so in harmony with life? Or is it something to do with being a druid? Are your beliefs as mysterious and confusing as men say?'

'Well, I suppose druids are like sea captains, Frii,' said Anroth. 'You never meet two who are quite the same. Is druidism confusing? No, not really. But, like the high-priest class of any religion, we're very good at making it mysterious.'

Frii smiled.

'At its simplest, it's about how we allow our lives to become part of what you were just talking about, the beauty that surrounds us,' continued Anroth. 'It brings with it an awareness of the Otherworld – of goddesses and gods as they reveal themselves through the animals and plants, the mountains, streams and rivers that run through our lives.'

'Yes, well, that all sounds pretty straightforward then,' retorted Frii, bewildered.

'It's best not to think of us as priests,' said Anroth. 'We're more a mixture of things: healers, law-givers, philosophers, storytellers, teachers and advisers to the high chieftain. The mix depends on what society asks of us.'

'Different times and places have differing priorities. I've just been discussing it with my novices. Most religions demand that their followers believe a fixed set of truths. Druidism is something I feel rather than believe in; it's a sense of spirituality. Anyway, tell me your news, I've heard nothing for months.'

"There's plague in Constantinople,' said Frii. 'And Totila the Ostrogoth has ended Byzantine rule in Italy. They say he plans to take Rome. Trade is unpredictable, with so many Saxon vessels further south.'

Anroth nodded. 'Are you trading with the Saxons?'

'No, not now,' said Frii. "They'd love to get their hands on my ship. Fortunately, they spend as much time fighting among themselves as they do attacking others. The word is they're buying up metal ingots. And the last time I was over their way, I noticed they'd felled a lot of trees.'

'Boats, weapons, that sounds like more trouble on the way,' said Anroth. 'Well, if they're going to make a move in our direction, it needs to be before the winter closes in. Can I ask you a great favour?'

'Anything.'

'Midar is a powerful and resourceful ruler, and we're reasonably secure. But if, one day, you sail in and find this place deserted, will you come back the following festival of Lunasa? If any of us are still alive, we'll be on Lindisfarne. There's a safe anchorage hidden on its northern shore. Please don't mention this conversation to anyone. Now we'd best be heading back.'

'You're right to worry,' said Frii, nodding. 'I've never known a time in my life when our world was so unstable, with one uncertainty heaped on another. If Northumbria falls, I'll come for you at Lunasa.'

Now the banquet had been prepared, a sense of calm had settled on the great hall. And, as the light faded, the torches made from Mullion stems, mounted on the walls, were lit.

Aine stood by the kitchen door, watching Cliona introduce Danu to the chieftains' wives. They showed her the food they had brought and laid it out on the tables. After the introductions the guests clustered in groups, eager for each other's news. Danu looked a little bit lost. Aine went across to her, greeted, by a chorus of admiration from the guests, anticipating another memorable feast.

Aine took Danu by the arm.

'Come with me, my girl, I need your help,' she said.

They went over to a narrow, heavily shuttered window.

'We need to open this,' said Aine. 'So, the Carnyx player can bellow out his war horn to welcome in the warriors.'

As they pushed back the heavy shutters, Danu saw the three princes waiting outside. The tallest one looked towards the window and smiled broadly, giving her a wave. Danu drew back and stood to the side of the sill.

'He's good-looking,' she whispered.

'That's Dian, the youngest,' said Aine. 'Sometimes I think he'll never grow up.'

Danu leant forward and studied the princes. Might one of them be able to give her what she was searching for? Then she remembered the advice of Damona, she with the horned serpent that heals. She had warned Danu never to become enchanted by the capricious allure of royalty, for it was improbable that it would provide either her or her lover with happiness.

'Who's the eldest, Aine?'

'Goibniu, the broad-shouldered one in the middle,' replied Aine. 'But, in his heart of hearts, all he really wants to be is a master blacksmith.'

'You mean he'd rather be a blacksmith than a warrior?'

'Oh yes,' Aine said. 'The red-hot alchemy of turning stone into iron and, as if by magic, into weapons has a powerful mystical meaning. None, save those of royal blood or druids like Anroth, are held in higher esteem. He prefers beating a sword into shape to battering someone's brains out in battle.'

Danu smiled.

'He's always inventing things, like new beers,' continued Aine. 'He calls his latest creation Dragon's Blood Barley Beer. It's too strong for my taste, my favourite is the one he flavours with heather, when it's in full bloom.'

'What's in those bags hanging from their waists?' asked Danu.

'Oh, trophies they've taken during the cattle raid,' said Aine. 'We'll get to see them at the banquet.'

'I like the bag the smaller one has.'

'That's Nuada'. 'Yes, it looks to me as if it's made from crane skin. If you ask him, he'll give it to you. He's very generous. A word of warning, though, my girl. If you've got your eyes on him, you'll have me to answer to if you don't treat him kindly.'

Danu laughed. 'You didn't need me to help you open the window,' she said. 'You just wanted to warn me off Nuada!'

Aine laughed and gave Danu a hug. 'I wasn't warning you off,' she said.

Cliona sent for Midar and his champion, Lugh, and gave orders that the princes were to assemble with the warriors outside the great doors. As Midar entered, his eyes lit up with delight, and he lavished praise on his queen and the assembled company.

Outside, Anroth bent down to pick up something half-buried in the dunes, holding it under his cloak then walking with Frii to join the gathering.

The Wave Wanderer's life had become increasingly dangerous wherever he traded, there were so few people he could trust. Tonight, though, was just what he needed: a relaxing evening among friends.

He had never been to a Celtic banquet before, but he knew the Celts' hospitality was legendary. He couldn't believe his luck. Anroth introduced him to Goibniu, Nuada and Dian, their enthusiastic beerful embraces, gave him a sense of belonging.

Goibniu arranged his brothers on his left and the sea captain at his right hand, with Anroth stood next to him. The five stood in line and faced the great doors, awaiting the call of the carnyx. When the mighty battle horn bellowed its welcome, the doors swung open. The three princes stood proudly in all their finery and, behind them, the clan chiefs, warriors, blacksmiths and the brew master, all lined up in honourable assembly.

The princes had longed for this night. Their fighting prowess, courage and status as proven warriors would at last be recognised, not just among the clansmen of the Brigantes, but among all the nations and tribes of the Celts. No other Celtic tribe had three princes, brothers who had trained together and fought as one. Kingdoms would fall before them. Nothing stood between them, their dreams and destiny.

Before they took their places, they bowed deeply to the high chieftain and his queen. Goibniu presented Frii; and Cliona, smiling graciously, thanked him for his gifts of fish oil and wheat, and welcomed him as an honoured guest.

Midar took his seat at the centre of the table, facing the great doors, with his back to the fire. At his right hand sat his champion, Lugh; at his left his queen. Beside the queen sat Danu then, next to her, Anroth and Frii. Behind Midar, his favourite hound Oengus lay stretched out on the warm hearthstones. Anroth slipped Danu's spear out from beneath his cloak and laid it under his chair.

The tables groaned with bowls and the platters of food Cliona's friends had brought for the guests to consume before the banquet proper began. Never had there been a finer choice: nuts, berries, oatcakes, bread to dip in salted duck's fat and herbs, cheeses, mushrooms mixed with mountain thyme, pickled eggs, smoked herring and mackerel, salmon, crab and lobster.

Danu was happy beyond all imagining, wide-eyed with delight, all the birthdays she'd never celebrated had come as one. Eagerly she chatted to Anroth, the queen and the princes. Each time she addressed Anroth, she would say,

'My lord Anroth'.

'On nights like these, Danu, we don't stand on ceremony,' he said eventually. 'I prefer the nickname the warriors have given me.'

'What might that be?'

'Snout!' he laughed. 'Just call me Snout, Danu.' She smiled.

Behind Goibniu, Nuada and Dian, the massive doors swung closed. It took two servants to lift the heavy crossbar and slot it into place. Goibniu introduced Frii to his latest heady brew, Dragon's Blood Barley Beer. The sea captain stretched back in his chair, drinking deeply.

Suddenly, the massive head of Midar's mighty hound Oengus appeared between his legs. It wedged him between the table and his chair. Frii felt rather than heard the powerful vibrations resonating from deep within the beast's great chest. The hound's lips rolled outwards in a scowl as he gave an ominously long and threatening growl.

'What's he doing, Snout?' asked Frii.

'Trying to work out if you're friend or foe,' said Anroth. 'He's probably a bit hungry, too. No one has thrown him a bone yet.'

'What do I do?'

'He likes to nibble nuts, Frii.'

'Nuts! Whose nuts?'

Anroth stretched across the table and pulled a large bowl, carved from a silver birch, towards him. Scooping up a handful of hazelnuts, he handed them to Frii.

Oengus smelled the nuts and his massive maw opened. He didn't seem to be the type of dog who'd nibble anything. What had been a muted growl grew louder. The beast's moist, malodorous breath enveloped Frii's perspiring face. Cautiously, he put two of the nuts on Oengus's tongue. They disappeared immediately. Oengus's growl grew louder. Impotent, Frii looked at Anroth.

'He thinks you're hanging on to his nuts,' Anroth explained.

'Me! Hanging on to his nuts!?'

'Just give him the lot,' said Anroth. 'Don't take your hand out of his mouth too quickly. Sudden movements upset him.'

After what seemed an age, Oengus slowly emerged from the far side of the table, wagging his tail.

'Oh look, he likes you,' said Anroth. 'Mind you, you can never really tell. It seems to take a long time for his thoughts to go from his brain to his tail.' Frii smiled weakly.

'Try the wine, my friend,' said Anroth, replenishing Frii's drinking horn. 'Goibniu's beer is stronger than you might think.'

'You know, Snout,' said Frii. 'Seeing Oengus's huge head suddenly rise up like that without a body attached gave me a fearful shock.'

'Yes, it's distressing,' said Anroth. 'But, on the other hand, how much more disturbing would it have been to see a headless body rise up and start running around.'

'Unless it was a chicken,' suggested Danu, who had found Frii's discomfort very funny.

She had been observing the queen, hoping to emulate some of her airs and graces; and, speaking in a somewhat affected voice, she enquired brightly,

'And tell me, Frii, does one have a dog on one's boat?'

The queen looked around the great hall; her life was laid out before her. Gaiety was there in all its clothes and bright colours; and, for a while, her guests drank the wine till their cups were emptied and only the dregs remained. If fine buildings and magnificent rooms might experience feelings or emotions, she thought, then the great hall was in a state of welcoming contentment and joviality that summer's night.

Cliona often recalled her life in frozen moments, remembrances that others had lost. They were a private source of pleasure, a distraction from the male-dominated topics of conversation she had spent so much of her life listening to. In the summertime, when Midar and her sons rode out on campaign, they were a means of keeping the company of old friends as she sat on the headland, looking out to sea; reassuring reminders of how kind and wholesome life had been.

She looked across at Danu, animated and so full of life, chatting away, asking Frii about his many voyages, or talking to Snout and the three princes. It was hard to believe, that same morning, she had been a waif and stray, blown in from the sea. For Cliona, Danu would always be that laughing, happy young woman who sat beside her on the night of the heroes' banquet. The days of Danu's all too brief and happy youth were rapidly drawing to a close.

7 The Goddess

Midar, the old warlord of the Brigantes, sat back in his chair. Soon everything he had dreamed about but had never quite believed in, would come true. For centuries, the restless borderlands had been a place of warfare. When that creeping contagion, Rome and her empire, had tried to subdue them, the emperor Hadrian, seeking respite from the loss of so many of his legionnaires, had drawn a line in the sand and built a wall.

This had divided the historical domain of the northern Brigantes, weakening their unity and power.

Hadrian had brought with him, young saplings of his favourite tree, which he planted. It was, the only good thing that Hadrian ever did. For it was a handsome tree with dense foliage. The tree prospered, and as its spinning seeds fell, carried by the wind they travelled all around; covering the ground throughout the land. And so, it spread from shore to shore, Hadrian's elegant Sycamore.

Not until the Romans had finally abandoned Britain could the Celtic border tribes in the east reassert their old tribal identity. During Midar's long reign, Northumbria had been blessed with a golden age.

In the early years of Midar's rise to power, he had forged alliances, fought many battles and united the disorganised tribal lands of the Brigantes. Many bold warriors had fought beside him and he had made eight of them his tribal chieftains, honouring them with land

and trusting them to rule large areas of his far-flung kingdom. Divided up by Northumbria's many rivers, their territories surrounded Midar's own large estates and rich pastures. He kept the greatest warrior of them all close by; his most trusted, friend and champion, Lugh.

The proud father looked across the table at his three sons, Goibniu, Nuada and Dian. Seeing Dian's pathetic little moustache, he suppressed a smile. Even without it, he knew his son was still the greatest warrior in the room, for Lugh's strength – like his own – was waning.

Like many a warlord grown old, he reflected on how he'd lost his appetite for further battles. Now, in the autumn of his years, the noble ruler planned a new era in the life of the Brigantes. A cautious man, he would take things slowly and relinquish his kingdom by passing it on to his sons.

Goibniu was a born leader, preferring peacetime pursuits to war, but once he was provoked proved a fearsome enemy, whose men would follow him anywhere. With Dian as his champion, the defence of the realm was assured.

Then there was his second son, Nuada, who was a brave warrior even though he hadn't been blessed with his brothers' strength. Midar had realised long ago that Nuada was possessed of a thoughtful, creative mind like Anroth's, seeing things his brothers missed. If they were wise, they would listen to his counsel, just as he'd always listened to the perceptive druid.

Resting on the table in front of the princes were three bulging leather bags. Midar wondered what trophies they had brought back from the raid. Seeing his sons together reminded him there was something else in their blood he did not recognise in his own – a cold, ruthless violence they revealed whenever they fought together. He assumed it came from their mother and the royal house of Rheged.

He looked across at Cliona, the refined model of propriety. Could it be, that beneath the veil of charm and sophistication she wore, lay hidden a pitiless, vicious streak she might one day reveal?

Watching his sons return from the raid reminded him that he, too, had once been young, thirsting for the violence and brutality of battle. Finding love with Cliona had changed him. Rarely did he draw his sword in anger, loath to waste his greatest assets, his warriors and their ponies, in avoidable conflicts or dubious enterprises. So, over the years, he had fostered the myth that he and his warriors were invincible, riding forth with no more than thirty men.

Danu was excited beyond belief, overwhelmed by the sights, and smells of a Celtic banquet. She drank it all in, savouring so many rich flavours. She looked up into the rafters, to the great bow that glowed in the firelight and swung slowly in the warm air. But then, without any warning, subtle changes to her body began to occur. At first, she barely noticed as her breathing grew deeper.

'Tell me about the great bow, Snout,' she said.

'It was a gift to Midar from Gaul,' said Anroth, turning towards to her. 'Dancer brought it back when he returned from his travels. He claimed it was magical and yielded its strength to no mortal. Many have tried, but no one has successfully strung the golden bow.'

'Did Dancer travel far?'

'Some say he went all the way to Galatia and lived with the Galatian Celts,' said Anroth.

'You Celts certainly get around,' said Frii. 'Not even I've been to those far-off lands. Who's Dancer?'

'It's a long story, Frii. Another time, another night…'

As Danu stared up at the bow, she felt the muscles over her shoulders and neck grow stronger, her breathing become slower and deeper. Her shoulders grew broader, her true nature was asserting itself. A malevolent humour was slowly seeping into the great hall. Something or someone was trying to steal what remained of her precious childhood. If the changes continued, it was only a matter of time before those present would notice.

Desperately, she tried to cling on to what was left of her childhood, to immerse herself in everything around her – the queen, Anroth, Frii, those outrageous bragging, boisterous princes. Discovering the life of a child, she had been thrown into a wonderful exciting world. Now, she was being dragged back into her old life, a shallow, one-sided, world, where all she ever got was adoration, worshipped on the basis of what others believed they needed. She'd realised something had always been denied her, the most precious thing of all: that uncertain exciting love, mortals shared.

Unaware of the battle Danu was fighting, Cliona looked around the great hall. Everyone was eagerly waiting for Midar to announce the Hero's Portion and for the meal proper to begin. This was not just the night when the three princes became recognised as chieftains in their own right, but it was the moment when the queen would relinquish all authority over her sons. There would be no more sharp words or attempts to influence them – a somewhat fruitless exercise of late – for, as her sons would take command of Midar's warriors, any critical comments from her about their failings would risk undermining their authority. Discipline and lives could be lost. In future, no one would expect her to deal with the princes' unpredictable antics. She was more than content just to play the part of the perfect hostess, a queen conveying a sense of gentility to the proceedings.

When the great boar was well-roasted, Midar stood and all the men rose with him as he toasted the Hero's Portion. The banquet master cut into the lower back of the beast and, removing the burnt skin and fat, ran the blade down the side of the beast's spine and placed the meat he cut onto a golden platter, in the middle of the table.

Midar called out his sons' names and asked if any other warriors laid claim to the Hero's Portion. None did. Goibniu stood up and untied the leather bag on his belt. Out of the bag he drew a large black war bonnet. Mounted on top of it was a raven with its hinged iron wings outstretched. Holding the helmet tightly, he punched the air three times. As the raven rose and fell, its wings flapped. There were gasps from all around. They recognised the helmet, for it belonged to Balor, the Pictish high chieftain. Everyone roared and banged the tables. Lifting the helmet once more and turning in a full circle so all could see it clearly, Goibniu laid claim to the Hero's Portion.

Whilst his elder brother was displaying his trophy, Nuada loosened the thongs keeping his bag closed. As the mouth of the bag opened, a malevolent miasma surged out and began to swirl around Goibniu. It assailed his senses, intent on insinuating dark and murderous feelings into his noble young mind. Danu's throat muscles tightened. Only she had noticed the source of the evil pestilence, for it was invisible, odourless and tasteless.

Nuada rose and drew a wondrous, sparkling black bowl from his bag. The highly polished vessel was fashioned from the mystical stone Obsidian, forged in a far-off land of ice and snow, and vomited out from deep inside the belly of an ill-tempered volcano. In the flickering light, the Black Obsidian bowl flashed brighter than any blade. Nuada held it high and turned it around, showing all the assembled guests its mirrored base. Those who looked, saw their reflected face.

Anroth's eyes widened in disbelief.

'The Darkness, a nemesis by any other name,' he hissed under his breath. 'He's stolen Birog's Black Obsidian.'

The high chieftain Balor ruled the Kingdom of Gododdin with his sister, the Black Druidess Birog, Daughter of the Unforgiven Dead. She was a shape-shifter that few had ever seen – not even Anroth. But just as Anroth used his magical cauldron as a portal to the Otherworld and for good, so Birog, mistress of the occult, used the Black Obsidian for all manner of evil. With the Black Obsidian in her hand, she sowed pestilence throughout the land.

Holding the Black Obsidian above him for the approval of the baying crowd, Nuada had no idea of the forces he had unleashed.

A shiver ran down Frii's spine, for only he had seen that sinister, menacing stone before. No sea captain would carry it as cargo. Those who tried rarely made landfall. His hopes of a relaxing evening were heading into stormy waters. Remembering a Snoutism, 'When things are going badly, they can always get worse', he drained his drinking horn.

Anroth looked up into the rafters where his cauldron hung, its golden panels embossed with magical symbols and images of the gods. For years the cauldron had helped protect them. It had been a constant struggle to maintain the fragile harmony of their uncertain lives.

And Lunasa, like every festival, brought with it further uncertainty. He had sensed it, that afternoon.

'Long runs the hare, there's evil in the air'. Whatever was unfolding had yet to run its course.

As Nuada held Birog's bowl above his head, the virulent miasma – the distilled essence of every evil curse Birog had ever conjured up from her spellbinder – continued to flood out over its rim. It seeped slowly down Nuada's arms and cascaded onto the table, where it squirmed its way over the surface and wormed its way across the floor. The secret of Nuada's procreation and Anroth's sanctifying ceremony when he was still a baby were to prove blessings. He was impervious to the evil influences others were soon to suffer.

The miasma wheedled its way towards the queen, its invisible tendrils seeking out susceptible minds, capable of subverting even Cliona's refined sensibilities.

Nuada sat down, there was a subdued silence. Dian staggered to his feet and fumbled with his bag before pulling out an aged, handsome head. He held it up. Blood and water dripped from the severed neck. Frii looked up into the rafters, only to discover more severed heads.

'More wine?' enquired Anroth, trying not to show any outward signs of the mounting sense of horror he felt within.

'Yes, fill the horn to the brim, Snout,' said Frii. 'In fact, just give me the jug.'

Lugh turned to Midar. Their disciplined minds protected them from the influence of the miasma, but even they were not impervious to the shock of seeing the head of their old comrade.

'Bres, they killed Bres,' muttered Lugh.

In their youth, Midar, Lugh and Bres had ridden together, undefeated, renowned for their courage. Many years before, under her evil spell, Bres had married the enchantress Birog and became Balor's champion. Forever the honourable man, he was forced to live his life in a dishonourable place. The fortunes of war had divided them, but the bonds forged by men of arms are rarely broken.

'You remember, Midar, all those years ago when he went to marry the witch Birog?' said Lugh. 'We made a solemn promise that, whatever happened in the years that followed, one day we'd meet again, riding, into our last battle. I never imagined we'd meet like this. He died without us.'

Midar put his head in his hands.

'Yes, Lugh, we have always believed, the three of us would leave life together in a golden twilight of myth and legend. But Bres is waiting for us now. Slaughtered by my own blood. Our last battle may not be so far away.'

'Balor will never forgive the princes for the death of his champion,' muttered Lugh. 'Nor Birog the death of her husband. This means all-out war.'

'When the banquet is over, let's speak to all our chieftains,' said Midar. 'We'll get them to send urgent messengers to the clans. I need as many warriors as they can muster. We'll assemble two days from now in the Valley of the High Waters above the waterfall.'

There was a hushed silence and they looked up.

Danu had climbed onto the table. Her feet astride the Hero's Portion, she looked down on the princes. 'I claim the Hero's Portion,' she said, her voice cold, and distant. There was a moment's silence followed by bellows of laughter from the princes.

'You? A hero? You don't even have a weapon,' sneered Goibniu giving her the evil eye. Malevolent feelings raged within him.

'Get down off the table before I cut your skinny little legs off!' Danu looked through him and stretched out her arms. The guests gasped as the golden bow floated down into her hands.

'I can string this bow,' she said. 'And, unless anyone else can, I claim the Hero's Portion.'

'Bows and arrows? Slingshots? Are you pretending these are real weapons?' taunted Goibniu as the malign miasma coursed through his veins.

'Warriors don't fight from a distance. Show me your sword and shield! Show me your axe!'

'Are you refusing my challenge?' said Danu. 'I am the bow, you are the bowstring, bend me to your will.'

Goibniu snatched the bow from her. He trapped one end between his feet and gripped the other in his hands. Using all his massive strength, he tried to bend the bow but failed. Taking the bow back, Danu called out, 'I claim the Hero's Portion.'

'I'll show you a real weapon,' shouted Goibniu.

Before anyone had time to realise what was happening, Goibniu had drawn his sword. In one movement he slashed wildly at Danu's legs, cries of consternation reverberated round the room.

Just as the salmon rises from the river in autumn, Danu's body ascended and Goibniu's deadly blade stroke passed harmlessly beneath her. Like the salmon, she seemed to hang in the air, - even when her feet alighted back on the table, she was taller. Her shimmering, blood-red cloak no longer fell to her milk-white feet, all could see, the hem now hung nearer the knee.

Confused and alarmed, Nuada rose to his feet.

'You may be able to string the bow but even if you did, where are your arrows?' he said. 'Goibniu's right. Warriors and heroes don't fight from afar. You are no hero Danu, sit down please, and hold your peace; sit down and let's enjoy the feast.'

Anroth reached beneath his chair and picked up Danu's spear.

Meanwhile, queen's mind was in the thrall of the menacing miasma, she decided to break her own strict rules. Disturbed by all she had seen, she decided to intervene. But when she made as if to stand, Anroth firmly stayed her hand.

As the Hero's Portion grew colder, jealousy and anger smouldered in the princes' hearts. Was their moment of glory, their coming of age as warriors, to be upstaged by a windblown waif from the sea, taken in and adopted by their misguided mother? Danu handed Nuada the bow. He tried but failed to string it, and sat down again.

The miasma swirled around Dian. He had failed to notice Danu was changing from a slim young girl into an awesome goddess. Unexpectedly Dian blew his own trumpet, the way nature – but not Dian – intended. Gripping the table, he staggered to his feet and wagged his finger at Danu.

'Where were you when we were on the raid?' he bellowed.

Before he could drive home his point, due to the significant number of onions he had consumed earlier that day, he was interrupted. Without warning, he delivered a discharge of downwind of truly heroic and epic proportions. Just for a moment, it broke the tension.

Goibniu could not contain a warrior's loud belly laugh.

'Well, that concludes tonight's discussion as to who deserves the Hero's Portion,' he announced. 'Dian may not be able to play the Carnyx but, friends and warriors, I defer to my youngest brother. He deserves the Hero's

Portion, for he's the only man I know that can play the battle horn through his backside without ever picking it up.'

The warriors roared with laughter and banged the tables. The palpable tension that had consumed the room seemed to ease. That should have been the end of the matter, but it was not to be. Forces more powerful and uncontrollable than Dian's bowels began to grow stronger. The great hall pulsated with a feeling of foreboding, an immense and expanding malign force.

Nuada stared into the base of the Obsidian and saw the mirror-perfect image of Danu towering above him. He realised the evil forces that threatened them were in some way related to his trophy. So, he returned it to his bag, then gripped the leather thongs, pulled them tight and knotted them, hoping to contain the evil.

It was too late. Dian appeared to be still in the grip of battle fury, devoid of all judgement and suffused by violent, uncontrollable belligerence. Furious that everyone was laughing at him, he grabbed a double-headed Saxon battle-axe from the wall. His head pounded and his nostrils flared; snorting like a stallion looking for a mare. He steadied himself and leant against the table. There was silence, the cowed guests fearful of his next move.

Crimthain sat unnoticed with some of his warriors at a table set back in an alcove beside the chimneybreast. Puzzled by the violent behaviour of the princes and their strange symptoms, he wondered if they had been poisoned – though he was at a loss as to what the poison might be. Then some of his men started choking.

He had heard rumours about a new, lethal choking poison that had been concocted by a putrid little gnome who held sway in the faraway lands to the east of the

Scythians. Rumour had it the meddlesome misfit was even worse than Birog and would never be satisfied until he had every land on earth at each other's throats.

Crimthain's thoughts were interrupted as he watched Dian, who slowly raised his head. The prince's eyes bulged and there was a sinister leer about his lips. Like a cornered wild boar, his body bristled with untamed aggression, he quivered and slavered like a rabid dog. In a frenzied state, he swung the Saxon axe and aimed at Danu's feet.

Just as the soon-to-spawn salmon jumps the waterfall, Danu soared upwards into the air and lifted her feet gracefully out of harm's way. With an ear-splitting crash, the heavy axe head split the long table from end to end and embedded itself deep into the wood. Such was the sound and fury of the blow that all the plates, the table and the seated guests jumped into the air as one.

Danu's feet floated back down astride the blade. By now, the hem of her cloak was above her knee. She stood there taller than the princes three.

Cliona's sincere desire to avoid rebuking the princes in public was about to suffer a severe setback. In all the hubbub, all the din, Dian had committed a mortal sin. The queen, all flushed with fury in her face, leant across the table space. Giving Dian a withering stare, considered hitting him with a chair. Grabbed him forcibly by the hair, decided to whack him fair and square. She slapped his face as hard as she was able. Slapped him for mutilating her banqueting table.

Goibniu groaned. 'When in public, we behave with dignity and decorum.'

Shocked back into reality, Dian looked at his mother, dismayed he had split asunder her cherished table. Once the deed had been done, Cliona crashed back in her chair, horrified by her behaviour. She turned to Anroth.

'I'll never forgive myself,' she said. 'I've brought shame on Midar and embarrassed the princes.'

'It wasn't you, Cliona,' said the druid. 'It was Birog, using your body. She draws her strength from the Black Obsidian. Don't be ashamed, your outburst has given Dian his sanity back.'

Seductively, the goddess Danu stroked the body of the bow. Though it swelled in strength, it became compliant to Danu's desire. It yielded as she arched the bow and slipped the noose of the bowstring into its groove. She had relieved the wood of its strength and independence, taken it into her own possession. All her power was harnessed within the bowstring. She stretched her left hand out behind her and took her spear from Anroth.

She turned and smiled at the three princes, but there was cold anger in her eyes. Loading her spear, in the angled groove at the bow's base, the goddess drew back the bowstring. A hushed silence fell on the hall. Nuada realised the power and poison of the Black Obsidian was undiminished. There was only one thing that might restore peace and harmony. He leant across the table.

'Snout, any moment now there'll be blood on the floor,' he said. 'I've an idea. I won't be long, please entertain the guests.'

Nuada slipped out to the kitchen. Without a moment's hesitation, Anroth rose to his feet and held his arms in the air until the room fell silent.

Danu relaxed the tension on the bowstring and listened. She was still in her goddess nature, but she desperately hoped her human side might yet return.

'My lord, my lady, friends and guests, we are honoured with the company of my old friend the Wave Wanderer, Frii, whose fine wine we are drinking tonight,' said Anroth.

There was wild applause, and plates and tankards were banged on the tables in appreciation.

'As you know,' continued Anroth. 'It's the long-standing tradition of the lords of Northumbria that, whenever we have a sea captain for supper, we always ask them if they wish to say a few words.'

'I prefer the pork; sea captains are too salty!' someone shouted.

There was even more laughter and violent banging of tables. Cliona's face froze, for she was perturbed by the thought of how much damage her guests were inflicting on her tables. Her eyes fixed on the deeply embedded Saxon axe, and the split in the table which ran from end to end.

Turning to Frii, who was not fully fluent in the Celtic language, Anroth explained what he had just said, and told him to say whatever he felt like in his native tongue. Anroth would then translate.

By now, much taken with the drink, Frii could have spoken all night. He was a down-to-deck sailor, who believed in telling things the way they were, straight from the shoulder. They would have been better coming from slightly higher up.

'Tonight, I was looking forward to a nice, relaxing evening,' he said. 'But a howling gale on the high seas would have been more relaxing than the way things have gone so far. You people have a real problem with heads, or the people you meet do. I am surprised that boar behind us, still has its head on – or me mine. For the first time in my life, I've lost something, my appetite.'

Anroth translated. 'The captain thanks you for your hospitality,' he said. 'He is very much looking forward to his supper. He says the ladies here are the most beautiful he has ever seen.' There was rapturous applause. Emboldened by his reception, Frii continued.

'If there's one thing that gives me the willies more than snakes, it's disembodied heads. 'But earlier tonight, out of nowhere, the high chieftain's hound from hell came up at me from under the table.

Snout told me it likes goolies then accused me of grabbing the dog's bollocks. Its breath smelt so foul that the fleas fell out of my beard. But there are no hard feelings, they landed on the dog. They're my gift to you all.'

'The captain says he's honoured to be allowed to transport the high chieftain's hunting dogs to Gaul,' translated Anroth. 'He has many rats on board his ship and he hopes that, on the voyage, the hounds can kill the rats, but not the ship's cat!' Frii sat down to more rapturous applause and banging of tables.

In the kitchen, Nuada found Aine dismembering a suckling pig. She looked up at him and smiled as he gave her a hug.

'Do you want a bite?' she asked.

'Aine, I've a very big favour to ask,' he said. 'When I was a baby, you used to sing me lullabies. Then one night, when I was getting older, you asked me what I wanted to hear. So, I asked you to sing whatever song meant the most to you.'

Aine smiled.

'You sang the most beautiful song I'd ever heard,' continued Nuada. 'I've never heard it since. Come with me to the great hall and sing your song once more. Sing it to the goddesses and the gods. Sing it for those now gathered at the feast.'

Aine dutifully put down the pig and followed Nuada. He turned towards her, held her shoulders gently and looked into her eyes.

'Aine, promise me that whatever happens in there, whatever goes on around you, you won't stop singing,' he pleaded. 'Sing your song right to the end.'

He kissed her softly on the cheek. 'Promise me, Aine.'

'I promise,' she replied, returning his kiss.

They entered the great hall just as Frii sat down and Anroth concluded with his final fictitious translation. Nuada turned his chair around to face the great doors and told his brothers to do the same. He sat Aine down on his chair.

Addressing the room, he simply said, 'As befits this special occasion, I want to share with you the most beautiful thing I've known in my life.'

Aine rose from the chair. She walked forward, ignoring everything around her. She seemed to be looking through the great doors.

8 Aine's Song

Aine wiped the fat from her hands onto her apron. Her unkempt, long blonde hair fell about her shoulders and her plump face was flushed from all the cooking. Aine, all alone, artless and sloppy, started to sing.

She sang in Goidelic, a Celtic language that only she, Danu and Anroth understood. The song started in a light-hearted, whimsical manner, and her voice was as pure and sparkling as a mountain stream – it tinkled down and relaxed in ebbs and flows, as each sequence was repeated with increasing emphasis. It stopped and rose again, then sank into a slow, swirling movement; each passage echoed with greater depth.

There followed a sense of urgency and alarm, moments of emptiness descending to despair, as the repeated sequences faded away. The pace quickened as the words galloped forth from her mouth, and rose and circled around, before her firm cadences moved the song off again then made it stand still.

Her singing was so beautiful, even her silences were pure music. The listeners in the great hall were spellbound. The sound of her singing knew no boundaries, it could not be constrained by the walls or doors of the banqueting hall. To the listeners, it seemed so exquisite that the whole world should stand still and listen, paying heed to something lost and beautiful.

Danu remembered the day Aine sang about, and she thought of the spell she had cast and how she had destroyed the love of a man and a woman. She had blighted their lives forever. It was too late now to return what she'd taken so long ago, and she was filled with remorse. She wanted the world to know the spiteful side of her seemingly sweet nature, so she drew back the bowstring to its limit. As she did so, she called out, 'Ibar!'

She watched the flight of the spear as it found its mark, in the centre of the door's crossbar. The bar shuddered and bounced upwards, then fell to the floor.

'Athibar!' called out Danu, and the spear flew back into her hand.

Midar watched, realising how easily Danu could become a lethal instrument of war.

Aine sang on, but now her timing changed. The song became wistful, lilting and natural as though it was a conversation. She was reaching out to the world beyond the great hall and, for the first time, she displayed the full richness, vibrancy and power in her voice. She wasn't singing to the enthralled listeners in the hall, but to another world where others had once listened to a song of lost love from long ago.

Aine willed the doors of the great hall to swing open and, slowly, they did so. Standing outside, lit by the half-light, was a three-horned stag and, beside him, snorting and pawing the ground, was the pure white bull Chillingo with his saviour, the alluring Celtic goddess of healing Sirona. Beside the bull stood Dancer with Snibo the raven on his shoulder. And, before him, with its long, thick bristles running along the length of its spine, was the enormous, blue-black wild boar Formael.

In front of them, the great god Cernunnos sat naked on the ground, with an elegant set of antlers sprouting from his head. His eyes were closed, his back was straight and his legs were crossed beneath him as if in meditation.

In one hand, he held a golden wand around which two snakes with human heads – one black and evil, the other silver and virtuous – coiled and uncoiled themselves. Sometimes they were apart, at other times they wrapped themselves around each other. In his lap sat the mystical blue hare of the winter. Many other creatures of the forest were gathered around them.

Dancer saw Danu and realised who she really was, for only a goddess could have strung the golden bow, the gift he'd given so long ago. Noticing Aine, his heart beat faster.

Singing her song to its conclusion, caressing, languid and low, she saw her lover from long ago. Then there was silence. It seemed to go on forever. To the audience, it became part of the song and they strained to drink in more of that breathtaking silence, the most beautiful sound they'd never heard. Across the void, Aine and Dancer shared a smile.

When the crowd eventually erupted with applause, Aine turned and looked back at Nuada. She had taken him back to his childhood. His eyes were closed and he was lost in a state of rapture, recalling the day Aine had sung her song to an adoring audience of one little boy. Life had been so beautiful and simple then. He opened his eyes in time to catch her eye, and he reached out towards her.

Aine turned her attention to the table and gathered together some empty bowls to take to the kitchen. One beerful young buck, protesting his undying love, grabbed her around the waist. When he refused to let go, she carefully put down the bowls and gave him a playful punch on the jaw, sending him sprawling.

Looking at all the wild animals standing outside the door and the weird, naked old man whose dignity was only hidden by a fluffy blue hare, Frii was alarmed.

'I hope Snout doesn't think he's having that chap sit next to me,' he muttered.

He was about to close his eyes, hoping the whole thing would go away, when Snibo took off, flew into the great hall, and landed on Frii's shoulder. The horned god Cernunnos opened his eyes. He raised his golden wand to the goddess Danu by way of greeting.

'Cernunnos!' gasped the watchers within.

'Cernunnos!' shouted Frii. He didn't know what it meant, but he hoped it would afford him some protection from the evil predations of the forces of darkness that now gripped his shoulder.

Anroth rose and took the golden plate containing the Hero's Portion, then walked over to Cernunnos. He bowed and set it down at the great god's feet.

Oengus, Midar's magnificent hound, followed Anroth. He lay down and stretched out beside Cernunnos.

Anroth turned to look at Midar, who nodded. Cernunnos kissed the tip of his golden wand and the two snakes disappeared within him. He handed the wand to Anroth.

Anroth presented his battered, old wand to Dancer, then bowed once more and returned to the table. Slowly the doors swung shut as the visitors departed, taking Oengus with them. He was too perfect a hound for the world of mortal men.

Peace and harmony had been miraculously restored to the great hall. The purity of Aine's song had destroyed the evil miasma, just as Nuada had hoped. Scarce believing what they had seen, the guests rose to their feet and cheered in homage to the goddess, welcoming Danu to the tribe of the Brigantes. She smiled and raised her arm to salute them. She climbed down from the table and handed her spear to Anroth.

'An unusual weapon, Danu?' he said.

'I borrowed it from a friend.'

'I fear you may well need it.'

The conversations resumed from where they'd left off, and the jovial chatter and sense of wellbeing returned. The roast pork and venison were duly carved and served, and the banquet began.

Danu pulled the Saxon axe from the table and placed her hands across the gap. She called out 'Athibar' and the long wound in the wood magically healed over. The polished surface was as good as new.

'Oh!' exclaimed Cliona. 'It's not as bad as it seemed.'

Believing what they had witnessed was some clever illusion dreamed up by Anroth, the guests all rose and applauded once more. Frii turned to the Druid.

'I'm baffled,' he said. 'Was everything I witnessed before Aine came in just entertainment or something more sinister?'

'It had nothing to do with entertainment,' said Anroth. 'What you observed was the lethal power of the black witch from Gododdin.'

'I'm beginning to understand your problems,' said Frii. 'Come the next festival of Lunasa, you'll find me moored off Lindisfarne.'

Though Frii was delighted Oengus had taken his loyalties elsewhere, he was perturbed by the bird perched firmly on his shoulder. Doing his best to make friends, Snibo affectionately pulled Frii's earlobe with his beak. If the superstitious sea captain had not tried to swipe the bird off, Snibo would never have inflicted such a deep gash and caused such profuse bleeding from the sea captain's ear.

Matters were not improved when the bird dropped like a stone onto the table between Anroth and Frii's plates. Cocking his head to one side, he seemed to be sizing up a particularly succulent piece of pork Frii had hoped to impale on his knife. The sea captain wondered if wringing the infernal bird's neck would be considered a departure from the social norms of Celtic table manners.

Something dripped down onto his plate and Frii put his hand up to his ear. When he brought it down again, he saw it was covered in blood, which he now realised was running down his neck. Trying his best not to be noticed, he licked the blood off his hand.

'Apart from a few nuts,' he muttered, 'I still haven't had anything to eat. Now I'm reduced to drinking my own blood.' Anroth tore a strip of pork from his own plate and fed the bird, then lifted it onto his shoulder.

'Snibo just loves pork,' he explained.

Taking a large chunk of bread, Frii rammed it against his bleeding ear and bloodied neck, and started to eat with his other hand. 'This pork is excellent, Snout,' he said. 'By the way, that chap with the horns, the one you gave the Hero's Portion to earlier, does he come around often?'

'No, I've never met him before,' said Anroth. 'We normally deliver our offerings to him at the sacred grove. It's the first time he's called here to collect.'

'Who is he?'

'Cernunnos,' said Anroth. 'He's one of my favourite gods.'

'It was nice of him to give you his golden wand, wasn't it?'

'The way things are going around here, he may well think, I'm going to need it,' said Anroth.

'You Celts aren't like the Greeks, are you?' said Frii. 'You don't stick your gods and goddesses on top of mountains. You have a very informal relationship with them.'

'Yes, we don't draw sharp distinctions between ourselves and the world of nature, as I was explaining this afternoon,' said Anroth. 'Our many goddesses and gods use animals, rivers, trees, all manner of things to cross the boundaries between their world and ours. Sometimes we do too. And it's not just for us; it's yours to share with us Frii. Brief, magical visionary moments of awareness are there for everyone.'

'Standing alone in the bow of my vessel, far out at sea, I have times like that,' said Frii. 'But though I experience a reawakening of my sense of being, I never have any new insights into my life.'

'Sometimes, Frii, that renewed sense of awareness provides solutions to problems you thought insoluble.'

Frii removed the soggy, bloodied bread from his ear and put it down it beside his plate. Snibo dropped to the table and picked it up, then flew up into the rafters. As the evening wore on, occasional showers of breadcrumbs fell into Frii's hair and over his shoulders. 'Great,' he thought.

'All I need now is for that thing to do what I've been trying desperately not to do all evening.'

'Do you ever run into Pictish pirates?' asked Nuada, leaning forward.

'Not if I can avoid it,' said Frii. 'They rarely leave their own waters. Mostly they just take inshore voyages up north, but sometimes they raid as far away as Gaul. They have a large fleet, and they're excellent sailors.'

'So far, they've left us alone,' said Nuada. 'But there's always the risk of attack.'

"They won't want to provoke too much trouble so close to home, Nuada,' said Frii. "They know how much damage you can do. However, Northumbria has a long and exposed coastline, so you're certainly vulnerable. Looking at things from the seaward side, your coastal settlements are impossible to defend.'

Balor's notorious fleet of sea raiders was one of the reasons he had grown so powerful. They were fearless and wild, regarded as the finest seamen ever to sail the seas. Part fishermen, part traders and part pirates, they were a law unto themselves. Sometimes they sailed alone, at other times they sailed out in fleet formation.

Their craft were unlike the traditional, broad, almost flat-bottomed, Roman-style vessels. Longer in length, thinner in the beam, they sliced through the waves, out sailing anything sent against them. They would carry cargo or travellers, and even warriors and raiding parties, for any warlord prepared to pay for the privilege.

What they were most feared for, were their random attacks on the settlements and vessels of other tribes. When times were lean, and the shoals of herring and mackerel deserted the sea, the Picts were not above taking hostages to ransom or to sell as slaves.

Balor ignored these nefarious enterprises, for he had profited handsomely from them, and, as the pirates' strength grew, so did the size of their fleet. Balor had built his kingdom on the power, wealth and influence the pirates brought him.

'Be good, lest the Pictish pirates take you,' mothers would warn their children.

Once Midar had ended the official part of the banquet, the guests circulated freely. Anroth asked

Goibniu to look after Frii. He whistled Snibo down from the rafters onto his shoulder, put the bag containing the Black Obsidian inside two others and tied each bag tightly. Then, taking his novices with him, he headed for his room.

'Keeva, go and find Aine,' he said. 'Ask her to make up two sets of provisions for a three-day ride. Be discreet, though, and ask her to bring them to me here. Then go down to the boats and find Danu's coracle. Take it to the Lake of the Dark Waters and stow it in my cave. Arm yourself, tread carefully and stay there a couple of hours. Get back to me before dawn.'

He handed the Black Obsidian to Sirona. 'Under no circumstances are you to open this,' he said. 'Take it to the circle of the Three Kings in the valley of the Rede. Bury it deep in the centre of the ancient circle. Take my pony. Luchtain can use one of Nuada's fresh ponies. And, Luchtain, take a sword and a couple of spears with you. Speak to no one on the journey. You leave tonight.'

On the walls of Anroth's room, alongside quivers of arrows, hung a number of bows he had hand-carved. He picked up a small quiver filled with short arrows and tapped it on Snibo's beak until the bird grasped it, then flew from his window. He handed a larger quiver of arrows to Sirona. 'Which bow would you like?' he asked.

When she had selected her weapon, he said, 'Luchtain, which roads will you travel?'

'We'll avoid the roads,' said Luchtain. 'The sky's clear enough tonight to use the stars. We'll travel southwest and cross the Glendale causeway, then we'll carry on until we reach the old hill fort above the river Breamish. We'll rest the ponies by the cup and ring rocks.'

'What else will you avoid?' asked Anroth.

'The wild white cattle,' said Luchtain. 'We'll follow the River Coquet west and climb to its headwater, then we'll cut through between the Hog's Lair and Bloodybush Edge. We'll turn south into the Redesdale Valley and follow the Ramshope Burn down to the river Rede.'

Anroth turned to Sirona. 'Where then?' he asked.

'We'll follow the river Rede east and cross to its southern side where it joins the Chattlehope Burn,' she said. 'Then we'll ride along the southern ridge of the valley until we reach the Three Kings.'

'Will you ride together?' asked Anroth.

'No, Luchtain will ride ahead,' she said. 'I'll carry the Black Obsidian and shadow him from a distance.'

'And how will you return?'

'We'll cross back to the north side of the valley,' she said. 'Then take the road to the old Roman fort at Bremenium. We'll rest up there for a while then head for home.'

'Why not take the easier way down the Redesdale Valley?' asked Anroth.

'Because there's a settlement lower down the valley,' said Sirona, 'where the Burn of the Otter joins the Rede.'

Aine came in and gave them both their provisions, she hugged them and left. Satisfied they had memorised the many trails they'd ridden together and were well-versed in how best to pass unnoticed, Anroth took them to the stables. Before they left, he took Sirona to one side and handed her two hazelnuts.

'Take these with you,' he said. 'On your journey homeward, when you've put many miles between yourselves and the Three Kings, rest and build a fire. Throw the hazelnuts in the flames and watch to see if they burn together.' Sirona hugged him and laughed.

'Even in these hazardous times, you remain a mischievous, romantic old druid!' she said. 'We'll have plenty to do before then, but I promise not to forget. I know what the answer will be anyway.'

'Safe journeys, and return as soon as you can,' said Anroth. 'One last thing, Sirona. If anyone challenges Luchtain, what will you do?'

'I have witnessed the evil and chaos that which I am carrying can cause. Until the Black Obsidian is buried deep in the ground, Celt or Pict, I'll kill anyone who stands in our way.'

With the moon and stars to guide them, Luchtain and Sirona slipped into the forest. Lugh, Midar's champion, rarely revealed his feelings, but the wanton slaughter of his old friend Bres had been a blow to the pit of his stomach. He was heavy with the drink, overcome with emotion. As the great hall emptied – he rounded on Dian.

'You disgust me,' he said. 'Have you any idea what you've done? Bres could have taken you any time. If you hadn't looked like your father, he would have done. You were on a punitive cattle raid; you should have known when to stop short of unnecessary bloodshed. There was no need to kill Bres. He was your father's friend and mine. Idiot, buffoon, you've just started a full-blown war.'

Dian's jaw dropped. Lugh was his greatest inspiration, he hero-worshipped him. Now he was overcome with remorse for an evil deed he could never undo. He had wondered at the time why Bres had seemed so loath to fight him.

'You don't deserve to be your father's son,' said Lugh. 'Thank the gods you're the youngest, because the makings of a high chieftain simply aren't in you.'

Nuada and Midar moved in to separate them. Midar put his arm over Dian's broad, sunken shoulders and took him out into the night air.

'You are my son and I'm proud of you,' he said. 'You're a warrior and always will be. In my time I've killed many men but, when the heat of battle has dissipated, there were some whose deaths I've bitterly regretted, even to this day.'

Midar's eyes opened wide. He stared into his shadowlands.

'There is haunted part of your mind that never sets you free, Dian, a place of ghosts.' He continued. 'You must learn to live with the uninvited living there, who without warning, wander through your mind. Never let anything distract you when you're engaged in mortal combat. Always carry through to the kill, lest one day you end up in the place of ghosts in another warrior's mind.'

Anroth returned and joined Frii, who was sitting with Goibniu and his warriors. The Celts' laughter and body language was all Frii needed to feel welcome. Seeing them together, Cliona called over to Anroth. 'Ah,' she said. 'Just the men I'm looking for.'

She had folded a thick, hooded, woollen cloak, renowned even as far away as Rome, over her arm. She walked towards them.

'Frii, we've so enjoyed your company,' she said. 'This is a gift to keep you warm and dry when the winter storms come. You must come and visit us soon, and, next time, I insist you come to stay.'

Frii felt the warmth of Cliona's smile; and when he saw the cloak, his eyes opened wide with delight. Taking it from her and ran his hand over the natural oiled finish of the wool.

'Oh, the famous Birrus Britannicus,' he said. 'I've always wanted one of these!'

He pulled it on and did a drunken dance of celebration. To a man alone, an outsider like Frii, this was the most precious part of a memorable night, for it was proof against the storms and of more value to him than the twig of hazel in his cap.

Cliona noticed the blood on Frii's neck and the deep cut in his ear. 'Snibo?' she enquired. He nodded.

'It needs stitching,' said the queen. 'Let me get my needle and thread, and I'll mend it for you in a moment.'

Frii smiled and held up his hand. 'Don't worry, I have good healing flesh,' he said. ''The salt in the sea air will help mend it on my journey homeward.'

What a capable, kind woman, he thought. Midar may be a great high chieftain, but Cliona was the perfect queen.

'What gift can I give Frii?' Midar whispered to Anroth. 'For, in his own special way, he's braver than any warrior of mine. He's a man of honour. I thought he spoke most eloquently at the banquet. Don't hold back, think of something special. His friendship could be of great value to the kingdom.'

Anroth smiled. 'I'm pleased you liked his speech,' he said. 'I've already organised a gift for you. I hope you don't consider it too generous.'

'Nothing could be too generous if it's a gift for my friend, Frii,' insisted Midar, his benevolence, due in no small part to his consumption of wine.

'You're giving him one of your hounds,' said Anroth. ''The beautiful bitch Nehalennia.'

'I'm doing what?' spluttered Midar. 'I'm giving him my precious Nelly? The man doesn't even like dogs!'

'He will when he sets eyes on Nehalennia,' said Anroth. 'She's the perfect gift. Nehalennia is the goddess of the North Sea. The seafarers from Gaul worship her. They have many statues and temples dedicated to her, and they always show her accompanied by an elegant hunting dog, just like our own Nehalennia. They believe the hound protects not just the goddess Nehalennia, but the cargo they carry on their hazardous voyages.'

'But, Anroth, she's pregnant by Oengus and we've already lost him to Cernunnos. Not that I begrudge it.'

'Frii lives a dangerous life, Midar,' said Anroth. 'He needs all the help we can give him. He's not the sort of man to ask for a favour but he's certainly the sort of man to do one. One day we might need him. I've already prayed to the goddess Nehalennia to protect him and bring him good fortune. You're not going to start an argument with a goddess, are you? We've had quite enough goddess problems for one night. It's far too late to change your mind now.'

'Change my mind, Snout? Change my mind!?' spluttered Midar. 'You've only this moment told me what my mind is.'

He paused and rubbed his chin. The noble code he lived by came to the rescue. 'Snout, you're right, give him Nehalennia,' he said. 'A gift is no gift at all unless it's something so precious you'd prefer to keep it.'

9 No Journey Finds Me Homeward Bound

Anroth, Frii, Midar, and Goibniu, walked towards the headland, followed by a slim, elegant hound, hesitant and unsure of herself, hanging back behind Midar's cloak. The warlord was usually a man of few words, but on those rare occasions when the wine took him, he could become quite effusive.

'Frii, we thank you for the honour of your company,' he said. 'Many times, I've stood here on this rocky outcrop and watched the storm rage, wondering how anyone could survive out there. Courage such as yours isn't given to many. Snout calls you the Wave Wanderer.

I say you are a warrior of the waves; your subjects are far more unruly than mine. In the eye of the storm, your authority over those who sail with you must be absolute,' he continued.

'I never fight my enemies alone. Courageous warriors like you never recognise themselves for what they are.'

'For a warlord, you're a thoughtful man,' laughed Frii. 'Each to his own, Midar. I was born with a gift, to sail the kingdom of the sea. It's all I've ever wanted to do. If I die doing so, then I'll die living.'

Midar nodded. 'It's the destiny of kings,' he said. 'If you had Snout forever sticking his nose into your business then you, too, would be a thoughtful man.'

'Ignore him, Frii,' protested Anroth. 'I've never accused him of being thoughtful.'

Midar whistled and Nehalennia, her shoulders dropped low, sidled around to stand beside him. He crouched down and stroked her ears, then invited Frii to do the same. And, on that windswept headland, Midar showed a side to his nature none could have guessed at. He spoke to the hound as a man might to his lover; softly, tenderly.

'She's beautiful, Midar,' said Frii. 'Such fine features…'

By way of enquiry, the gentle bitch pushed her wet nose into Frii's face and slowly licked the dried blood from his cheek and neck. He couldn't help but make a fuss of her. The times in his life when anyone showed him much physical affection were all too few. A lick and the feel of a dog's wet nose on his cheek rated quite highly.

Somewhat taken with the wine, Anroth chuckled. 'There you are, Frii, Snibo the raven, has brought you good luck,' he said.

'Had it not been for the little scratch on your ear and a bit of bleeding, then Nehalennia would never have made friends with you. Rest assured; I'll thank the bird on your behalf.'

Frii's brow furrowed and he shook his head. 'If that was what you Celts call a little scratch on my ear, I'd hate to imagine what you'd call a cut on the neck.'

'Decapitation,' suggested Goibniu, entering into the spirit of things.

Nehalennia's large, trusting eyes looked up at Frii as she licked him clean, encouraged by his warm welcome. His clothes still retained the strong smell of her recent lover, Oengus. Reassured by something so familiar and powerful, she curled up on his feet, pushing her back against his sea boots for comfort.

'She's my gift to you, Frii,' said Midar. 'She'll be your guardian, and keep you safe on land and sea.'

'But, Midar, I can't accept her. She's too beautiful, too precious,' said Frii. 'I possess nothing I could ever offer you in recompense. She's far too valuable a gift.'

'She's yours, Frii,' said the high chieftain. 'It's important you accept her, for chance favours the moment. Her name is Nehalennia. She'll bring you good fortune and safe journeys, and she'll be a reminder that you're always welcome at my table. Don't be too surprised if you find she's pregnant. Oengus has been paying her a great deal of attention of late.'

Embarrassed by Midar's generosity, Frii wanted to refuse the gift, even though he already adored the bitch, but when Midar told him her sacred provenance and that she was named after the great sea goddess Nehalennia, he knew he had to accept. To refuse would bring misfortune.

'I cannot begin to thank you for such riches,' said Frii, stumbling over the words.

'Think of the pleasure you've given me, Frii,' said Midar. 'It's a fine gift to honour a valiant hero.'

He stopped and sniffed the air. 'I smell the coming storm,' he said. 'But from where?'

'Fear not the storm you expect, Midar,' said Frii. 'Beware those unpredictable winds sweeping in without warning.'

Together, they looked at the stars and watched as Orion's belt crossed the southern sky. The wind blew full in their faces.

'And beware this southerly,' cautioned Frii. 'When the wind changes like this, it's one of three winds. To the south of us, the old wind from the west is doing battle with the younger wind from the east. And, as the younger wind grows stronger, so the older wind fails. Come tomorrow, I'll be fighting an easterly on my journey home.'

'Let's hope the easterly doesn't bring unwelcome strangers with it,' said Anroth.

Midar said his farewells, then left them and walked back to the great hall but, before he did so, he patted Nehalennia's head. He stretched out his hand to stroke Oengus, too, before remembering the hound had left him for the gods. As the others walked towards Frii's ship, one of the huntsmen and the three hounds leaving for Gaul joined them. Beside the ship, a driftwood fire burnt. Some of the crew huddled around it. The tide had turned and, from time to time, the sailors would push the boat back out into the water so it didn't become embedded in the sand. Frii always insisted his ship was ready to cast off at a moment's notice.

'I will sail tonight,' he said, melancholy creeping into his voice.

'Your leaving tonight bodes well,' said Anroth. 'Our seabirds and their ghosts won't follow you in the dark.'

Goibniu tried to cheer the sea captain up. 'The journey homeward is always shorter than when the wayfarer is outward bound,' he said.

'No journey finds me homeward bound, Goibniu,' said Frii. 'I never knew my parents and I was just a boy when first I took to the sea. It's all I know and the closest thing to home I possess. I love the feeling of the wind in my sails and a stout boat crashing through the waves. The sea will always be my mistress, but she leaves me no bed to lie on. I'm forever on the road to nowhere and wherever she takes me is where I wander.'

'It's time you settled down with a wife,' said Anroth. 'Why not consider this your home? Before your next visit, I could talk to Midar. I'm sure he'd confer the rights of clanship on you and give you lands, barns for storage, men to sail with you. My offer isn't an idle gesture or an act of generosity. In these uncertain times, your alliance brings with it many benefits to the tribe of the Brigantes.'

'It's weird and wonderful, Snout,' said Frii. ' I always feel I am the outsider, forever the stranger passing by. But tonight, I felt myself accepted; at home.'

Tears filled the weather-beaten seaman's eyes and Anroth patted him on the back. 'That's the second time you have cried tonight,' said the druid. 'I was watching you when Aine sang and tears streamed down your face. You couldn't possibly have understood a word she was singing about.'

'I wasn't listening to the song,' said Frii. 'I was listening to the most exquisite musical instrument the gods have ever made. I doubt I'll ever hear anything so beautiful again. It was a memorable night. How often do you have your banquets?'

'Every other Thursday,' replied Anroth.

Frii laughed. 'Let's be serious for a moment,' he said. 'I've heard tell of a young Saxon war-band leader. His name is Ida. He's been south of here in Deira. He's the son of a powerful warlord and is carving out quite a name for himself.'

'I'll remember the name,' said Anroth. 'But young heroes come and go. Most don't last long.'

Frii bent down, lifting Nehalennia gently, nuzzling softly into her neck, before setting her down on the ship's deck. His men loaded Midar's other hounds, then pulled Frii aboard. The sailors bent their backs into the oars and the boat slipped out into deeper waters.

'Have a safe journey,' called out Anroth. 'See you a week on Thursday!' They heard the sound of Frii's laughter as the sail caught the wind.

'Tonight, could so easily have ended in disaster, had it not been for you, Nuada and Aine,' said Goibniu, as they walked back up the beach. 'Praise the goddesses for Aine. Nothing disturbs that woman; she takes everything in her stride.'

'The Picts brought the raid down on themselves, Goibniu,' said Anroth. 'But it was far too successful. There'll be a backlash.'

'What about Danu?' asked Goibniu. 'Why's she suddenly arrived, Snout? Where does she fit in?'

'I'm trying to work that out,' said Anroth. 'These are precarious times, and walking in the shifting sands between being a goddess and a mortal is a dangerous game.'

The Second Day Of The Festival Of Lunasa

10 Crossing The Threshold

It was the second day of the festival of Lunasa and Anroth rose before the dawn. He sat on the headland and looked out on a dark and restless sea. Waves of thought rolled in and out of his troubled mind. Keeva came to join him.

'Good to see you,' said Anroth. 'How was your journey?'

'I've learnt many things,' said Keeva. 'Do you remember that, yesterday, you said those who travel the furthest have the shortest journey?'

'That isn't precisely what I said.'

'Well, last night I made that short journey,' said Keeva.

'Tell me.'

'As I made my way to the Dark Waters, I knew I was being followed, the hairs rose on the back of my neck; there were the sounds of a struggle, then silence.' Anroth nodded.

'Two people followed you, now one of them is dead.' Keeva shuddered and continued.

'Walking the night alone in the moonlight cleared my troubled mind. I needn't waste words telling you what you already believe. Life as we've known it is drawing to a close. The days of the tribe of the Brigantes are dwindling.'

'You and I share the same thoughts,' Anroth said. 'You possess a rare and special talent. It didn't come from me; it came from within. You have the gift, but foretelling the future is both a blessing and a burden.'

Keeva's mind was filled with haunting images, and he couldn't wait to unburden himself.

'After I'd stowed the coracle in your cave, I went to Brigantia's Grotto, set high in that rocky place,' he said. 'I rested below the mother goddess and lay my head down at her feet. She shared her fears with me, so I might better see the darkness, and she bid me bathe in the Dark Waters. To swim down to where there was no light. She promised that, when I rose again, I'd have the answer to that which troubled me.'

Anroth nodded.

'Well, I slipped into those cold waters,' said Keeva. 'And I swam down deep but never reached the bottom. I washed away the confusion of days. As I returned from the depths and floated slowly to the surface, my mind was illuminated by a golden moon shimmering above me. I rested against the sacred oak and listened to the gentle rustle of its leaves.' Sensing his excitement, Anroth took Keeva's hand and motioned for the novice to sit down beside him.

'In that luminal place, I knew I'd set out on my final journey. 'For years, I've toiled and travelled towards it but, in that moment, I realised just how short the journey is when first you cross the threshold. A form of completeness came to me, a ruthlessness against myself, a new confidence, a momentous purpose to my life.'

'Last night, Keeva, you changed from being a novice to one who has attained druidhood,' said Anroth. 'It's not a calling that always needs to be bestowed. What a novice doesn't know and understand after seven years of study is unlikely to be grasped in three times seven years. This means our relationship has changed from one of dependency to one of equality. I'm proud of you but have a care, attaining druidhood sometimes weakens your grasp on reality.' Keeva ignored the advice and changed the subject.

'What about Sirona and Luchtain?' he asked. 'I have judged them harshly, for they are as deserving of druidhood as I, if not more so.'

'Your brother Luchtain and sister Sirona are more than ready to walk the world without me,' said Anroth. 'All they need is to discover is the threshold, which I don't expect them to do soon. I fancy they're preoccupied with exploring other posterns and passageways.' Keeva smiled, Anroth drew closer.

'Keeva, my final lesson is that you do not confuse some of your strange thoughts with religious truth. As your friend, I must warn you that the way you interpret druidic teaching worries me. I trust age and time will change the nature of your understanding.'

'Do I have to leave you?'

'No,' said Anroth. 'One day you will, but not, I suspect, in the way you think.'

'I'll never leave.'

'There are many ways of leaving, Keeva.'

'To return to my story, Anroth, what happened next was stranger than anything I've ever encountered,' said Keeva. 'One moment, as my heart grew heavy with the burden of destiny, I was all alone. Then, from nowhere, Dancer appeared and knelt in front of me, shining like silver in the moonlight, blood running down his chest. He gave his usual crooked, little smile. He could read my mind and it caused him great pain, for he stared at me in disbelief. He knew what I've dared to think and for the moment dismissed.' Anroth nodded, Keeva continued.

'He stroked that thick band of red fox fur he always wears around his left upper arm,' continued Keeva. 'And he undid it and tied it around my arm as if it were a cherished parting gift. Then, with tears streaming down his face, he held out his arms towards me and stood up, before fading away through the trees' swaying branches.'

'He has the gift, he's one of us,' said Anroth. 'What more can you tell me?'

'I wish I'd returned knowing where the greatest danger lies,' said Keeva. 'But I'm certain we must make a move soon. We need to conjure up what we can from your cauldron.'

'Divination and the interpretation of omens is always like this, Keeva,' said Anroth. 'You may feel the malevolence drawing ever closer, but from which direction? When what's revealed is still not enough, we're forced to play a dangerous game. After you've rested, go to the forest and gather what we need. You and I will decide tomorrow how best to cast the cauldron's spells. Now you've attained druidhood, you'll make me guilty of giving in to the weakness of pride if you stay much longer.' Keeva smiled.

'Oh, before you go,' said Anroth. 'Did you manage to work out my riddle?'

'About truth and wisdom?'

'Yes.'

'The answer is, if belief is what you think is true and knowledge is knowing what you don't know, then wisdom is deciding which to choose,' said Keeva.

'But you've answered my riddle with a riddle!'

'I know,' laughed Keeva. 'That's what druids do.'

Anroth threw his hands in the air, admitting defeat. 'Go and get some sleep,' he said. 'At least we can still laugh.'

When Keeva departed, Anroth continued looking out to sea, wondering how Frii and his crew were faring. With the wind now blowing towards them, he could imagine the boat bucking up and down as it crashed through the waves, with the spindrift wetting their faces and bathing Frii's torn ear.

11 All Beauty On A Summer's Day

Anroth felt a hand on his shoulder. Danu stood beside him, radiant and smiling.

'Do you usually get up this early?'

'Always, Danu, it's good thinking time,' he replied. 'After last night I've much to ponder, including you. Let's walk together.'

She pulled him to his feet; her strength surprised him. They headed north along the drover's trail.

'What a lovely morning,' she said. 'I want to live here forever.'

'It's not so good for our friend Frii,' said Anroth. 'The wind has changed.'

'Is that bad?'

'Yes, in more ways than one,' said Anroth. 'He'll be making heavy weather of it and it may bring us unwelcome visitors from the sea.'

'Can I hold your hand, Snout?' asked Danu. 'I adore all these innocent forms of physical contact that mortals indulge in. We don't have anything so casually intimate in the Otherworld.'

A raven hovered in the sky above them, riding the strong easterly wind, which blew sand up from the dunes.

Further along the trail, a man came out from beneath the trees with a short quiver of arrows hung from his belt and a body over his shoulders. It was Dancer. Looking up, he saw Danu and Anroth, and tossed the body down in front of him. Like a deer, the warrior of the wildwood stood motionless, half hidden by the bushes.

Anroth waved in salutation. The woodwose waved back before melting into the forest.

Danu shivered.

'Does Dancer normally go around killing people?'

'Not very often, he's one of us,' said Anroth. 'He's placid unless roused, so don't make fun of him.'

'I wasn't planning to,' said Danu. 'With a brute like that on your side, you don't have too many worries.'

They walked over to the body. It was that of a well-built Pict, whose long red hair was tied back in a ponytail. There were deep, penetrating wounds in one eye socket and the other eye had been plucked out. A short arrow protruded from his throat.

Anroth shook his head. 'There's more trouble in store,' he said. 'That's Mechi – Balor's youngest son. They must be desperate to get the Black Obsidian back.'

Shading his eyes with his hand, he scanned the trail to the northern horizon before deciding it was safe to continue.

'Let's get down to the water's edge, away from this sand blowing in our faces.'

Cutting through the dunes, they continued north.

'I walk here most mornings,' said Anroth. 'This beach is always so beautiful, every day it's refreshed, but its nature never changes. Imagine Danu, hundreds of years ago, the sun shone as it shines today and others walked here. Perhaps they walk beside us still? They might even have found as much happiness as I have walking beside you.'

'Oh, Snout, don't stop,' said Danu. 'No one talks to me this way in the Otherworld.'

'One of the great joys of growing old, my dear, is that you can say nice things to a beautiful young woman without being misunderstood.' She stopped walking and leant on his shoulder.

'Yes, just imagine,' she said. 'In another thousand years, people will still be coming here to walk and talk just as we do today.'

'Indeed and, who knows, our spirits might return to join them,' said Anroth. 'When I die, it'll be sufficient just to become part of the beauty that surrounds us. I've no desire to be reborn into the Otherworld.'

'No Otherworld will serve you better,' said Danu. 'You're already in paradise.'

They walked the tide line, picking up the occasional small treasure that the sea had left behind, until they eventually came to the large log with its roots embedded in the sand. They sat on its smooth, bleached trunk.

'I call this log Journey's End,' said Anroth.

'Journey's End?'

'Think of all the journeys this log has made since it fell into a river and was washed out to sea, then came to rest here,' he said

'Here we are, on this lovely day, sitting on a fine seat. I often sit here. It's the last resting place of a once-mighty tree from who knows where. Season by season, it grew in strength and size. Then in old age, as the winds howled around it and the rains came down, it fell into a river in full flood. Some would say it died that day. Yet, many years later and far away from where it once grew, it provides us with this admirable seat.'

Danu smiled.

'I used to think it was dead, Danu,' continued Anroth. 'Now I wonder. This log has become my friend. I look forward to meeting it on my walks. It waits for me here and shares my life as once it shared its life with the leaves that adorned it. Is life entirely lost when the last leaf falls or the last breath is drawn?'

Danu got up and stood behind the druid, resting her hands lightly on his shoulders. She looked out to sea.

'You have beautiful ideas about things most people can't even imagine,' she said. 'I wonder if beautiful ideas come from beautiful places? Sorry, I'm interrupting…'

'Not at all, I'm talking too much. One of my many failings,' said Anroth, slapping his log with his hand like a man astride his pony. 'This may not be the first beach our venerable seat has graced, nor necessarily the last. Who can say? The waves may one day choose to take our seat away. When the tree fell into the river, the nature of its life changed, but did it die? Does its physical presence or even the memory of its existence confer on it a form of life?'

Danu sat down beside him. Do you think my friend knows we're sitting on it? I'd like to think so.' She laughed.

'You talk to your old tree trunk when you're all alone, don't you?'

'I most certainly do,' said Anroth. 'And where's the shame in that? If you were a tree trunk, I'm sure you wouldn't mind me talking to you.'

'Very true,' said Danu. 'But I doubt I'd like you sitting on me. On the other hand, I could sit beside you and listen to you all day, which leads me nicely into what I want to talk to you about. Unlike this tree, my life will be nothing when I die.'

'How can you talk of dying?' said Anroth. 'You're immortal and a renowned mother goddess. Does this have something to do with why you've taken mortal form?'

She nodded; her raven-black hair rippled. There was no disguising the sadness in her smile. 'I've been a Celtic goddess for thousands of years,' she said. 'But the glory of the old Celtic kingdoms and our culture are withering away.

Our civilisation is dying by degrees, fading into the twilight. Your gods and goddesses will fade and die when those who once worshiped us are no more. All that'll remain will be stories retold or invented by those who never knew us. The strength I once possessed grows weaker. I used to think it would last forever, but there's no infinity of existence.'

'Well, I agree with you about infinity,' said Anroth. 'If there were such a thing, how could anything have started in the first place? The only certainty in our lives is change.'

'Where are the gods of the Babylonians now?' she said with anguish and urgency in her voice. 'Where are the goddesses and gods of the Pharaohs? You won't find them in the Otherworld, for they died with those who worshipped them. I looked on, as they were sapped of what had once sustained them. Their power and strength withering on the vine of celestial life. I watched their slow and bitter end as they died unloved. All that remained swirled away as clouds, falling to earth as rain.'

Anroth stared at her.

'There is so much more to your mortal love than the pale, cold, loveless world of a goddess,' continued Danu. 'Before I die, I want to discover real love. That's why I've come here. I don't want the impersonal, meaningless love that I give in dribbles to everyone who asks for it. I want to feel love gushing out of me. I want to love just one man and I want to feel his love flowing back into me. I'm lonely. How utterly worthless my life as a goddess has become.'

'Half the world is lonely, Danu; probably more,' said Anroth. 'Our world still needs you as a goddess.'

She looked down at the sand and slowly shook her head, then she reached out and took his hand.

'All you've ever given me is adoration, my eternal life has become a form of death.' she said.

''Through so many centuries, you've stood before my stone-cold statues and left your precious golden gifts in those ice-cold waters where you worship me. Where's the love? Why was I never allowed to be loved as a child? Why have I been denied the frailty, the intimacy and happiness that comes from one eager soul finding completion in another?'

'In your long life as a goddess, you must have known love much more powerful than ours,' said Anroth.

'No, gods with absolute power bequeath nothing of themselves when they make love,' said Danu. 'I can't claim to understand mortal love, but it seems to be the opposite of celestial love, which is devoid of tenderness. The love I seek is about sharing feelings of strength, weakness and dependency. Please don't laugh at me. I don't pretend to understand your love. I can only hope I'll meet a man who can find something in me to love.'

'I'm not laughing,' said Anroth. 'I hope you find what you're looking for. I admire your courage, but I confess that, when I think of the selfish, self-centred, bad-tempered behaviour of gods and goddesses, it's hard to imagine they're capable of mortal love. Real love, Danu, will never shine through unless you control that side to your nature.'

Danu nodded in agreement. 'I wouldn't know where to begin.'

'At the banquet, your dreams of coming to us as a child and slowly maturing into womanhood were cruelly destroyed by Birog's Black Obsidian,' said Anroth. 'It's changed you into a chimera – part goddess, part mortal. Where this will lead you, I can't tell. But I do know that, today, sitting with me on my log, your warmth and affection, makes an old and sometimes lonely man very happy. You're adorably human, Danu.'

She smiled, gently holding his hand.

'Are you sure you can forget your past?' asked the druid. 'After all, you're the mother of many gods. The Dagda is one of your sons and he, in turn, has fathered many more – including Brigantia, the goddess of the Brigantes.'

'Yes, Snout, The Dagda has a prodigious sexual appetite,' said Danu. 'I've no idea where he gets it from, certainly not from me. Not only was he one of my sons, but he also persuaded me to become one of his lovers. I don't know what I was thinking of. Who in their right mind goes to cloud with a pot-bellied dwarf?'

It was Anroth's turn to smile.

'As I've tried to explain to you, it's a myth that the gods make good lovers,' she continued. 'The gods don't cope well with emotion. Sadly, the stories you tell, about me making love to the sun god Mog Ruth are true.'

'Come now, Danu,' said Anroth. 'The sun god is a glorious being. He drives his golden chariot across the sky each day.'

'Oh, he's fine from a distance, but close up he only has one eye,' said Danu. 'And that's in the middle of his forehead.'

She paused, worried about confiding any more of her grievances to a mere mortal, quite forgetting she'd become one.

There was an embarrassed silence. Anroth stood up.

'Shall we walk on?' Danu pulled him back down again, as her frustrations and anger at the inadequacies of her celestial partners boiled over.

'I suppose it's too much to expect the gods to know where the goddess spot is,' she said. Anroth's eyebrows rose.

'The goddess spot?' he said, feigning ignorance as to what she was talking about.

'My granddaughter Brigii told me about it. Though I didn't dare ask exactly where it is or how she found out about it.'

'Enlightening,' said Anroth. 'I thought the Christians had turned Bridget into one of their saints?'

'They will do one day,' said Danu. 'But she's having such a wild time as a Celtic goddess that she's going to delay changing into one of their saints for as long as possible.'

'Explain.'

'Well, as a goddess she gets into all sorts of mischief,' said Danu. 'Out of curiosity, she bluffed her way into the Christians' heaven and had a look around. Compared to the Otherworld, she found it a pretty miserable place. She never heard the sound of laughter'

'It's true, no one ever laughs in heaven,' she said. When Saint Peter discovered who she was, he refused to let her out unless she promised to come back again as a saint. She promised she would one day,

Anroth raised his eyes.

'They steal our deities and call them saints,' said Danu. 'They adopt our veneration of bones – or relics, as they like to call them – and they take our festivals and call them feast days. When Brigii complained to Saint Peter about it, he just shrugged his shoulders and claimed we probably stole the ideas from some other religion in the first place.'

'Well, Danu, whatever you think of Christianity, I must tell you I admire Jesus, he will always be one of my gods,' said Anroth. 'Is Brigii annoyed about Saint Peter forcing her to be a saint?'

'No, she adores him, he's promised to take her fishing,' said Danu

Anroth laughed. 'I am not in the least surprised Peter is attracted to Brigii if she's anything like you.'

'She says that when I'm no longer worshipped and nothing more than a faded memory, she'll still be good for another few thousand years. She'll be worshipped as a saint until Christianity eventually goes the way of all religions.'

'I'm surprised and disappointed to hear your revelations about celestial love,' said Anroth. In fairness to the gods, though, some men make hopeless lovers – particularly warriors taken by the drink. But most of us have a great deal more respect for making love, delaying its inevitable conclusion and prolonging the precious time a couple share.'

'Go on, Snout,' implored Danu. 'Fill me in.'

'Pardon?'

''Tell me more,' she said.

Anroth breathed a sigh of relief. He stooped forward, picked up part of an old branch, worn white by the tides, and drew a straight line in the sand. 'Imagine this is a god and goddess making love,' he said.

Danu watched as Anroth continued to draw. His line rose up to a short, sharp, little peak before it dropped straight down again.

Danu studied it. 'Yes, I suppose that looks about right,' she said. 'But some gods don't even manage as long as that. Blink and you've missed them. Come to think of it, your picture looks a lot more exciting than the real thing, Snout.'

Beside his first drawing, Anroth began to draw another. This time, his line started to rise very slowly then, instead of falling down again, it continued straight along in a plateau. Then, without warning, it shot up again before collapsing completely.

Danu noticed Anroth was becoming animated.

'Good grief,' he whispered. 'I've not felt so excited in years!'

Proud of his artistic endeavours, Anroth pushed his stick into the sand. ''The long, raised plateau signifies the beautiful feeling of heightened sexual awareness you ought to feel before orgasm overwhelms you,' he announced. ''That, my dear, is mortal love as it's meant to be. It's best you find some muscular young man so you can discover the reality for yourself.'

Danu looked at him and smiled. 'I'm older than you, Snout,' she said. 'I think I need an older man to teach me. A man just like you, in fact.'

Doing his best to look disinterested in the proposition, Anroth turned towards her.

'Danu, I don't doubt you have enormous power,' he said. 'But not even you could resurrect my little warrior.'

'Are you getting embarrassed, Snout?'

'Indeed I am.' He started to draw a third picture.

'Are there three ways of making love?'

''There are doubtless a hundred ways, Danu,' said Anroth. 'My doodle in the sand doesn't depict what you're actually doing, but the delightful feelings your body and mind conjure up in response to the act of lovemaking. Remember the Celtic magical number three? There may be a third response. Let me attempt to introduce you to the Mindglow. Who knows, Danu? You may be one of the few to find it.'

'The Mindglow?' she said. 'Are you making fun of me?'

'No,' said Anroth. 'There are those who believe that, in certain circumstances, the act of lovemaking can overreach its normal limitations and rise to otherwise unattainable plateaus of intimacy and ecstasy.'

Anroth returned to his third drawing in the sand and drew his first plateau. But, instead of a sharp peak that fell away towards the end of lovemaking, his line began to slowly rise a second time and became a second plateau. This eventually rose to a second, even greater peak before the point of his wooden stick plunged right back to the baseline. Danu could see that Anroth was getting agitated; his hand was trembling. As he stabbed his stick forcefully into the ground, it snapped.

'I'm too old for all this nonsense,' he said.

'Making love?' Asked Danu.

'Drawing pictures,' said Anroth.

'But not for making love?'

'For making love and drawing pictures.'

Danu bent forward to study the picture in detail. Feeling flushed, Anroth went for a paddle in a rock pool. When he returned, she said, 'I don't think I'd be keen on that. It looks as though they fall off a cliff in the end.'

'True, with so much overarching stimulation, their minds would be fractured into many parts,' said Anroth. 'It's at this point, though, that Sirona, the goddess of healing, puts all the bits back together again. She breathes new life into the lovers and makes them whole once more. But, in doing this, she mixes parts of the two minds, so that each now possesses fragments of the other's mind. Love's shared perpetual embers now glow within them, hence the Mindglow. They've discovered sublime harmony.'

'It may sound sublime,' said Danu. 'But what's it really like?'

'I've no idea,' said Anroth. 'I've no experience of the Mindglow, nor have I met anyone who has – or who, at least, has been prepared to admit to it. I can't pretend to fully grasp the idea. Many believe there's no such thing.'

'True or not, it's a magical idea.'

'Well, Danu, if the Mindglow does exist and you were to succeed in finding it, then you'd have discovered mortal love in its purest form,' said Anroth. 'But if you do, have a care. Ask yourself why is it so elusive?' Danu smiled.

'I just wonder,' pondered Anroth. 'Is it really a blessing? Our world can be such an uncertain, unforgiving place. How can you protect yourself against evil if all you can feel is love? And something else troubles me. If two lovers spend their time looking inwards and are devoted only to each other, how much use will they be when it comes to sharing their love for the greater good, which is one of the most important things we do in our lives?'

'I don't know,' said Danu. 'I understand so little about your lives. You mention men may prove poor lovers, but what of women? My attempts at making love your way might be a disaster.'

'Improbable,' said Anroth.

'Anyway, let's not worry about the Mindglow,' said Danu. 'Do you know anything about the G spot?'

Anroth raised his hands in alarm. 'Don't ask me, Danu,' he said. 'You look so young, so beautiful, and I have to remind myself you are thousands of years old. We mortals don't wear so well when it comes to making love. I fear my old horn has played its last long song. I can no longer hold the notes, with no more tunes to play.'

Danu burst out laughing. 'I don't believe it,' she said. 'I've managed to embarrass you!'

'I don't believe it myself,' he replied, sharing her laughter.

If you want to experience our love, then you must also learn to grieve, for the love between a man and a woman often ends in tears.'

'Tears! When you're in love you can cry, how exciting!' said Danu. 'Goddesses rarely cry. We find it difficult to release our fears and frustrations that way. Instead, we just end up being nasty. Anroth paused and wondered how best to break unwelcome news.

'Danu, much as it pains me to say so, you must leave us,' he said. 'When I was young, I regularly prayed before your sombre statues, but found no comfort in them. Meeting you in the flesh is so different and invigorating. You make me very happy, but your safety is more important than the pleasure of your company. We live in dangerous times and this is neither the time nor the place for you to take mortal form.'

'I know the risks,' said Danu. 'This isn't just about love, it's also about atonement. I've a reputation as a river goddess of benign abundance, someone who protects the harmony of nature. The truth is different. I've found myself envious of what's been denied me. Once, in a fit of jealous rage, I destroyed the precious gift that two innocent young lovers shared.'

'The song Aine sang last night, she was singing about you, wasn't she?' Danu bowed her head in shame.

'Go back, I beg you,' said Anroth. 'We're about to engage in an uncertain, brutal war. Many will die. I've read the omens. If you die as a mortal, you'll lose your life and your immortality.'

'I'll never go back,' said Danu. 'And you can't make me. For the first time in thousands of years I feel alive. Everything within me is rejuvenated and now, at last, I think I understand. The frailty and uncertainty of human life makes every moment precious. Immortality as a goddess is a pale shadow of your life. Immortality is a glorified form of death. Only when death becomes a reality, can you really be certain your love was ever alive.'

'How so?'

'Part of every fibre that spins, weaves and informs the transient fabric of mortal life is that knowledge that one day you'll die,' said Danu. 'My life as a goddess never seemed that precious. Try to understand me. There must have been a time you were in love with a woman.'

'There was,' said Anroth. 'She died in childbirth, the saddest way to watch a woman die.' Visibly distressed, Anroth changed the subject.

'I know she'd be pleased you've come to see me and become my friend. Had she lived, our daughter would have grown to adulthood by now.'

He stood up and wearily plodded forward. Danu heard Anroth sigh, then he slowly shook his head.

'No one ever knows how much you love them, till they are dead.'

He stared blankly in front of him. Danu ran after him and slipped her arm into his, then held his hand. They walked in silence. A cold wind blew within him as he wiped his eye.

'If you should ever lose someone you love, Danu, bury them in the warmth of your heart,' he said. 'Talk to them, make them welcome. Never leave them to lie among strangers in a cold and lonely graveyard.'

She held him closer. 'In our world, we're incapable of hanging on to feelings the way you do,' she said.

'But you're not in your world now, you're in mine,' said Anroth. 'And since I can't persuade you to return to yours, nothing would make me happier than to welcome you to ours, and to adopt and love you as my daughter. Let me love you as the one I lost. Let me love you as I love Sirona. For, in our world, love and sometimes sadly hate transcend the generations. When the one you love dies, their love lives on within you. It becomes part of your love.'

Danu squeezed his arm against her body. 'Oh, that's beautiful,' she said. 'I'll be your daughter. I can think of no nicer way of feeling mortal. You're making me all emotional.'

Anroth looked in her eyes, which were brimming with tears. 'Danu,' he said softly.

'Yes, I know, I'm going to cry,' she interrupted triumphantly.

'But surely you must realise, Cliona has already adopted you as her daughter?' She kissed him gently on his forehead, and stroked his hair.

'But it is different having a father, I can mother you as well.'

'I know it sounds a silly question, but apart from sharing a father's love, how may I recognise my love for other men?'

'Mortal love, my dear, is a confusion of imperfections.'

'Stop talking in riddles.'

'Let me put it another way,' said Anroth. 'One day, you may meet a man who makes you laugh, makes you happy and secure, a man you can't imagine being without. If you wonder if his strange attraction really is love, you know you can always tell?'

'How?'

'If you find him an irresistible confusion of imperfections, then you're definitely in love with him.'

They rounded the headland. The island of Lindisfarne rose out of the sea in front of them.

'Can we go there?' asked Danu.

'I hope so,' said Anroth. 'Like many mystical places, it looks closer than it is. It wouldn't be safe to go today.'

Danu nodded.

'You know, we could walk all the way to Lindisfarne and back, talking of nothing but love, and try to define it but never quite grasp it,' said Anroth. 'There are as many ways of sharing love as there are lovers. Look for friendship, let love find you.'

'Just imagine, there might be someone who could love me for what I am, as a mere mortal,' said Danu. 'What a beautiful idea. The risk of death doesn't seem too high a price in exchange for love. Even if I died, my love could live on in his heart. That's such a precious idea.'

'Precious?'

'It's precious because others might also love the man I love,' said Danu. 'And when he died, his love and mine would endure in the hearts of those who loved him. My love would become part of love's immortality.'

'One day, I'd love to walk with you to Lindisfarne and talk of love, but I don't need to go there. You've taught me all anyone really needs to know about love.' She stopped in her tracks, holding on to him, looking into his eyes. 'It is not my life which needs to be immortal,' Danu said, 'but the love within.'

They walked on in silence, then Danu hesitated. 'Please don't tell me if it hurts too much,' she said, 'but why have you never loved again?'

'How do you know I haven't?' he said. 'Let's just assume that, at my age, I prefer friendship. Love offers the promise of perfection, and sometimes finds and sustains it. Friendship is less fickle, usually more dependable and enduring, but don't assume you can always tell the difference.'

'I like friendship, Snout,' said Danu. 'I could fall in love with friendship!'

For a goddess, she was almost childlike. He reminded himself that, had it not been for the night before, she might never have lost what was left of her childhood.

'I wish we could walk all day together,' he said. 'But I'm expecting visitors. We really must get back.'

Danu continued to hold the old man's hand and lackadaisically swung it backwards and forwards, and sometimes gaily skipped along beside him. They did not do friendship like this in the Otherworld.

12 The Peace Delegation

Later that morning, a Pictish peace delegation arrived. Crimthain and his men made them welcome, setting up a table and seats. As the serving maids brought out cold meats and other victuals left over from the banquet, Midar, Lugh, Anroth and Goibniu joined them.

The delegation was led by Strebo, a fat, self-important, sweaty little man, who introduced himself as Balor's counsellor. Most of his men stayed at a distance, resting in the woods. Midar noticed Strebo wore an ornate gold ring inset with a large red garnet, clearly the work of a Saxon master craftsman and far too large for the leader's podgy finger.

Strebo had brought with him a magnificent hound, with a silver torque around its neck. The delegation came prepared to bargain, and carried a heavy wooden chest and on top of it, wrapped in a tattered, bloodstained red cloak, a long, thin bundle. Once they'd been suitably fed and refreshed, the negotiations began.

Strebo conveyed Balor's greetings to Midar. He regretted the unruly and unjustifiable behaviour of the three princes and the consequent loss of life, but he recalled that, when younger, they had all been prone to youthful exuberance. Lugh looked at Strebo in disgust, he couldn't imagine him ever being prone to youthful exuberance.

Strebo emphasised that Balor was a magnanimous man. And, in the interest of restoring harmonious relations, he was prepared to forget the insult and injury to the Picts, under certain conditions.

He then launched into a Pictish version of events with regards to their common border and the historical causes of their differences. He was a self-confident, verbose man, at ease with recalling the dates, places and outcomes of previous encounters. At times, he became breathless, but only because he found breathing an unfortunate intrusion to his continuous flow of rhetoric.

Anroth knew as much as anyone about Midar and Balor's shared history. As a man who had spent his life weaving words, he had to admire the pompous little man's ability to manipulate facts, and the way he glossed over Balor's treacherous, ruthless nature.

Goibniu had never sat in on a peace negotiation before. At first, he was reassured by Strebo's manner and apparent grasp of the situation but, as he listened to the torrent of misinformation and to numerous inventions, he concluded Strebo's verbal skills bore a striking resemblance to a bull moving its bowels.

When Strebo eventually ran out of words, Midar spoke.

'Your name – and the way you pronounce it – interests me,' he said.

'I'm frequently asked about my name, lord Midar,' said Strebo. 'My grandfather, on my mother's side, was a Greek mapmaker so my name sounds different because the Greek alphabet is different. In any case, what's in a name? You're proud to trace your lineage back to the tribe of the Brigantes, but others call you the Bernicians and your lands Bernicia.'

Anroth interrupted. 'Strebo, you will no doubt concede that lands change hands and their names in the wake of war,' he said. 'Whereas a man's tribal beliefs and background cannot be written out of history by the slash of a sword.'

'Oh well met, my lord,' said Strebo. 'Well spoken! You're a man of extreme erudition. Your wine commends itself to me, might there be more?'

Anroth recharged Strebo's goblet, as the fatuous little man's torrent of misinformation continued.

'I was very fond of my grandfather, on my mother's side. 'But, interesting as maps are, I don't think they're reliable or have much of a future. My great passion is digging up old bones and working out how ancient societies lived their lives.'

'Did you know I once dug up the big toe of a Hittite? I was able to prove his toenails grew inwards. He was a warrior, but he didn't die in battle. I can say, without fear of contradiction, he choked to death on a fish bone.'

'Amazing,' said Goibniu.

'You talk of restoring harmonious relations,' said Midar. 'But, if you knew anything about our past, instead of wasting my time with pure invention, you'd have conceded at the outset that we've never had harmonious relations. You've stolen or butchered my fine longhorn cattle when they graze the high pastures.'

'You've blighted our crops, slaughtered my herdsmen and burnt down their summer shielings, and our northern trails remain hazardous for travellers. Tell your warlord Balor, a man with only one tooth left in his mouth, not to nibble away at my northern estates lest ambition get the better of him.'

Strebo seemed hurt and surprised. He assured Midar that if there had been any unruly behaviour by the border

Picts, he was sure that, once it had been brought to his attention, Balor would find and severely punish those responsible.

'I can say with some confidence that heads will roll, it's in all our interests to find agreement.' Midar sighed, but before he could reply, Strebo carried on, with his misguided nonsense.

'None of us wants the Sword of Ramses hanging over our heads now, do we?' he said, turning to Anroth, who had casually removed, Cernunnos's golden wand from his belt. Strebo looked at it, but before he could say anything, Goibniu, without a flicker of insincerity in his face, interrupted.

'Don't you mean the Sword of Socrates, Strebo?' he enquired.

Beneath the table, Anroth delivered a warning nudge rather than a full-blown kick at Goibniu's shins.

'Thank you for correcting me,' replied Strebo. 'You are highly educated, doubtless by my lord Anroth. It was indeed the Egyptian Socrates not Ramses the Greek. You must forgive me, but it's all ancient history now and, as such, will soon be forgotten.'

'Was there anything else on your mind?' asked Anroth, leaning forward. As he did so Cernunnos's golden wand slipped from his grasp and fell onto Strebo's hand. Strebo jerked his hand back and Anroth apologised.

'No, nothing else,' said Strebo. 'Oh, actually, there was just one thing.'

'One thing?' challenged Lugh, who was getting increasingly irritated by the obnoxious little man.

'Don't waste any more of our time talking rubbish. My mother used to say that what people don't know, they make up. I fought in all the battles you've mentioned.

Nothing you've said so far coincides with the truth. Get to the point!'

Unruffled, Strebo continued. 'Your mother was clearly a highly intelligent woman,' he said. 'I wish I could have met her, for one gets so few opportunities to indulge in sophisticated conversation in this part of the world. Your mother was not alone when she made that observation. It was one of Cicero the Elder's favourite sayings, when he fought the third Punic war in Anglesey.'

'Where did the Punniis come from and what were they doing in Anglesey?' asked Goibniu.

'That's exactly what Cicero the Elder asked,' replied Strebo.

'Tell me, Strebo, did the Punniis ever wage war against the Hittites? And, if so, who won?' asked Goibniu. He was in grave danger of receiving a kick from Anroth beneath the table.

'Indeed, they did,' said Strebo. 'I personally negotiated the peace settlement. Let me tell you about it.'

Lugh banged the table. 'I've already asked you once to get to the point, Strebo!'

'Indeed, you have,' said Strebo. 'Let's return to our discussion. During your raid, my lord Balor dropped his helmet. As a sign of goodwill between our tribes, he hopes you can see your way to returning it to him.'

'No,' said Lugh. 'His helmet is a weapon of war as much as any sword, and it's a justifiable trophy for the victor. Tell your master he was fortunate to keep his head.'

'Oh, talking of heads, there was something else,' said Strebo. 'Among the dead was my lord Balor's champion, Bres. You have his head.'

Goibniu pointed out that the head had been taken honourably, and that it would always be treated with honour and respect.

''The great hero and warrior Bres has returned to his true friends,' added Lugh, to Strebo's thinly disguised fury.

Midar interrupted. 'If we were to consider your requests, what compensation would you offer for our losses?'

Strebo turned and motioned to his men. Lugh half-drew his sword.

'My lord Balor has authorised generous compensation,' said Strebo.

Two of the Pictish warriors carried the wooden chest over to them and put it down on the table. Strebo opened it. It was full of gold Roman coins.

'Can we agree to these requests?' asked Midar. Lugh disagreed, and Goibniu and Anroth said nothing. Midar looked across at Strebo's magnificent hound, which was asleep and stretched out on the grass.

'You can have the head and, in exchange, I lay claim to the beast,' said Midar.

'I can't agree,' Strebo said. 'He's been with me since birth. He's like a son to me.' Concerned by the mounting hostility, Anroth rose from the table.

'In view of the difficulties of our negotiations, I'm sure we'd all benefit from a libation of our new barley beer, flavoured with wild mountain thyme. We do find other things to do, Strebo, when you're not provoking us to take up arms. Excuse me while I arrange for it to be served.' Strebo was sweating profusely, Midar pressed home his advantage.

'Well, Strebo, it's your hound or nothing, make your mind up.'

Then, like Anroth, Strebo called for a break and walked across the headland to calm down and consider Midar's request. He was joined by two of his men, after a short conversation, he followed them along the trail before returning to the table.

'My men have found a body,' he said. 'I can only apologise and confirm he's one of ours. I've no idea what the man was doing here. He wasn't part of my delegation.'

'Take him home with you when you leave,' said Midar, who was by now becoming increasingly exasperated at the way things were unfolding.

Both he and Strebo knew the meeting was futile, a prelude to inevitable war. He wanted the Picts out of the way, but he'd set his heart on the conniving little man's hound. Strebo didn't deserve such a fine animal.

Anroth returned and the servants brought out the beer. Midar looked up and breathed a sigh of relief, for perched on Anroth's shoulder was Snibo the raven. From past experience, he knew that, when Snibo ended up on Anroth's shoulder, negotiations soon came to a rapid conclusion. Strebo looked at the bird, only to discover the bird was already looking at him. And however much the bird moved its head from side to side, his bright, beady little eyes continued to watch Strebo.

'This is Snibo,' said Goibniu, 'a much-loved family pet. He's such a funny, unpredictable old bird.' He added confidentially, 'he can be quite naughty.'

Strebo, who was visibly startled, knew all about Snibo. The raven had a gruesome reputation for swooping down on any Pictish spies and assassins who ventured onto Midar's lands, and pecking out their eyes. Sweat beaded on Strebo's brow and he cleared his throat.

'Before we consider the tribute for Bres's head, there's one other thing I've been asked to mention. My lord Balor's late wife once gave him a fruit bowl. He still grieves over her tragic passing and losing such a personal possession has caused him great distress. Should you find it in your heart to return it, then he offers you this trophy. We acquired it many years ago when we wiped out the ninth Roman legion.'

The odious little man paused. This was meant to be the highlight of his negotiations. He looked up to see the infernal bird still staring at him, slowly moving its wings up and down as if about to take flight. There was a sense of shared foreboding, they all knew the innocent fruit bowl was in fact the Black Obsidian.

Hands shaking, Strebo unwrapped the old bloodstained Roman cloak to reveal a golden standard – the famous, long-lost Eagle of the Ninth.

Lugh stood up to admire it.

'We'd be more than willing to trade a fruit bowl for such a famous trophy,' he said. 'But we have nothing to trade. What colour was the bowl?'

'Black.'

'We brought back no black fruit bowl,' said Goibniu.

'So, all that's outstanding is the price of Bres's head,' concluded Midar.

Strebo tried to persuade him to accept ever increasing amounts of gold in settlement, but Midar refused and insisted on the hound.

'You can't return to Balor empty-handed,' he said. 'Accept my terms and take the head, lest Balor sees to it that you lose your own.'

Strebo hesitated and rubbed his chin. 'We might be able to agree terms,' he said.

'If the beast proves unsuitable, I'll return him and you can keep Bres's head,' said Midar. 'What's his name?'

'Ominnios, my lord Midar. I call him Ominnios.'

Strebo seemed unable to make up his mind. Midar was on the verge of flying into a rage, when Anroth slowly stretched out his arm and pointed at Strebo's ring. Snibo watched, his beady eyes fixed on the ring.

'Your ring is most unusual, Strebo,' said the druid. 'It looks Saxon to me.'

'Quite right, my lord Anroth,' said Strebo. 'It was a present from a grateful Saxon high chieftain to one of our heroic sea captains, who rescued his daughter from a sea monster.'

Lugh's eyes rolled up in exasperation at Strebo's latest lie.

Before Strebo could further embellish his deceit, Snibo struck. Swooping down, his claws gripped Strebo's hand and penetrated the skin as he grasped the ring in his beak. Petrified by the hideous sight and fearful he was about to lose a finger, Strebo let out a high-pitched shriek and fell backwards off his chair. Snibo ripped the ring free.

Anroth stood up and leant over the table. 'Oh dear, I must apologise, that was entirely my fault, Snibo just loves brightly coloured, shiny things.'

By now the bird had flown off in the direction of the wildwood.

'He normally just hides things like that under a stone,' continued Anroth. 'He's quite shy, your shouting must have frightened him away. I fear the ring is gone for good now. Can I make good your loss?' Strebo staggered to his feet, furious and flustered.

'Forget the cursed ring and keep the confounded hound,' he spluttered. 'It's late in the day and I must return to Gododdin.'

Anroth helped him onto his pony. 'It's been an honour meeting you, Strebo,' he said. 'Please don't hesitate to come and see us again, if we can help you in any other way.'

The Picts departed with their dead warrior and Bres's head, the latter immersed in cedar wood oil and sealed in a clay pot. Midar was delighted he'd won his prize The queen came down with Danu. Aine brought out more food and wine.

Snibo returned, swooped down and landed on the table beside Danu. Crouching down and chuntering triumphantly, he dropped the gold and garnet ring in front of her. When she didn't respond, he pushed the ring towards her hand with his beak. She picked it up and put it on her finger.

'Did anybody see when I dropped Cernunnos's wand and it fell on the back of Strebo's hand?' asked Anroth.

'No,' said Lugh.

'Then you probably didn't notice the skin on the back of his hand when he left?' said the druid.

'No.'

'It was badly blistered and getting worse,' said Anroth. 'Strebo is not the man he claims to be.'

'Birog the Black Druidess, the daughter of the Unforgiven Dead,' said Cliona. 'That treacherous shape-shifter!'

She looked at Anroth. 'It was her, wasn't it? She of the Deplorable Mind?'

He nodded. 'Once I realised who he really was, it was easy to prove,' he said. 'No black druidess can touch anything that once belonged to a god. The actual purpose of her visit was to retrieve the Black Obsidian. I hope she fell for our story.'

'In spite of his ridiculous behaviour, he was so convincing. I can't believe Strebo wasn't a man,' said Lugh. 'If you knew it was Birog, why didn't you expose her? She's the real cause of most our problems with Balor. I'd have killed her there and then.'

'You can't kill her,' said Anroth. 'Had you tried, she'd have killed you. She can only be killed when she reveals her true self, not when she's shape-shifted.'

'Not even by me?' asked Danu.

'In your present state, even you might be powerless against her dark magic,' said Anroth. 'She can turn herself into far more gruesome creatures than Strebo.'

'Well, what does she look like, in her true form?'

'Nobody knows, Danu,' said Midar. 'None of us have seen her.'

'Oh, I've seen her,' said Cliona quietly.

Everyone looked at the queen.

'It was before we married, Midar,' said Cliona. 'She attended my father's court in the days when she was still young and beautiful. They say that, since then, she's shape-shifted into many different creatures. And no one's seen the real Birog for years.'

Midar shook his head. 'Well, how did we fall for that today?'

'Because she disarmed you from the start,' said Anroth. 'She made herself an object of ridicule. She came out with so many obvious lies. And, because we saw through these petty falsehoods, we failed to noticed the one big lie, which was who she really was.'

'What put you onto her?' asked Midar.

'She had to be there somewhere in the delegation,' said Anroth. 'I knew she'd be desperate to get the Black

Obsidian back, for it's like my cauldron - without a way of concentrating your magical powers, you lose a lot of them. Then, simple things like table manners are difficult to disguise.'

'She's of noble birth. And, although she had the thick, broad hands of a man, I noticed that during the meal she couldn't help but eat her food in a refined, dainty manner. I had my suspicions then that Strebo was Birog. And I knew that Cernunnos's wand would burn her skin if I was right.'

As the others left, Anroth took Midar to one side to give him some unwelcome news.

'She made one other slip,' said the druid. 'Realising the wand had burnt her, she was desperate to get away.

When you said, "It's the hound or nothing" she lost her concentration and replied, "But he's been with me since birth, he's like a son to me".

Despite her protestations that she wouldn't part with Ominnios, it was always her intention to give him to you. She was determined she'd leave you with an enemy within.'

Midar looked at Anroth. 'It isn't a hound, is it? 'It must be Cu Roi, her idiot son. Why didn't you warn me sooner?'

'You made the right choice anyway,' said Anroth. 'If you'd chosen the gold, it would probably have turned to dust by now. I suspect the only way we can destroy Birog is to use the one thing she loves as much as herself – her son. Give me time to think about it. We can't be complacent, bear in mind, Birog, is returning to Gododdin with her husband's head and the dead body of her brother Balor's son. Not that there was any doubt, warfare is certainly inevitable now.' Midar shrugged his shoulders.

'There's one thing the young don't understand about border warfare, and that's when to stop and go home, having made your point,' he said. 'And on top of all that, we've now got Birog's son in the form of a hound wandering around all over the place. Someone might well talk about last night and the Black Obsidian in front of the beast.'

'I hope not,' said Anroth. 'When I made the excuse of going to get the beer, I went to Cliona and Nuada, and told them to talk to the servants, warriors and everyone else who'd been at the banquet. No one is to breathe a word about last night or the Obsidian.'

'Good, I've had my fill of meetings for one day,' said Midar. 'This is getting more complicated by the moment. Tomorrow, we plan for war.'

13 The Lama

Cu Roi was surprised how easy it had been to make the transition from Birog's weak, snivelling son, a young man who still clung to his mother's cloak and was scared of his own shadow, into the monstrous hound Ominnios. He was even more surprised how easy it had been for his mother to persuade Midar to accept him into his family.

Now, he lay contentedly in front of the fire, feigning sleep and listening to their conversation over supper. Dian suggested they should organise a hunting trip, so Midar could put the hound through his paces with the rest of the pack.

There was a difficulty here, for the snivelling, weedy Cu Roi had never been hunting, nor did he understand how a pack of hounds worked together in a group. He had devoted most of his life to showing off without anything to display or, alternatively, moaning, making an exhibition of himself and generally embarrassing his mother.

Blissfully unaware of what would be expected of him when out hunting with the other hounds, Cu Roi lay there relishing the prospect. He decided he would leap into a lake and kill a few swans. That ought to impress them.

He fell to wondering why his mother had never worked her malign magic to improve his scrawny body in its human form. He could so easily have been big and strong like his recently departed father, and just as considerate and kind.

That was one of Cu Roi's problems. There was a side to him that liked the idea of being nice, at least in theory, but he'd never quite grasped the fact that the only magic his mother performed was intended to make life worse for her victims.

Crimthain stood up, stretched and walked towards him. He began to talk about the new storage pits they'd dug in preparation for the harvest. He suggested that Anroth sacrifice a couple of dogs and put them at the bottom of the pits as an offering to the gods so they'd protect the crop.

'If this brute turns out to be a useless hunting dog, we can always kill him and throw him in,' he said, kicking Cu Roi in the haunches.

To Cu Roi's surprise, another side to the beast's nature revealed itself. He was able to sense something predatory and intimidating about Crimthain. It was a similar feeling to the one he got when he saw a strange shadow on the moor or felt something menacing and unseen following him through the forest.

The hairs on the back of his neck stood proud and his head went up. He looked into Crimthain's eyes. Mother had told him to be on his best behaviour, but he couldn't help himself. He lifted his head to its full height, and drew his legs up under him, preparing to attack Crimthain. As he did so, he let out the blood-curdling, deep-throated growl of a dog of war.

Crimthain didn't move, he just stood there looking at the hound.

Was it just the firelight or did Crimthain's dark-brown eyes burn within? Cu Roi had already noticed, now that he had been changed into a hound, he could hear sounds, that would be impossible for him to hear as a human. Everything sounded louder. With his highly developed hearing, no one other than Cu Roi heard Crimthain's response – the howl of a wolf calling to the wolf pack. It sent shivers down Cu Roi's spine.

Then, out of the darkness, he saw what no one else in the room seemed to be able to see: in the shadows around him, other fiery, dark-brown eyes, which watched and waited for him to make his move. Fearful, Cu Roi fell silent and rested his head back on the floor. He was cowed into submission. The bravado of the brute and the bully couldn't compensate for the coward within.

After supper, Goibniu took Cu Roi for a walk.

'The beast is twitchy,' observed Anroth. 'They must be planning something. Crimthain, hold your men in readiness through the night. If Birog comes looking for the Black Obsidian, this could be my chance to kill her.'

When they retired, they left a guard to keep watch over the hall. Cu Roi stretched out on the hearth. He'd been much taken by a young serving maid named Soay with amber, curly hair. Her facial features brought back fond memories of his less-than-savoury country pursuits, he started to count sheep in his head, who knew where idle minds would wander?

He assumed, once he'd done what his mother wanted, he'd be released from the body of the beast and would return to human form. He could hardly wait. Then he could take Soay for himself, and ravish and despoil her. Lustful feelings filled his mind. How frustrating it was to have paws and not hands.

Relief from his carnal frustrations came in an unexpected way. What if the soft and gentle Soay was not what she seemed, but Crimthain's daughter – a wolf in sheep's clothing? Tormented with self-doubt and terrified by things only he recognised in Crimthain's nature, Cu Roi's horny thoughts and intemperate anatomy deserted him.

The guard paced up and down, inside the hall. He found a stool and decided to sit with his back resting against the closed outer door. Later, he heard the sound of Midar's large pack of hounds barking in their kennels, followed by just a few brief yelps and growls before an ominous silence.

Something unspeakable was in amongst the pack of hounds. Having bitten two of the dogs' heads' off, swallowing the heads whole, it cowed the rest of the pack into submission, and departed, heading for the great hall.

Ominnios raised his head. He could hear an almost imperceptible, slithering sound coming closer. He heard it worming its way up the wall of the great hall onto the thatched roof. Tearing, tugging sounds followed and he watched as straw began to fall beside him onto the floor. His tail wagged slowly.

'Ah, good evening, mother,' he whispered.

Looking across to the doors, he saw the guard had fallen asleep. One tallow torch still spluttered and burned weakly on the wall. Through the hole in the thatch, a large head with bulging, grotesque eyes and a mouthful of monstrous teeth squeezed its way into the great hall. Gobbets of foul mucous slobbered from its mouth and slopped onto the floor below.

Birog had shape-shifted into the Lama. Every springtime, this loathsome behemoth – half slime-covered worm, half venomous snake – would ravage the countryside, slaughtering shepherds, sheep and cattle along the borderlands of the Brigantes.

The Lama's thick warty neck, which was coated in a greenish slime, twisted and turned. She was looking for something. There was a satisfied hiss when she found Anroth's golden cauldron hanging from the rafters. Grasping it tightly in her mouth, she shook the it free.

The guard awoke and struggled to his feet, drawing his sword. He tried to raise the alarm, but Cu Roi, in the body of Ominnios, the horrific hound was upon him, and ripped out his throat. All that was heard, was a strangled scream as the guard crashed to the floor. Standing on his hind legs, Ominnios, pushed up the crossbar, the creaking doors swung open, and the beast was lost to the night.

Lugh, Danu and Anroth arrived, roused by the sound of the doors, the Lama was pulling back through the hole in the thatch, crushing the cauldron gripped in her mouth.

'The Lama!' yelled Anroth. The others rushed forward.

'Avoid standing in that slime,' shouted Anroth, pointing to the mucous on the floor. 'It's poisonous!'

The head disappeared and Lugh ran outside to grapple with the beast as it slithered down the wall. A battle of giants ensued. Lugh attempted to use his colossal strength to squeeze the life out of the Lama, hoping it would drop the cauldron, but it responded by coiling itself slimy body around him. Crimthain and his men joined the fray, hacking at and attacking the beast from all sides, but their swords and axes simply slid off the slippery Lama. However, since it refused to release the cauldron, it was somewhat disadvantaged, unable to bite them.

Awoken from her slumbers by the rumpus, Aine came storming out, armed with two of her heavy, clay cooking pots. The first pot she threw went awry, but the second hit the Lama full force in the eye.

The Lama's body writhed as it let out an ear-piercing shriek. Aine had no intention of taking singing lessons from the hideous maggot. Hands on her hips, she screamed right back at the witch, louder than the Lama and at a higher pitch.

Disconcerted by the din, unable to see properly, and worried that the wily druid Anroth, must have discovered how to turn himself into a monster even more frightening than herself, the Lama took flight. It shook itself free of Lugh, tossed him to the ground and slithered away. Lugh staggered to his feet, covered in the creature's foul-smelling slime and decomposing skin.

Those were two of my best pots,' Aine tutted, as she returned to her bed.

There was the sound of a galloping pony as Birog made good her escape with the cauldron. Anroth was distraught.

'She outwitted me,' he said. 'Lugh, go down to the sea, throw all your clothes away and wash all that slime off. It's poisonous when it dries. Danu, go down with him, but take your spear. That hound will still be out there somewhere, hungry for another kill.'

As it happened, they were safe enough. Fearful of Crimthain and fed up with the frustrations of a dog's life, Cu Roi was bounding after his mother, pleading with her to take him home.

Lugh and Danu walked down to the sea. He undid his belt with a buckle that resembled the intertwined talons of the sea eagle, stripped off his foetid clothes and bundled them together, then hurled them far out into the water. Rinsing his golden torque and belt, he handed them to Danu.

His skin was beginning to feel hot and swollen. Those areas that had come into contact with the Lama's body throbbed and he felt as though he'd been stung by a swarm of bees. He swam out into the bay to wash away the creature's decomposing skin and thick mucus. The saltwater refreshed him, soothed his skin and eased the pain.

When he returned to Danu, his hands were shaking so much that he couldn't put the torque back around his neck. Danu did it for him, before covering him with her cloak and walking him back to the stronghold.

The Third Day Of Lunasa

14 The Council Of War

It was the third day of the festival of Lunasa and Midar and the council met in the great hall. As the blood on the floor and the gaping hole in the roof testified, the honour of the tribe had been defiled. Midar brought the meeting to order.

'It would be easy to imagine that last night was the consequence of our successful punishment raid on Gododdin, but that would be to misunderstand the cause of all the conflicts plaguing our northern borders,' he said, remembering the headstrong days of his youth and stopping short of blaming the three princes.

'Retaliation has long been overdue. The battle we must now prepare for was always inevitable. It's a conflict that's been many years in the making.' Those present looked up at the high chieftain.

'The black druidess Birog's jealous eyes have fuelled her brother Balor's lust for our northern estates,' he continued.

'She's pumped him full of her poison and persuaded him our northern borderlands are rightfully his. I've always hesitated to strike at the heart of his kingdom because, if we do, there's a danger his northern neighbours will be threatened by our advance and join forces with him in an alliance against us.'

'We've yet to see warfare on such a scale, and neither side could be certain of success. Don't forget that Balor is a great warrior. He's welded together and ruled his far-flung lands for longer than we've ruled the Kingdom of Northumbria.'

Lugh nodded. He had spent a restless night, tormented by images of the Lama worming its way through his window and he'd woken several times in a cold sweat. In the morning, much to his relief, his skin had returned to normal.

'Just because Balor's rule is a byword for brutality and duplicity, do not make the mistake of imagining his subjects are his enemies,' said Midar. 'He leaves most of them untroubled, and he's bestowed on them the gifts of peace and stability. It matters not to them if their ruler is good or evil, for what eats away at the heart of any people is uncertainty. A high chieftain is admired and respected above all things for his strength.'

Lugh grimaced.

'Balor is acknowledged throughout his kingdom as the greatest high chieftain of them all,' continued Midar. 'He's bestowed more than just peace and stability on his people. He's made them proud to belong to the tribe of the Gododdin. Our cattle raid was well planned. Speed and surprise gave us a well deserved victory. But don't imagine the battle before us is a foregone conclusion or make the mistake of underestimating Balor. His life is proof of the perversity of war. Remember that success is not the sole privilege of the righteous and those of noble intent.'

Lugh could not find a comfortable position in his chair and spasms of pain shot up his spine. Danu watched him.

'Recent events have left us no choice but to attack and destroy the high chieftain's stronghold, Balores,' said Midar. 'The deaths of Bres and Mechi have ensured that, as we speak, Balor will be calling in favours from his northern allies.

It's our good fortune that these matters should present themselves when we're all together to celebrate the festival of Lunasa. It means we have the ability to move fast and take Balor by surprise. I've already ordered my friends and fellow chieftains to send all their available warriors to the Valley of the High Waters, close to his kingdom, Gododdin.'

Lugh gripped the table. His head spun and the sound of angry bees buzzed in his ears. His throat parched, he attempted to stretch out his arm for the jug of water that sat in the middle of the table, but he changed his mind.

Danu poured him a goblet. Only she noticed that, as she handed it to him, his hands shook.

'We'll meet in the woods west of the waterfall,' continued Midar. 'From there its but half a day's journey through Gododdin, to his stronghold, Balores. Until we're all assembled, no one must cross the river, as the next river to the north defends his stronghold. Before this festival of Lunasa has run its course, Balores will be razed to the ground, Balor's fleet of pirate ships will be ablaze and those who seek to destroy us will either be dead or will have fled.'

Midar stood up. His penetrating eyes and grave countenance matched the cold, considered way he came to his conclusions.

'There are other matters to mention,' he said. 'Balor has an elder daughter, Eithne, and another son. A year or two after his wife gave birth to their fourth child – a boy – she died in mysterious circumstances, as did the son. His sister Birog then took Balor's children under her dark wing, and raised them in her own image and likeness. She has made their minds a mirror of her own.'

'They say that Eithne, should she ever master the powers of a black druidess, will prove even more evil than Birog. If we don't succeed in rooting out and killing not just Balor and Birog, but the whole family, then Birog and her brother will live on in their children. The evil in Balores will endure.

'Difficult as it may be for you to believe, Balor and I could have come to an agreement if it hadn't been for Birog's malign influence. Both our kingdoms would have prospered. In a lifetime of treachery, weasel words and deceit, that one woman has brought down discord and the seeds of destruction on both our houses. Why has she devoted her days to the destruction of Northumbria? My home has been desecrated by the Lama and insults so inflicted must be washed away in blood. I've seen her falsehood in her rotting flesh, listened to her last lie. Birog and all around her will die.'

An eye peered through a hole in the kitchen door. Occasionally it disappeared, to be replaced by an ear pressed against the roughened edges of the wood. Once there had been a large wood knot where the hole was, but it had loosened and eventually fallen out – with a little help from Aine – and now there was a hole in the door.

When the carpenter had been summoned, Crimthain had told him to plug the hole with a peg. But Aine had fed the carpenter a fine meal and, when he'd finished, she'd asked him to leave the hole be. The carpenter had fitted his peg above the hole, so Aine had somewhere to hang her cloak.

Long before the council of war had concluded, Aine had marshalled her troops in the kitchen. She declared war on every available morsel of uncooked food and whatever else she could lay her hands on, including some unfortunate chickens that strutted outside the back door and scratched for grain in the courtyard.

All available hands were pressed into service. Soon they were baking breads and biscuits, roasting meats on spits and heating cauldrons full of vegetables, freshly killed fowl and leftovers from the larder. While they waited for the food to cook, they set up tables outside.

Long before the council of war had been concluded, news that the Brigantes were going to war had spread around the settlement. The common fighting men sharpened their weapons and gathered together all they needed to take with them. The meal before their departure would be the best Aine could manage for her boys. No man leaving her care would do so with an empty belly. It might be the last decent meal they ever had.

Aine pressed her ear hard against the hole, and heard Anroth speak.

'I must take the blame,' he said. 'I could so easily have killed Birog last night. If Danu and I had waited in the shadows, she could have killed her son, Cu Roi, with the spear of Assal while the Lama was hanging down from the rafters. Seeing her son mortally wounded, she would have returned to human form and fallen to the floor below. Birog's magic would have been no match for Cernunnos's golden wand.'

The high chieftain leant forward, clearing his throat.

'This conflict is much more than just a clash of arms, Midar,' said the druid. 'There's an added dimension to all this. Birog's dark powers were enhanced by the Black Obsidian we stole from her, as mine were by the golden cauldron, but neither Birog nor I now possess our most trusted means of channelling either her dark desires or my means of repelling them.

'However, there's another much more deadly game she can play,' he continued. 'Birog's greatest inspirations are the Morrigan, those battle hags of the ancient tribe of the Tuatha de Danann. In times of war, they take to the air as three black carrion crows and feed off the dead and the dying. If we can't catch Birog off-guard before battle commences, the outcome will hang on the thread of a spider's web. Once she starts shape-shifting from one hideous creature into another, she'll prove impossible to kill.'

There was a stunned silence.

Cliona nodded in agreement. 'She of the Deplorable Mind always was a repulsive creature, even in human form.'

'Why is she known as "She of the Deplorable Mind"?' asked Goibniu.

The queen stiffened and looked him in the eye. Her countenance did not invite further discussion.

'Her behaviour and exploits are not the stuff of idle gossip cultured young men like you should be listening to,' she said.

Undeterred, Goibniu pressed her. 'Well, if her behaviour is so reprehensible, how come you seem to know so much about her, mother?'

Lugh, mercifully relieved of his afflictions, stepped in.

'Let's not get too bogged down with Birog's background,' he said. 'The important thing to remember, as I know to my cost, is that the creature is more monster than woman, and she's lethal. Anyone going up against the fiend will be dealing with something extremely dangerous.'

'My chance of killing her must be better than anyone else's,' said Danu. Worried by Danu's intervention, Anroth cautioned her.

'She'd have to be in human form for you to have any chance of succeeding,' he said. 'She's more than capable of killing you.'

'Let's not forget Cu Roi in all this,' said Danu. 'He must be out there somewhere, still transformed into Ominnios, waiting to run back to Balores the moment he sees us setting out for battle.'

Anroth sat in silence, with his head back and eyelids closed, unable to comprehend how Birog's many powers could be counterbalanced without his cauldron. It had been both his crutch and his shield through many perilous battles of the mind.

'If Birog lives long enough to wreak havoc among our warriors, we could be beaten before we've even begun,' said Midar. 'Without the element of surprise, she sounds invincible.'

'How would it be if, without warning, Birog found the hound Ominnios dead?' asked Danu. 'If we somehow managed to bring the two together, then Ominnios the hound, would be transformed back into his human form, Cu Roi, her son and, once she'd seen his dead body, so would she.' Anroth opened his eyes. A glimmer of hope returned.

'Yes, under those circumstances, she'd inevitably revert to her human form, even if was only briefly,' he said. 'We're assuming of course that she possesses a maternal instinct.'

Cliona insisted that not even Birog could fail to care for her child.

'Let's assume, Danu, that somehow you got them together,' said Anroth. 'You'd be alone with precious little time and only one chance to inflict the fatal blow. Remember what I told you yesterday. You're in a state of flux and are part human, part goddess. You're no longer immortal. If she kills you, you'll forfeit your life forever.'

Seeing a solution, Midar was quick to interrupt.

'How might you achieve this Danu?'

'I'll leave for the Valley of the High Waters as soon as our meeting has ended,' she said. 'Cu Roi may not know who I am, but he'll have realised by now I'm both a threat and a prize he'd dearly love to destroy. If he sees me head north to Gododdin, he'll almost certainly follow me, which will give you valuable time to make your preparations and set out in secret. When I reach the Valley of the High Waters, I'll kill him. It's too soon to know how I'll achieve the rest.'

'I fancy you'll find a friend along the way,' said Anroth. 'You met him yesterday. If anyone can help you in this hazardous undertaking, he can.'

'Dancer?' she asked.

'He has his own way of doing things,' Midar reassured her. 'He's a good man, one of the best and one of us.'

Dian spoke up. 'When we talked with Frii at the banquet, he warned us how formidable the Pictish pirates have become,' he said. 'They may not be warriors as we know them, but they're well-trained and lethal with the spear and bow. They sleep in their ships. On the cattle raid, I saw many vessels moored up by the mouth of the river. We rode down the bank of the estuary, intending to destroy them, but I withdrew when I realised what we were up against.'

'And what was that?' asked Midar, surprised by this unwelcome news.

'Each vessel was like a small fortress, bristling with weapons,' said Dian. 'They stick to those ships like limpets. It'll be a costly encounter if they're expecting us. The moment Danu has dealt with Birog and before you launch your main attack, we must strike hard at his fleet. Otherwise, they'll slip the net and put out to sea to ravage our coastline.'

Midar nodded. 'They could wipe out our coastal settlements,' he said. 'They'd have nothing to lose. We have warriors coming up from the south. So, in addition to your own men, Dian, you'll command these reinforcements. Wait for them here, they should arrive tomorrow morning. You'll need to move quickly, to catch up with us.'

Midar stood up, his brooding presence like thunder clouds hovering on the horizon. 'Before I launch the main attack,' he continued, 'deploy your warriors as close as possible to the fleet. We can only make more detailed plans once the area has been scouted.'

Dian nodded.

'One more thing,' said Midar. 'Balor is mine.'

Anroth intervened. 'Unless Birog is already dead, on no account should you attack Balor on your own,' he said. 'Whenever Birog sees her brother fighting another warrior, she finds ways of protecting him. He never really fights alone. How do you think he's defeated so many great warriors over the years?

'She can shape-shift into all manner of fearful things, including a massive swarm of flying ants,' he continued. 'They cover the warrior's head, sting his eyes, and fly into his nose, mouth and ears. Balor waits until Birog's victim has fallen to his knees, then he decapitates him.'

Anroth looked at Lugh, Goibniu and Dian. 'If you do attempt to kill Balor while Birog still lives, all of you must attack at the same time.'

'There's something else to discuss,' said Nuada. 'At the banquet, Frii suggested the Saxons may be planning further expansion. They could attack us here.'

Crimthain agreed. 'It's true, their reach has never been this far north, but my spies inform me they've gained a foothold in Deira to the south. Before we commit too many warriors to Balores, we need to ensure we're able to adequately defend the stronghold in your absence.'

Anroth suggested that Midar made Nuada the commander and Crimthain should choose which warriors would stay behind. The rest of the meeting involved planning the rapid deployment of Midar's army. Goibniu and the master blacksmith would be responsible for the distribution of any additional weaponry, and the queen would oversee the provisioning of the troops. Lugh would organise the movement of the warriors heading north, as well as their ponies and the baggage train.

They planned to leave that evening and travel through the night.

As they left the meeting, Dian turned to Goibniu. 'Is it wise to leave Nuada behind and divide the three of us up?' he asked.

'We'll be fighting separately in this encounter anyway,' said Goibniu. 'Midar's only trying to protect Nuada. He's our weakest link.'

'He may be,' said Dian. 'But he's never let us down and we've been able to protect him. If things go wrong down here, he'll be much more vulnerable than he is when he's with us. Once he starts, he doesn't know when to stop. Neither of us will be around to yank him back in line. We should speak to father.'

Goibniu thought for a moment and looked across at Midar.

'He doesn't look to me, as if he's in the mood to discuss anything.'

Before leaving, Danu talked her mission through with Anroth.

''There are two important things to avoid on the journey, Danu. 'When you walk beside a river, you might see the Washer at the Ford. But even if you hear her weeping, don't venture nearby. She's an omen of death. She washes the blood from the clothes of those about to die. Don't look her in the eye. Have a care, beware her empty, cold and soulless stare, lest it be your clothes she washes.'

Danu nodded.

'And, as you walk through the woods, keep clear of the enchanted white cattle,' he continued. 'Long ago, their great herds roamed the length and breadth of Northumbria. They're the oldest cattle in the world and they're ruled by the magnificent great white bull Chillingo. You saw him at the banquet, standing behind Cernunnos. Of all the wild, white cattle, he's the most dangerous. The rest of his herd are small and beautiful to look upon, with milk-white coats and placid faces, but don't be deceived. They're the most violent beasts of the forest. Without warning, they'll attack anyone who ventures near. Many a hapless wayfarer has ended up skewered on their horns.

'If you try to escape by running into the sea or a river, they'll follow. As they hit the water, they change into seals with pure-white fur, large dark eyes and horrifying teeth. They tear their victims to shreds, leaving the victim's bones to slowly sink below.'

Thanking the druid for his ominous warnings, Danu picked up her provisions and left. Anroth waited until she was some distance away, then called out to her.

'Danu,' he shouted. 'When you meet Dancer, remember that he hasn't always been that way. He'll do everything he can to help you. I hope you can find it in your heart to help him.'

She waved, wondering what he could possibly mean, and headed north with a confident spring in her step, disguising her apprehension. The life of a mortal was so different from the world of the gods. The importance of loyalty to the clan and putting the greater good of others before all else had never occurred to her as a goddess. It was a life more precious than anything she had known before, and it was worth fighting and dying for.

Her heart thumped. Was she frightened? Oh yes, she was terrified. To defeat Birog would require all her skill and a fair measure of good fortune, but something else drove her on. Something she well understood as a goddess – revenge. Birog existed to make as many people as unhappy as she could. The pernicious gift to create misery that she possessed gave her a sense of fulfilment and power in her empty, loveless world.

Birog was not to know she had stolen what remained of Danu's precious childhood. But, if she had known, she'd have been delighted. And though killing Birog would not give Danu her childhood back, it would bring an end to a life incapable of anything but evil.

Danu turned around for one last, wistful wave goodbye. Out of the corner of her eye, she saw a flash of silver. Cu Roi in the form of Ominnios had taken the bait and was following her. Killing Birog's son would whet her appetite for the real revenge she sought.

When Danu was completely out of sight, Anroth went and found Midar.

'What are her chances?' the high chieftain asked him.

'Better than anyone else's,' said the druid, weighing his words carefully and looking him straight in the eye. 'But one thing troubles me – this idea that all women have maternal instinct. I don't believe a word of it.'

'I agree with what you're doing, Midar, you have no alternative. I tell you what I foresee with regret. It won't change your mind, but you still need to know.

'Yes, you will kill Balor and, if Danu doesn't lose her life in the attempt, she may well kill Birog. Yes, you'll burn Balores to the ground. But though you won't die in the battle, you are riding to your final clash of arms. Be warned, if you win a battle but lose a kingdom, then where does victory lie? No man's head should lightly rest upon another's thigh.'

'Thank you for the warning,' said Midar. 'It's the destiny of kings. The day good fortune no longer fights beside me draws ever closer.'

By the time the council of war disbanded, men were already congregating around the tables outside the kitchen. Aine's helpers handed out as many dry provisions as the men could carry in the leather pouches hanging from their belts. There was a cheer as the roasted meats, the simmering cauldrons of thick broth and the freshly baked breads were set down among them.

Aine moved through the excited throng, speaking to them in song. Some songs were soft and loving, others bold and strong, songs to shed a tear by, songs to march along. Before they left, she embraced them all, for she desperately needed to share her love. She wished she could fight beside them.

It was a fine thing for a common fighting man to leave his home with a full belly and the remembrance of Aine's affection. They had grown up with her. She had mothered them all. They recognised it was their honourable duty to fight for the noble warlord Midar, but, above all, in the tumult and bloodletting of battle, they fought and died for Aine and the world she represented. In their eyes, she was the goddess of all things bountiful.

That evening, Anroth walked out alone to look for Ollathir. He found him talking to his children.

'Olly, you'll know by now that Midar and his men are to ride north to fight Balor,' he said. 'The expedition is beset with problems, one of which seems insoluble. How do we draw the Pictish pirates away from their ships? We may well win the battle for Balores, but we're in grave danger of being mortally wounded in the process.'

Ollathir leant on his club and shook his head.

'I agree, it's hard to think of any solution other than a costly frontal attack on their fleet,' he said. 'If the tide is high, many ships will slip anchor anyway, so nowhere will be safe. Give me what time we have left to think about it.'

Drastic measures were called for. When Ollathir went to bed that night, he realised he needed the help of his massive and magnificent lady friend Bebhionn. What was required was quality thinking time and, while most would say their best thinking time came when they rose early before the dawn, Ollathir was different. His best thinking time came when dusk had fallen and he retired to his straw-filled cot. It was a special treat to snuggle up to that patron of pleasure, Bebhionn, she of the rusty red hair and bright-red ears. As he lay awake trying to think, he listened to the soothing sounds and contented grunts of her dreamtime.

15 She Of The Deplorable Mind

She of the Deplorable Mind, the black druidess Birog, was the younger sister of Balor – the high chieftain of the Picts in the Kingdom of Gododdin on Northumbria's northern borders. By all accounts, in her youth, she was blessed with fine features: a wide-eyed, innocent beauty that men in their misguided dreams associated with a sweet and virtuous nature. This might explain why, from an early age, she had deluded herself that every man she ever met fell madly in love with her. Some undoubtedly did fall for her shy, seductive smile and ominous, come-hither charms.

It would be misleading to say she had been disappointed in love, for there was no love in her, and had there been, she would have saved it for herself. Nothing had been allowed to intrude on her ambition to, one day, obtain wealth and eminence by marrying a powerful warlord.

Her decision to be taught the skills and arts of a druidess was down to her compulsion to control and dominate everyone she encountered. Her motives were hardly unique, for how many of those attracted to the priestly classes are also driven by the desire for status, and the acquisition of authority and power?

Birog had left Gododdin to train as a druidess in the Kingdom of Rheged. Not long after she'd arrived there, Midar had visited the court to reaffirm old alliances and treaties between the two powerful kingdoms. To further demonstrate the importance, he placed on this alliance, he hoped to find a wife from amongst the nobility of Rheged.

Though he was still young, he was already much celebrated among all the Celtic tribes. The storytellers sang the praises of 'Midar of the thirty battles'. And with his two famed warrior companions – Bres who rode on his right and Lugh who rode on his left, he had proved invincible. When Birog heard of his visit, she set her sights on snaring the renowned warrior.

Even in the days of his youth, Midar, tall and commanding was a man of just a few, well-chosen words. He was of a somewhat solemn and sombre countenance, and respected as an even-handed and honourable ruler. The isolation and loneliness of his high calling did not sit well with his sometimes melancholy nature.

In honour of Midar and his warriors, all the great and good of the kingdom gathered together in Rheged's magnificent hall. Birog, marriage on her mind, stalked him around the room, worming her way through the crowd towards Midar.

Before Birog reached him, Midar's eyes fell on Cliona. Almost in the first flush of womanhood, the future queen's features were already famous, her beauty the pride of Rheged. She tried to hide her insecurity and shyness by remaining aloof. When she felt the noble warrior's eyes resting upon her, she made as if to move away. But in her moment of hesitation, she found him standing beside her.

She turned and he saw, a rare vision of beauty that made him shy and stumble over his words. He only had to look into her tranquil, pale-blue eyes and he was under her spell. He ached inside with a desire to share her dreams and sought only to please her.

Midar had found a prize far more precious than his kingdom – someone to walk besides, to love, cherish and honour. The chieftain was a man who usually planned his moves meticulously but, in that brief moment when she first turned her face towards him, he knew she would be his bride. His behaviour was completely out of character; however, his instincts proved him right. For the first time in his life, he knew happiness. He worshipped the ground she walked upon. And, as she gave him her love and fed off his, Cliona grew gracefully into an admirable queen.

Not many men can carry the heavy burdens of being a warlord while, at the same time, respecting everything they rule. But Midar strove hard to govern and serve in equal measure. He was duty bound to the territory he had taken by strength of arms, accepting responsibility for the care of those lands. Just as he'd trusted Cliona would prove fruitful, he trusted in his kingdom. He knew that, in summer, his meadows must be bountiful, swaying with the harvest; and in autumn, his storage pits must be filled with grain.

He suffered, when the rains came down, and the harvest was spoiled and beaten to the ground, for he knew even a noble tyrant is held to account for the failures of his land as he is praised for his success in battle.

Midar was a man who could be driven to despair, fearful of the failure of his fields. Only Cliona could soothe and mollify his unpredictable moods of brooding melancholy. He would come to rely on her. But he had yet to discover this side to her character.

When Birog realised Midar only had eyes for Cliona, she had melted back into the crowd. In the heady magic of that first meeting between the chieftain and his future queen, Midar had never even noticed the black druidess.

There were so many guests, many were gathered outside the hall. Hearing bellows of raucous laughter, Birog went out to join them. She saw Bres loudly affirming his adoration for a buxom Rheged maiden, much to the amusement of his admirers. Now there was a prize worthy of her ambitions. As an act of vengeance, she decided to cut off Midar's right arm and steal Bres away from his warrior friends. Biding her time, she watched and waited, and wondered how best to relieve Bres of his freedom.

She remembered days gone by, a terrifying time from long ago. Her mother had taken her on a hazardous sea voyage to the far-off island of ice and snow, a place of sinister sagas where only the daughters of the unforgiven dead could go.

She recalled standing on crumbling wastelands of hardened lava, where nauseating mists belched up from fissures in the ground and provided portals to that Otherworld of evil. She had watched her mother stand on the edge of a chasm as mists and steam bathed her face. Savouring the moment, the evil hag's features had briefly been transformed into the beautiful woman she had once been.

Without warning, her mother had thrust her hands deep into the turbulent vapours. And, as she withdrew them, Birog saw her mother fashion the swirling mists, conjuring up a magical fabric, creating a wondrous, iridescent scarf.

Birog remembered the exquisite sight – icy blue, shimmering white, lava-grey and as black as the night.

The scarf billowed up, it moved with a life of its own, and transfixed, unable to take her eyes off it, Birog felt her thoughts being sucked out of her, until her mother started to fold it.

With a whispering hiss, her mother gave it to her and promised that 'whenever you wear this scarf, it will give you everything you desire.'

Before going to the great hall of Rheged, the day Midar came to call, remembering her mother's words, all those years later, before leaving her room, Birog placed the folded the scarf, in a pocket deep within her robe, intent on wedlock.

Birog looked at Bres, then turned away, drawing the scarf from within and casually covered her head, so it fell shimmering over her shoulders. She walked over to the warrior and stood in front of him with her back turned towards him, until he noticed the scarf, alluring, unable to take his eyes off it.

She turned her face towards him and let the scarf slip slowly down over her hair. She smiled and tied it loosely around her neck.

Bres was mesmerised. It seemed so innocent as he fell under her spell, and so she was able to fill his, by now subservient mind, with promises she would never keep. She persuaded him to become her brother Balor's champion, and assured him of fame and wealth equal to that of Midar. Later, she took him back with her to Gododdin and married him, and so Midar's comrade in arms became his enemy. But he wasn't the only one. Even stealing Bres away wasn't enough to assuage the insult to Birog's pride that Midar had unknowingly inflicted on her.

When Birog heard Midar and Cliona were married, she swore she would never rest until she had reduced the

Kingdom of Northumbria to ashes. The fall of the house of Midar was always somewhere in her nefarious schemes, the faded, putrid perfume of her fruitless dreams.

Someone less versed in the evil arts would have assassinated Cliona, but that would never have satisfied Birog. Only when she'd widowed Cliona would she rest, for hadn't Midar made Birog a widow of her own possessive mind? There would be time enough to plan Cliona's humiliating demise once the high chieftain was dead.

Birog's mother had introduced her daughter to the seductive skills of a black druidess. When Birog began training at Rheged, she put these skills to good use. From the start, she set about gaining as much knowledge as she could by taking many lovers. She claimed this bestowed upon her, important insights into druidic visionary understanding.

Whenever she made love to a fellow novice, she could gain access to his inner thoughts in no time at all. The amorous confusion of a man's mind at such times allowed Birog to suck it empty and memorise everything he knew.

Mysteriously, novice druids began to disappear and no one in Rheged could understand it. But if they'd have looked closer, they'd have found that, on every occasion, Birog had taken them to her bed the night before. Since she was discreet about her affairs, no one ever made the connection.

Before long, her knowledge was such that she became celebrated as the most gifted of all the novice druids. And though she was despised by some for her seductive behaviour, and blatant promiscuity, she was admired by many others.

They would have been surprised to know that, despite her many dalliances, Birog had never actually climaxed. While Birog had enjoyed remarkable success as a sexual predator, she had remained orgasmically innocent, until – that is – she encountered the young Dancer.

Some years after Midar's visit, Dancer was sent by Anroth to Rheged. Birog was very excited. At last, she had a chance to learn everything she could about Midar, discover his weaknesses and plan his assassination.

Dancer, who by nature was something of a rebel, never really settled down in Rheged. Compared to Anroth and his more intuitive methods, he found his druidic teachers overbearing and pompous. Most of a druid's skills involved debate, deduction and a good memory, but, in Rheged, they were also taught manual skills: healing, sacrificial throat-slitting and other ceremonial procedures, including woodcraft and the cutting of the mistletoe.

Dancer particularly struggled with the 'Lighting the Sacrificial Fire,' a ritual where any fires used in sacrificial ceremonies could never be lit using the embers of other fires. The flame had to be pure and created by the druid specifically for the sacrifice, and this involved twiddling and twisting one long, thin bit of wood – the firestick – inside a hole in another piece of wood with some dry kindling tucked in around it. When the kindling started to smoulder, you blew on it until it burst into flames. But, try as he might, this skill eluded Dancer.

His teacher was a skinny, cantankerous old druid, who, in spite of his twisted arthritic fingers, could produce a fire every time. He would say to Dancer.

'Imagine you're making love to a woman. Caress the wood, twist and twiddle your firestick so it tickles the hole and starts to smoulder within. Blow softly on the hole until the kindling bursts into flames.'

Anroth never bothered with such niceties. Dancer knew he just took embers from the kitchen, to light his sacrificial fires, yet Anroth's magic was better than anyone's. When the old druid realised, he was getting nowhere with Dancer, he took him to one side.

'You need to reconsider your decision to become a druid,' he said. 'Your life might be better spent as a potter or a swineherd. I'm going to give you one more week, then I'll test you again. If you still can't light a sacrificial fire then you're not fit to be a druid and will be expelled.'

Not wishing to let Anroth down, Dancer spent the next week frantically blowing, twiddling and twisting his little stick, but all to no avail. He promised himself that, if he ever did manage to create a sacrificial fire, the first thing he'd set alight would be the wizened old druid's gown, though which particular deity would find the miserable old goat an acceptable sacrifice he simply couldn't imagine.

Day after day, he twisted, twiddled and blew. It came between him and his wits. As the fateful day drew nearer, the more fixated he became. He could do or think of nothing else.

Unbeknown to Dancer, Birog had been sizing him up, patiently pursuing her prey. He was young and tasty, she considered him easy meat, a meal to be savoured after she had drained his mind of everything, he knew about Midar. The night before his final Lighting the Sacrificial Fire test, Birog finally made her move and took him to her bed. He offered to bring some food with him they could share, but she politely declined, explaining that she expected to eat later.

Dancer did his best to kindle Birog's spirits. But, having spent a week trying to light a fire while imagining he was making love, he now found that all he could think about was how to light a fire, when he should have been thinking about how to make love to Birog. Unable to forget about twiddling his little fire stick and blowing softly, his unusual foreplay was more prolonged than it might have been. Birog adored it. She had a splendid time, and found it so exciting and delightfully new.

Though she wasn't a virgin, her orgasmic innocence made her vulnerable to Dancer's oddly appealing, unconventional and earnest endeavours. Aroused, Birog became tantalisingly tumescent and completely forgot to access Dancer's mind. To his surprise, he realised Birog's fire was smouldering. If only the old goat could have been there, Dancer was sure the druid would have passed his fire-lighting skills on the spot.

At that critical moment, Birog remembered to try to drain Dancer's mind. He, on the other hand, was still preoccupied with lighting her fire, and hoped his little firestick, which had grown to the family size, wasn't about to burst into flames. Disaster struck as she climaxed, all she was able to see was an impenetrable wall of fire. To confuse matters further, a scraggy, semi-naked druid rushed past with his gown in flames, shouting, 'Stop blowing!'

The sensory and mental overload was all too much for Birog, who was in a state of unstable ecstasy. Instead of her sucking up information from Dancer's mind, she transferred every last iota of the knowledge she had painstakingly extracted from everybody else directly into Dancer's brain. Overwhelmed, he fell back into a state of confused soporific contentment. Unaware she had lost all her knowledge, Birog was overjoyed with Dancer's performance. But she had a lethal surprise in store for him. Feeling hungry, she licked her lips and shape-shifted into a gigantic, hairy, black spider. It was time for her supper. Dancer hadn't needed to bring a meal; he was the meal.

He felt her scuttle up over his body. She seemed to have acquired rather more legs than he remembered. Birog bit into his neck but, bewildered by all the knowledge that had overloaded his brain, he didn't feel a thing. His neck just went numb. It felt quite nice when she started to wrap him up. How kind, he thought, for the night was unseasonably cold.

'That was so nice, Dancer,' she whispered in his ear. 'You gave me so many lovely little things: your kiss, your fingertips, your lips, all of you. Promise me I can start my meal with just one little thing, Dancer, it belongs to me now and nobody else.'

As her fangs hovered over it, she added, 'You won't be needing it anymore.'

Dancer opened his eyes and found himself trapped within the eight hairy legs of a gigantic spider and partly cocooned in the web she had spun around his body. Barely awake, but ever the man of action, young Dancer made a critical decision. He closed his eyes again.

When Birog saw the petrified look on Dancer's face, she relented. She could always eat him on some future occasion, she decided, but not now. Making love with him was too much fun.

Dancer's semi-conscious mind retreated into that confusing place where fact and fantasy are bedfellows and logical thought doesn't intrude. He prided himself on his powers of observation, but now they failed him. He was annoyed with himself.

'How come,' his muddled mind demanded, 'I've known Birog all these months and I've never noticed she had hairy legs?'

When he opened his eyes again, she was back in human form, looking coy and cuddly. She dismissed him with a languid wave of her hand and gave him a vacuous grin before falling fast asleep.

As he walked back to his cell, it dawned on him that his mind had become the receptacle of an enormous amount of knowledge that didn't belong to him. It could only have come from Birog. Feeling guilty, he wanted to return her knowledge. He wondered if tossing a pitcher of ice-cold water over the sleeping woman would refresh her memory and restore what she had lost. But he abandoned his plan, worried that the sudden shock of the cold water might freeze her mind or shut it down completely.

Still confused and giddy, he felt quite favourably disposed to the evil sorceress and, for the briefest of moments, he even thought he might be in love with her. People could say what they liked about Birog but, when it came to making love, she really was something else. However, her appetite for his modest little warrior, perturbed him. Aware of the rumours that Birog was a black druidess with a vindictive streak, he decided to leave Rheged that very night.

Birog woke the next day in the very best of moods. She hadn't a thought or a care in the world – until she realised, she'd lost all the knowledge she'd stolen over the years. Her fury knew no bounds and she swore that, one day, she would kill Dancer.

The disastrous decline in Birog's mental capabilities did not go unnoticed by her tutor, the cantankerous old druid, who reported her to the high druid of Rheged. She could provide no explanation for her ignorance.

Protecting the reputation of Rheged's druidic school took precedence over establishing the truth, so Birog was dismissed. Since she was of royal blood, the high druid had to tread carefully. He found her a position at court, where she attended to the queen, and the whole affair was hushed up. In time, she returned to Gododdin, married Bres, and plotted revenge against Dancer and Midar. Serpents swam within her heart.

16 Departure

Cliona's father, the high chieftain of Rheged, shared a common border with Northumbria to the east of his kingdom. The alliance between the two great kingdoms was important and they provided each other with mutual protection. To the west was the Irish Sea, from which Rheged was frequently attacked by seaborne raiders. Given the uncertainty of the times, it was a long-established tradition to train not just the sons, but also the daughters of the high chieftain of Rheged in the arts of war.

Cliona's mother was well-versed in such matters, for her own father and later her brother had been the champions of Rheged. Although Cliona had moved to Northumbria, she remained her mother's daughter. Often, she would sit on the headland and look out to sea, searching for make-believe enemy raiders and imagining herself a warrior queen.

She confided her ambitions to Anroth, expecting him to laugh at her, but he took her very seriously. He was well aware their own borders could never be completely secure. Crimthain, who was her bodyguard in those days, was more than happy to undertake her training.

Over the years that followed, Crimthain taught her how to defend herself and she became proficient in many disciplines. An excellent horsewoman, she was experienced with bow, spear and sword thanks to his patient guidance. He taught her how to kill simply, without embellishment, hiding a dagger up her sleeve or in the folds of her dress; and how to slide a thin, long blade up from the stomach and behind the breastbone into the victim's heart. Skilfully performed, the enemy barely felt a thing.

He taught her to kill with poison and also how to spare someone's life while rendering them senseless. He showed her how to use her feminine charms to distract, and how to feint an attack in which she would dance around a warrior's shield arm, then run her blade into his armpit and straight into his heart. She never asked him how best to strangle someone. One day, when Crimthain was instructing her, he suggested the garrotte, Cliona blushed.

'I've thought about it,' she said. 'But it seems such a common way of killing. It takes a long time, and it isn't very ladylike, unbecoming of a queen.'

'It's a lot less messy than stabbing people.'

'I don't mind blood, Crimthain,' said Cliona. 'It has a certain nobility about it. I'm used to blood, I've seen plenty. Don't forget, many times I've helped Anroth stitch up our warriors.'

'Only you, my lady, could make that distinction.' Crimthain laughed. 'Please reconsider, strangulation is a useful method of killing, particularly for a woman. Say, for example, someone arrives unexpectedly when Midar and the princes are away, and you've good reason to believe the visitor may be planning to assassinate you.'

'Tell him you're just about to eat, few men can resist a good meal and fine ale. Most will defer your murder till after they have eaten. Come to the table wearing a girdle round your waist, with a fine rope concealed within it.'

'Insist he leaves all his weapons at the end of the table. Then during the meal, when he's relaxed, rise from the table on the pretext of filling his goblet. Stand behind him, loop the girdle around his neck and pull it taut before winding it around the back of his chair. That technique saved your mother's life more than once.'

'Oh, I see!' said Cliona, excited by the idea. 'Oh, you mean I should serve him a fine meal first, then strangle him during the meal? Oh yes, I think that would be perfectly acceptable. It's a form of hospitality. There's nothing more delightful than a memorable meal.'

So Crimthain had his way and Cliona became proficient in strangulation.

Even when Crimthain considered the queen to be well-versed in the arts of war, they continued to practice regularly. Now, for the first time in her life, Cliona wondered if all her training might soon be needed.

As she busied herself organising supplies for Midar's journey north, Goibniu came in, carrying a breastplate and a golden shield for his mother, and two matching swords for Nuada. 'These were meant to be your birthday presents, mother,' he said. 'I made them for ceremonial purposes. But, with the threat of Saxon invasion, now seems a good time to give them to you.'

Aine buckled Cliona into the breastplate.

'Does it fit alright?' asked Goibniu.

'It's perfect,' said Cliona. 'I love it.'

'You're a warrior queen now,' said Aine admiringly. 'And if you fight, then I'll fight beside you.'

Cliona nodded and turned to Goibniu. 'This shield is stunning, but I wouldn't use it in battle,' she said. 'Take it with you and give it to Danu when you see her. Send her my love.'

Goibniu turned to his brother. 'Nuada, you're handy enough with both hands,' he said. 'I can never tell if you're left- or right-handed, so I've made you a matching pair of short swords.'

Nuada was delighted. Goibniu had fashioned the weapons like a Gladius, the Roman sword, and they were wide at the base with extended guards around their handle. The blades tapered sharply to their points.

Nuada handed his old sword to Goibniu. 'They're perfect,' he said. 'Please give my old sword to Dancer, for it has served me well.'

Anroth needed time alone. He went to the dark waters and stood below the statue of Brigantia, looking up at her disfigured, lichen-covered face. As usual, she failed to inspire or comfort him. He walked to the welcoming entrance of his cave and rested against the rock, looking out at the water.

He remembered resting against the same rock many years before. His wife was been in front of him, her back against his chest, as they'd looked out at the lake. His arms encircled her, his hands resting on her heavily pregnant belly. He recalled the pure joy as he'd felt their child vigorously kicking inside her.

'I want our child to be born here,' she'd said. 'To be welcomed into this world by all the happiness we've shared here.'

It was a place their child was never to see, for she had died inside her mother's womb, shortly before her mother. He buried them still together, close beside his cave, forever keeping him company.

He climbed to the plateau above the cave and sat on his favourite rock, looking out over the lake, the gently swaying canopy of trees and, beyond, to the stronghold and the beaches. Above the calm, blue sea, long, low clouds, tinged by sunset's shades of gold and soft purple underbellies, hung motionless in the otherwise clear blue heavens.

Anroth reproached himself, guilty of the delusion of possession. He had come to assume a sense of ownership of all he saw before him, but it was nothing more than an image fleetingly bestowed on him. He was just one of many who had sat there over the centuries and admired the same view.

Down below someone moved.

Keeva stood in front of Brigantia's statue. He left her looking rejuvenated and confident. And, when he caught sight of Anroth, he waved enthusiastically and climbed up to join him.

'Sirona and Luchtain are back,' he said. 'Everything went as planned.'

'How's Sirona?'

'She's pleased with herself,' laughed Keeva. 'On the journey home, they camped at the old hill fort and she threw two hazelnuts in the fire. They burned together brightly.'

'Gratifying.'

'She said she got lucky,' said Keeva.

'And how's he?'

'I've never seen him so fulfilled, he tells me he and Sirona dream the same dreams.'

'Come and sit beside me,' said Anroth.

There was an over-enthusiasm about Keeva that seemed misplaced. Sitting in silence, they admired the careless way nature created splendour. And, the longer the silence lasted, the more Anroth's fears grew.

'You know what I'm going to do, don't you, Anroth?' said Keeva.

'Don't even think about it. There's no need for you to prove your bravery, Keeva.'

'Before your cauldron was stolen, I was uncertain about what I should do. 'Now my future is revealed. Losing the cauldron proves I'm right.'

'I've warned you about believing your own deluded prophecies,' said Anroth.

'But that's the point, they're not just mine, they're yours,' said Keeva. 'Why won't you just come out and say it? My lord Midar, his lineage and everything we feast our eyes upon will all be swept away.'

'No, Keeva, everything we see before us will remain,' said Anroth. 'We will be swept away. Why don't I say anything? Because we could be wrong.'

'You taught us that we were warriors of the mind,' replied Keeva. 'A warrior dies for what he believes in. It's too late in the day for uncertain sacrificial gestures. Nothing will be gained by slaughtering the white bull. There's only one sacrifice left – that of my own life.'

'What purpose can it serve?' asked Anroth. 'You can't wage war on what you can't see. You've lived here far too long. Do what I did at your age: travel the world, deepen your understanding, widen your horizons. Go anywhere, - but go!'

'No, the life I give will help prepare the way for those who take up arms.'

'And just what do you expect me to tell Sirona and Luchtain?' said Anroth, spitting out the words.

'I've already told them. After they shared their news with me, I shared mine with them. They're distressed beyond measure and spent ages trying to dissuade me. And, when they failed, they sent me to you.'

'You'll get no blessing from me,' said Anroth. 'Human sacrifice is a pathetic, empty gesture that achieves nothing. It's a rejection of all those who love you.'

'I've been to see Midar.'

'And?' asked Anroth.

'He forbids it. He sent me to you.'

'Well then, you've done everything within your power, but you've tried and failed. You were misguided, for which I blame myself. In some ways, I admire your courage. But you can hardly expect me to preside over your ritual murder.'

'I told Midar I didn't expect to get your approval. He has reluctantly agreed to put the matter before the council.'

'When?'

''They're waiting for us now.'

As they walked down to the great hall, Anroth did all he could to reason with Keeva.

'After everything I've taught you over the past seven years, it comes down to this,' he said. 'Our time together was time wasted.'

'No, Anroth, you're wrong. When I first came to ask if you'd accept me as a novice, you knew I didn't come from a well-born family. You ignored my status. All you've taught me has been good. You told mc thcrc are many ways of interpreting druidic belief. And though my ritual death was never part of your teaching, it is nevertheless rooted in druidism.

You and I think the same thoughts, yet we've always been different. I knew I could never become you. The careful, considered way you think, and the simplicity and humility of your life are all beyond me. You're a man informed by your feelings, but in a state of private self-doubt.'

'Keeva, don't delude yourself that the beliefs we put our trust in are inherently good,' said Anroth. 'Each generation of religious leaders changes the message to their own liking. And the flawed tradition of human sacrifice is a practice from our past, the deranged delusion of a high druid from long ago.'

'Anroth, not once in the seven years you've been teaching me have you ever suggested ritual human sacrifice was evil,' said Keeva. 'You can't suddenly condemn it now. I love my life. I don't relinquish it because I'm weary of it. That would be a hollow offering. My life is a gift I choose to return so it may serve a greater purpose. It's all I have left to offer. May my death help protect you.'

Everything was wrong with Keeva's judgement and intent, but, for some disturbing reason he failed to understand, Anroth found himself almost persuaded. He reminded himself that, just because a man's mind is clearly deranged, it doesn't necessarily mean the conclusions he comes to are wrong. Insanity might well have its own unique insights into the truth.

As they approached the hall, Crimthain opened the door and welcomed them. The others were sitting around the table eating, as if it were just another meal, and Goibniu stood up to give Keeva a hug and hand him a goblet of beer. He liked Keeva. They had grown up together and the prince had appointed himself as Keeva's protective elder brother.

'Drink and celebrate our friendship,' said Goibniu.

Cliona rose to greet Keeva and proffered a bowl filled with choice cuts of pork in honey, arranged on a bed of stewed apples and berries. She held on to him tightly, willing him with every bone in her body to change his mind.

'Eat, my son, let me go on sharing my love with you,' she said. 'Is there anyone else you want beside you?'

Keeva remained composed and assured, and thanking them for the warmth of their welcome, he ate, drank and asked for Aine. Nuada went to fetch her. She came and sat quietly beside him. Cliona tugged frantically at the hem of Midar's sleeve.

'You've got to do something,' she hissed into his ear. 'Do something!' When Keeva had finished his meal, Midar spoke.

'Keeva, how have I failed you?'.

Keeva shook his head.

'No, my lord, you've never failed me,' he said. 'No high chieftain could have made me more welcome in his home. What I do, I do because of my love for you, your queen and the kingdom.'

Aine stood up.

'Am I the only person in this room who understands what Keeva is trying to say?' she spoke in a dull monotone, tears streaming down her face. 'Keeva and I have something in common. We're both low-born and came into a world where whatever we did made no difference. We were born to be used, and to remain passive and obedient. Most of our kind accepts that, but I never did, and neither does Keeva.'

Midar and the queen looked at her.

'Keeva has always seen more than you and I see,' continued Aine. 'He couldn't be speaking more clearly – not in words, but in what he believes he should do for the kingdom. I think he's terribly wrong. He breaks my heart.'

Keeva, who had remained calm and assured until this point, began to squirm uncomfortably in his chair.

'Do you think we don't notice things in the kitchen?' asked Aine. 'Do you think the farmers on their steadings or the shepherds on the hill don't feel how cold and threatening this uncertain festival of Lunasa has proved to be? On the night of the banquet, when Nuada came to me, we knew something bad was brewing. I'd been watching you all through my hole in the kitchen door. It's not for me to entertain you, but Nuada asked and I agreed, for he's loved me faithfully, like a son.'

Cliona bowed her head.

'I had to endure standing before you all,' continued Aine. 'I heard the sniggers, I felt myself ridiculed. But, like Keeva, I didn't care what anyone thought of me. I did it for love. When Keeva first came here, many years ago, he was awkward and shy.'

'I'd find him standing by my kitchen door, inventing some excuse for being there, and I'd bring him in, feed him and make a fuss of him. I loved having him around. I still do. He'd talk to me about everything, and share his fears and dreams. I was so proud he'd adopted me as his mother.'

Aine looked at Keeva and smiled, then put her arm around his shoulders. He looked up at her as tears filled his eyes and ran down his cheeks.

'Telling you was always going to be the hardest part, Aine, and leaving you, the cruellest thing I do.' Aine continued.

'After I sang that night, the goddess rewarded me with harmony instead of bloodshed. I've listened to you Keeva, now you must listen to me. Long ago, you promised me you'd do anything I asked you to. I never asked, but I'm begging you now. Please don't do this to me! There's been more than enough grief. I've lost so much in my life and too many of those I've loved have been taken from me.'

'I wish I could change my mind, Aine,' said Keeva. 'But the voices in my head that call me, will not set me free.'

Aine sat down and blew her nose loudly into her apron.

Lugh spoke. 'Keeva, I don't doubt your bravery or resolve,' he said. 'If we deny you, what will you do?'

'The ceremony of the three different degrees of dying is important to me, Lugh,' he said. 'We've shared our lives together for so long and I hoped you'd make my journey to the Otherworld a fitting, decent way to die, a dignified way to say goodbye. But, if you deny me, I'll hang myself from a tree.'

Lugh groaned. 'Keeva, no one has even talked about, never mind actually done this sort of thing in years.'

'Centuries, more like,' added Anroth grimly, realising this was an argument they were steadily losing.

'Keeva, what's the matter with you, man?' asked Dian. 'They tell me I'm the headstrong one in this family, forever rushing into things. When we were younger, we were the best of friends. You need to spend more time in our company.

You spend all your time with druids, so it's no wonder you've ended up with weird ideas. Let's all get drunk together. I promise to find you a good woman to take you in hand and look after you, one way or another she will make you see sense.'

'Dian, don't be coarse,' said Cliona. 'You're offending dear Keeva.'

Dian smashed his fist down on the table, the dishes danced. 'Will you shut up, mother?' he said. 'You're worse than he is! You pretend to be so pious, but you're as loose-thinking if not as loose-living as the rest of us. Don't you understand? We all love Keeva and I'm trying my hardest to help, the only way I know how.'

Midar looked at his three sons and felt pride. He wondered if they mirrored the three different sides to his character. He wasn't blind to Dian's failings and was grateful he was the last-born, rather than the first. Unlike Goibniu, he was headstrong failing to convey a sense of authority, and he lacked Nuada's patience and eye for detail.

Midar looked at his queen. Was it possible he loved Cliona more now than the day he'd first seen her? He knew he wasn't the easiest of men to be married to. But, in all things, Cliona had proved to be the perfect companion and wife. That didn't mean he found being married to her easy. He happened to agree entirely with Dian's furious outburst.

There was an awkward silence. Goibniu stepped in.

'Keeva, my good friend, I agree with everything Dian says,' he said. 'Don't let's consider doing this today. How do you expect us to fight well and win if all we can think about is helping you die?'

All nodded in agreement. Quietly weeping into her apron, her eyes red with rubbing, Aine implored him to stay his hand. Keeva shook his head.

'Those who choose to give, then hesitate, have left intention far too late'.

Midar's warriors assembled and waited outside the stronghold for the night march north, their ponies champing at the bit. But in the sacred grove, beside the Dark Waters, Lugh lifted the wooden cover off the pit that was their portal to the Otherworld. Those who loved him clustered around Keeva, and he spoke for the last time.

He said, 'Let my eyes no longer see, my mind no longer be, so that others may see more clearly. Let the strength of my beating heart be stilled and pass to others. May the blood that flows from me purify those who walk beside me.'

Midar stepped forward and placed his hands gently on Keeva's shoulders. 'Soon I must leave with my warriors,' he said. 'Must the bravest of the brave leave me?'

Keeva nodded.

Midar took off his heavy, gold-studded belt and buckled it around Keeva's waist. Anroth made one final attempt.

'The gods are watching you,' he said. 'You've done all you set out to do. They've already accepted the sincerity of your sacrifice. There's no more power or proof to be gained by dying.' Keeva remained unmoved. Anguish in his eyes, Anroth asked.

'What separates us, Keeva?'

'It's the difference between being a true believer and someone who knows what they believe, but never knows if it's true,' he replied.

There was a sickening thud as Lugh brought down his club on the back of Keeva's head and sent him to oblivion. As the body sagged backwards, Crimthain twisted a rope tightly around his neck and garrotted him. Then Lugh and Crimthain held the body away from the pit. Anroth slit his throat.

When the blood had drained away, Midar climbed into the pit and the others lowered Keeva's body down to him. He curled Keeva up like a baby on the ground and, as those above him handed down their gifts, he carefully arranged them around the body.

Aine went last. She passed down a bowl of porridge to sustain Keeva on his journey and a small, wooden bucket of butter she'd made as a gift to the goddesses.

Midar stood there alone, upright and silent, deep in the pit of his private loneliness. He turned to the east then raised his arms. Lugh lifted him out. Cliona buckled a belt around Midar's waist, then hugged him and wished him a safe journey.

Midar mounted his pony, then turned to Goibniu.

'Let that be a lesson to you, too much religion rots the brain and confuses the mind.'

'Why did you allow him to do it?' asked Goibniu. 'You could have stopped it any time you wanted.'

'We're in all sorts of trouble,' said Midar. 'Anything can go wrong and probably will. You and I were born to be warriors, that's all we're capable of, but Keeva was born to be a druid. How could we be certain that what he asked us to do was right or wrong? It doesn't do to upset the gods and goddesses in times such as these. We need all the help we can get.

In the end, I couldn't even be certain that Anroth found fault with his reasoning. Do you want to know what real courage is, Goibniu, not the beer sozzled bravery of a warrior in the warp spasm, but calm, carefully considered bravery, the lonely courage of the thinking man? You've just witnessed it; well, that or insanity. Pray you never have to find it.'

'Lugh certainly cured him, if he was mad.' said Goibniu gloomily.

Midar kicked his pony in the flanks, and cantered into the night.

The Fourth Day Of Lunasa

17 The Waterfall

It was the fourth day of the festival of Lunasa when Danu reached the waterfall, situated at the top of a deep valley. Anroth had suggested it would make a useful base while she planned her attack on Birog. She had worked her way through the wildwood and avoided open land whenever she could. She'd fallen in love with Northumbria, with its forests, rivers and valleys, and its rolling, open lowlands with cattle and steadings from which lazy smoke wafted out of thatched roofs. Occasionally she noticed a glint of silver shining through the bushes as the sunlight caught the torque around Ominnios's neck.

On her journey, she'd seen a number of dead Picts. All of them had Dancer's mark: an arrow through the neck and Snibo's deep, penetrating stab wounds in the eye sockets. She wondered what manner of a man Dancer really was, he seemed so cold, so lethal, and was grateful they were on the same side.

The limitations of Danu's background as a deity had quickly become apparent. She'd run out of food after a day and had no idea how to live off the land. Numerous opportunities to use the spear of Assal to kill a stag or a wild boar had presented themselves, but the idea of ending up with so much meat had offended her, so she had gone hungry. There were other practical difficulties. She had no idea how to butcher the meat, cook or light a fire.

Danu removed her cloak, for it was a warm, humid day. As she rounded a bend in the river, she saw the waterfall. Not looking where she was going, she almost tripped over the body of a man on the edge of the bank. He lay motionless on his stomach and one of his arms had fallen over the side, into the water. At first, she thought he must have been another Pictish spy, but then she saw Snibo sitting beside the body. The bird looked up and made excited little guttural croaks. He sounded pleased to see her.

Then, to her horror, she realised the body was that of Dancer. The Picts had finally killed him. She had thought him invincible, but he'd turned out to be as mortal as any other man. The real meaning of Anroth's warning on the beach hit home. Deities might die gradually over centuries but they would never perish like Dancer, in one brief, brutal moment.

What if the Picts had been watching her and were hidden in the bushes close by, waiting for their moment? She could hardly believe her stupidity. She had walked straight into a trap, knowing Cu Roi stalked behind her in the form of Ominnios and would cut off her escape.

On her journey north, her powers as goddess had been waxing and waning. And now, just when she needed them most, they had deserted her. Was she out of her mind? Did she really want to be a mortal whose life could soon come to a miserable, irredeemable end? With Dancer dead, her mission seemed doomed.

A twig cracked behind her. She froze, terrified to turn around. The swaying bushes had taken on a sinister appearance. They seemed to be moving closer to the river, hemming her in and hiding her enemies.

Danu heard a deep-throated growl.

Desperate to scare Cu Roi off, she shouted Dancer's name. The body on the bank never moved, Dancer was dead.

The beast broke cover and ran towards her.

Without warning, Snibo rose in the air. Just as Cu Roi closed in for the kill, the bird swooped and embedded its sharp claws into the hound's neck, savagely stabbed its beak into the back of his head and tearing at his ears, petrified and, bloodied, the beast retreated to the bushes.

Whichever way Danu looked; she felt the Picts closing in. Gripped by uncontrollable fear, she crouched on the edge of the bank and looked for any evidence of life.

Suddenly, like a flash of lightning, Dancer scooped his hand out of the water and rolled over. A bar of silver flew towards her, hit her full in the face and knocked her backwards into the river. Dancer stood up and looked apologetic. He held out his cold, wet hand.

Still somewhat off balance, Danu stretched out her own hand and Dancer pulled her out of the water. She felt in perfect harmony with the powerful grip that held her and, in that miraculous moment, released from the fear that had consumed her, she forged an unbreakable bond with the woodwose. Still in a state of panic, she peered frantically into the bushes, then threw her arms around his neck. She closed her eyes and clung to him.

'Dancer will look after me, Dancer will protect me,' she told herself.

He held her tenderly and stroked her hair. She stood quite still, unwilling to let go until the warmth of his body had melted the ice-cold fear within her. Then, cautiously, she opened her eyes. The bushes had retreated back from the banks of the river.

She rested her head on his shoulder, surprised by how gentle he was. But then, mortified by her behaviour, she pulled away and stood back. She was so confused, but could feel her confidence returning.

Before their dramatic meeting, Danu had only ever seen Dancer from a distance. Close-up, he was nothing like she'd imagined. She'd expected him to be muscular, thick-set and coarse-featured. But he was slim, almost as tall as her and had a prominent nose. He wasn't the least bit good-looking and was the last person you'd notice in a crowd. But, when she stood close beside him, she noticed his gentle blue-grey eyes, his long eyelashes, and his thick, black, wavy hair that tumbled over his forehead, trivial features, casually combined, which much pleased her to look upon.

Her thoughts were interrupted when she saw the large salmon, he'd tickled from the river still gasping on the grass. Dancer knelt down and dispatched it with a stone.

'Can I have some?' asked Danu, pointing to the fish.

Dancer looked flustered, then, pointing at himself, he stuck his fingers in his ears and shook his head, looking very sad. He covered his mouth with a hand and shook his head again. Then it dawned on Danu. Why, she thought, hadn't anybody told her?

He was deaf and dumb. For some reason, probably a combination of the relief she felt at finding Dancer alive, as well as being hit by the salmon and ending up in the river, she burst into a fit of laughter. Being beside Dancer felt wonderful. He made her happy.

Dancer looked at her and his face emptied. It crumpled in front of her. His shoulders sank, his head hung down and, with a resigned shrug, he started to turn away. The brutish, cold warrior, the beast of the forest, didn't look so frightening now.

Danu was horrified. Too late, she realised he thought she was ridiculing and rejecting him.

'No, no, no,' she shouted at him. 'I wasn't laughing at you!'

She grabbed his arm and the empty, flattened face turned towards her. 'I was worried,' she said. 'I thought you were dead, then you hit me in the face with the salmon and I ended up in the river. You made me laugh; you made me happy.'

She realised he couldn't understand a word she was saying. Her shouting, must look to him as though she was being domineering and aggressive. All she wanted was to be friends.

Dancer stood there, closed his eyes and took a deep breath. He sighed. He had lived a lifetime of 'Oh well, never mind.'

On the day Danu had been with Anroth and she'd watched Dancer as he casually walked out from the forest with the dead Pict across his shoulders, he'd seemed so powerful, almost monstrous.

Now she realised he wasn't so big or strong. She didn't know why he lived his twilight life, but perhaps the situation wasn't of his own choosing. He put on a fearless face to a world he did his best to avoid, but she could tell his confident manner was a lie.

Without thinking, she stepped forward and hugged him, then rubbed her hand around his shoulders before gently patting him on the back.

He didn't respond, so she rubbed her nose against his in a hesitant, enquiring manner. Such innocent intimacy wasn't something you did in the Otherworld, where deities moved straight from the vertical to the horizontal, and nothing preceded their brief and often loveless conjugation.

Hugging was nice, she decided. So, she did it some more, increasing in confidence and very much hoping he liked it as much as she did. He might do it to her. That would be nice.

Some warmth and a sense of worth seemed to be seeping back into him. But she feared that, if she let go, he'd slip away and lick his wounds alone. What a strange dejected creature he was. Answerable to no one, he lived in a fragile world, all alone in a thousand ways. Maybe his sad and isolated life was something he'd prefer to share. Poor Dancer, she thought; it wasn't fair.

Tears ran down her face and nose, dripping onto Dancer's cheeks. Without trying, she was crying. How exciting, tears!

He opened his eyes and looked into hers. Her tears surprised and upset him. He gave a little shake of his head, then brought his hands up, held her head and gently brought it back towards his. There was kindness and concern in his expression.

Resting her head on his shoulder, she closed her eyes.

Dancer softly lifted her face and kissed her eyelids, first one, then the other. Then forgetting himself and the fact she was a goddess, he kissed her on the lips. It was just a little kiss. If he could, he'd have just said, 'It's alright'. That's all the kiss said.

So soft upon her lips, so sweet in the receiving, warm sunshine slowly spreading. How beautiful this place, with its bright and sparkling stream, and his kiss slowly trickling down to her feet. So soft the grass, so green and meadow-sweet, his kiss still flowing, where not knowing.

Danu smiled and opened her eyes.

Dancer bent down, retrieved Danu's spear and cloak, and handed them back to her. He picked up the salmon and hooked his finger under the gills, then beckoned her to follow him along the fox trail, where the occasional wolf pack still ran, to walk with him towards the waterfall.

She saw his camp beneath some spreading oaks. Snibo flew high above them and perched in a nearby tree. Dancer fed his fire with dry branches. What little smoke it produced filtered away to nothing in the dense canopy of leaves above.

As they waited for the fire to burn down to embers, Dancer set about preparing the meal. He took the salmon to the riverbank to decapitate it, gut and clean it, and wash away its blood and entrails.

Danu took off her wet clothes and stretched them out to dry on the surrounding shrubs, then wrapped her cloak around her. Many burdock plants lined the bank and Dancer cut down several of their large, heart-shaped leaves and sliced off the thick stems. When he'd tucked a couple of the leaf edges inside the body of the salmon, he wrapped the rest around the outside. To hold the leaves in place, he coated it all with a layer of thick river mud. He fashioned a bed for the fish deep in the embers of the fire and heaped more embers on top.

It had been a season of plenty and the wild fruits of the forest bent the bushes low. Dancer had collected nuts and berries earlier. Together, they shared the forest's bounty. Realising Danu was starving, Dancer stopped eating and fed her all that was left.

When the salmon was cooked, he filleted all the flesh from the spine down one side and gave Danu the lower half, so she didn't have to worry about the bones. Then he carefully rewrapped what was left in the burdock leaves and stored it in a hole in a tree, hidden from any passing otters.

Down by the banks of the river, shafts of sunlight shone through the branches and the foliage of the little alder trees, and, in that sunshine, columns and clouds of insects aimlessly spun and sauntered up and down, performing their last, dwindling dance of love before life's leaving.

Beneath the surface of the river, brown trout patiently waited and watched from far below, their tails wafting to and fro, holding position against the river's flow. They lingered until they saw the spent, struggling bodies of the insects float towards them and then, with a flick of the tail, they rose to the surface and sucked in the tasty morsel.

A lonely, late-summer butterfly fluttered in the clearing and came to rest beside Danu. She scooped it up in her hand. Its orange-and-black wings fluttered briefly as if were ready to fly away. But, tired of its fruitless efforts to find a mate, it gave up. Its wings closed. Danu searched the foliage for another, but she found it was alone. Feeling sad, she looked into Dancer's eyes.

Dancer drew Anroth's old wand from his belt and sucked its bulbous tip, slowly rolling it around his lips. Then he placed its moist tip into her empty hand and closed her fingers around it before withdrawing the wand. Danu felt a faint flutter and slowly opened her hand.

There within, was another orange-and-black butterfly. It rose in the air and fluttered above the first until, without warning, it flew up to join the wand's gift. Together they fluttered upwards, their flight disjointed in a joined-up sort of way.

Danu watched, wide-eyed and smiling, as the two butterflies flew higher and higher, and eventually disappeared from view in the canopy of the trees. She looked at Dancer. Why couldn't he hear, or speak? It was so sad not to be able share the magic of the moment with a few words.

On the other side of the clearing was a sprawling dog rose, its hips fully formed but not yet swelled to ripeness. Dancer walked towards it, holding out his wand, blessing the bush. Defying the season, the rosehips were reborn back to the delicate pink-and-white blossoms they had once been, much earlier in the season. Danu clapped her hands. She couldn't remember a time she'd felt so happy, since setting foot on the beach at Bamburgh.

Dancer kissed the palm of his hand and softly blew kisses towards her. As they left his mouth, the kisses turned to butterflies of many a different hue: pink, yellow, green and blue. Butterflies fluttered all around, butterflies landed upon the ground. And, where they landed, flowers grew: pink and white and yellow and blue.

Never had there been a more bountiful bower. He sat beside her as they savoured the perfume. And, in that place, the first delicate flowers and shades of love began to bloom. Danu, feeling a new life dawning, drank it all in deeply, seduced by the simplicity of happiness and Dancer's mysterious humanity.

18 Releasing The Serpent

Arising from her slumbers on that fourth day of the festival of Lunasa, Aine found her normally benevolent humours had deserted her. She felt irritable and overnight, her body had become bloated. She had a headache and sore breasts, and her nipples tingled. None of these problems were new to her, for they occurred every month.

In the past she'd sought Sirona's advice on the matter. She'd hoped a suitable spell or potion would ward off such diversions from her otherwise harmonious nature. Sirona had reassured her and explained that women who became tense and bad-tempered before their courses and flow were revealing the goddess side of their nature. Goddesses, she pointed out, were often ill-tempered.

Sirona had suggested drinking a warm infusion of Sulis Jove's Wort. She'd shown her how to concoct such a brew from the dried yellow flowers and leaves of the mystical plant, which Sirona also used for the treatment of wounds. She explained to Aine that her mind suffered a fleeting wound every month and, if she drank the potion early in the morning, it would relieve her distress. Thereafter, Aine kept a supply in a pot by the kitchen door.

That morning, she brewed and drank the infusion. Refreshed but her composure in no way restored, Aine set about her duties. On the seaward side of the kitchen, a door opened out onto a small courtyard that overlooked the cliffs. Once she'd gathered together all the rubbish that even the pigs wouldn't eat, Aine would toss it over the cliffs to the beach below. What the gulls didn't pick clean would be washed away by the tide.

But that morning, when she forcefully threw open the kitchen door and banged it on the outside wall, she was confronted by a Saxon warrior standing in her courtyard. Infuriated by his impudence, she hurled the rubbish at him and shouted for the guards. Completely taken by surprise, the warrior made as if to draw his sword. But Aine charged towards him, bellowing her head off. It was an intimidating sight, and sound. The Saxon dropped his guard.

Many years of regularly turning the kitchen millstone had left Aine with a muscular right arm. And, blazing mad that an intruder had the cheek to invade her space and upset her routine, she thumped him on the jaw. As the intruder reeled from the blow, he staggered and fell backwards over the cliff. When the guards arrived, they caught sight of two more Saxons running south and gave chase.

Crimthain and Dian arrived. Looking down over the cliffs from the courtyard, they saw the warrior spread-eagled below. They strained their eyes, searching the empty beach and sea.

'They must have landed somewhere,' muttered Dian.

When Nuada, Luchtain and Sirona arrived, Crimthain and his band of warriors were already riding south, pursuing the Saxons. They arrived on the far side of the southern headland just in time to watch a Saxon ship put out to sea.

Nuada sent Luchtain north to look for any more ships and asked Sirona to alert the settlement. Then, joining

Dian, he made his way down to the beach. The Saxon was conscious but badly injured. They helped him to his feet. Although he was tall and well-built, he was little more than a boy. He was barely able to walk and dragged one leg which was oozing black blood.

His finely wrought sword, his belt buckle and the intricate decorations on his shield boss suggested he was the son of a high chieftain. Organising a litter, they carried him up to the great hall and laid him out on the banqueting table. The colour had drained from his face and he shivered uncontrollably. His body had shut down from the shock of the fall. Cliona came in and, realising how badly injured the youth was, sent for Anroth.

When Aine saw the Saxon was barely more than a boy, her maternal instinct got the better of her. She mulled some of Goibniu's Dragon's Blood Barley Beer with honey over the fire and, setting a bolster behind the warrior's head, she poured the warmed, sweet concoction down his throat while softly singing a lullaby. His shivering subsided and some colour returned to his drained features, but his fingers and hands remained ice-cold.

Anroth arrived. He could see that both the Saxon's wrists were broken and he realised the boy was a great deal sicker than he should have been, even if he had fallen from a cliff. Whatever he was dealing with was a lot more serious than just a couple of broken bones.

'The last time we went fishing, Nuada, you asked me if, one day, I'd teach you how to heal people,' said the druid. 'This is a good time to start.'

Anroth spoke to the Saxon for a considerable time. The boy stared into the old man's eyes and did his best to listen through the pain. When Anroth finished, he patted him gently on the shoulder and smiled. The boy smiled back weakly.

'I didn't know you spoke Saxon, Snout.'

'I don't, Nuada, I was speaking Friesian,' said Anroth. 'But it's close enough for him to understand me. His name is Ida.'

Anroth put the palm of one hand on the boy's forehead and the other on his chest, and asked Nuada to do the same.

'What do you find?' asked Anroth.

'His forehead's red-hot, he's burning up,' said Nuada. 'I can barely detect his heartbeat, but it feels very fast.'

'Yes, that's not the result of him breaking his wrists,' said Anroth. 'Something festers within him. What was he like when you found him?'

'He was dragging his left leg and could hardly walk.'

Anroth pulled back the Saxon's bloodstained cloak, which had become stuck to his left leg. There was an old wound across the front of his thigh. The force of his fall from the cliff had split it open and black blood oozed from the wound. A green, foul-smelling pus ran between the chunks of clotted blood. Someone had made a crude attempt to stitch the edges tightly together, which had only made matters worse.

Nuada gasped. 'How could he have been so stupid as to go on a raid?' he said. ''The only wounds I've ever seen like that, ended up killing the warrior.'

'Nuada, never display your feelings in front of the person you hope to heal,' said Anroth. 'Always remain impassive and relaxed. Even if he doesn't speak your language, he'll understand the significance of the way you've just reacted.'

Nuada bowed his head.

'When this boy left home, he probably thought the wound was getting better,' continued Anroth. 'This is an old injury, which has got a great deal worse. His thigh is full of poison and, like a nest of vipers, has slithered and spread out of the leg. The viper within that finds the heart could kill him. Let's see what we can do with his leg, then I'll show you how to mend his arms.'

Dian had been watching in an apparently disinterested way. 'Why don't we just leave his arms?' he asked. 'That way, he won't ever be able to fight us.'

'Trying to kill someone and trying to cure them have one thing in common, Dian,' said Anroth. 'You never do things by halves. Would you fight half a battle? If you decide you're going to heal someone, then you must heal the whole. You'd be insulting the gifts you've been given if you refuse the sick any part of the help you can give.'

Goibniu's Beer was now working its way into the boy's system. Ida had a great deal more experience fighting other warriors than he did doing battle with ale. It was beginning to relax him. Despite his pain, he at least felt safe and knew now what was happening. The old man had explained to him, he was very ill from his leg wound. He'd known that, but hadn't dared tell his fellow warriors for fear of being thought a coward. The old man had caring, kind eyes and he trusted those eyes more than anything the old man had actually said.

Through the red mist of his pain, something soothed him, Aine's soft lullaby. She continued to pour the barley beer into his mouth, just as she'd give milk to a baby.

His head nestling between her fulsome, warm and welcoming breasts, he realised Aine was the most wonderful woman he had ever met in his life. Her husband must be a lucky man. Why didn't Saxons have women like that? She had such power, such strength; one blow from her right fist had knocked him clean over the battlements. Now there was a woman you'd be proud to call your wife. She had him at her mercy yet she chose to fill him with the milk of human kindness.

Inebriation was getting the better of the young Saxon. He wished he could lie there for ever, he'd met the perfect woman: strong, and violent, with a pure, haunting voice. He could listen to her sing forever. Bearing in mind his youth, Ida decided she might make a better mother-in-law and wondered if she had a daughter.

Anroth stood quite still, his breathing slow and relaxed, as he wondered what he might find in the wound. He reminded himself to be extra-vigilant if he felt an arrowhead or part of a spear embedded inside. Were he to cut his own hand trying to pull them out, he could fall victim to the same contagion and die. Many years before, he had suffered such an accident. A few days later, his injured finger had gone black. The blackness began to spread; to save himself, he'd cut his finger off.

He had no illusions about what he was up against. The wounds he'd be forced to inflict might prove too much for the Saxon. At least the boy knew they were trying to save him, and there was more love in life than hatred. Once he started, there would be no going back and, the longer he took, the less the chance of survival. Everything he might require had to be close to hand.

He turned to the queen. 'Cliona, we'll need plenty of long strips of cloth. Please can you find or make some?' he asked her.

'Aine, leave the boy and go to the potter to ask for a large bowl of his thickest clay. Go to the weavers' cottages and tell them to bring at least an armful of coarse, uncarded wool. Go to the carpenter, for I need two slats of wood as long as the lad's forearm down to his fingers and as wide as your hand. I'll also need a pot of honey.'

'Aine, you stay put,' said Cliona. 'I'll attend to all that. Nuada, come with me and help get everything we need.'

Anroth turned to Dian. 'Ask the girls in the kitchen to make me a cauldron full of piping-hot porridge,' he said. ''Take a couple of those daggers off the wall and stick the blades in the fire till they're red-hot. Fill two pitchers with pure water from the spring and bring me a beaker.'

Before she left, the queen spoke to Dian.

'Now, Dian, I need hardly tell you that what Anroth is attempting is extremely difficult. You must do everything you can to help.'

Dian nodded, but he was uncharacteristically nervous. He'd never seen Anroth try to save someone's life before.

'I'll do everything I can do to help, mother,' he stuttered.

'Make sure that matters proceed in an atmosphere of calm and due decorum,' she said.

'An atmosphere of calm and due decorum,' he repeated. 'Yes, mother.'

Anroth spoke to Ida again and explained he was going to do his best to drain away as much of the poison as he could. He told him to fix his eyes on the shiny brass raven that hung from his neck.

The boy nodded his head, and smiled up at Aine. She smiled back and ran her fingers through his hair, then gave him a warm, casual kiss on the forehead as she squeezed his shoulders. She put on a brave face, but she felt sad. She expected him to die.

It didn't take long before most of what Anroth had asked for had arrived. All save Cliona had returned. Word that the great man was shortly to perform one of his miracles had spread throughout the settlement and a large crowd gathered around the banqueting table. The potter had arrived with his clay and some of his apprentices. All of the weavers were there with their wool and some of their friends. The carpenters came with the slats of wood, and they were joined by the blacksmiths.

As Anroth requested, a serving maid brought in a large cauldron of hot, steaming porridge. Many of those present had been roused from their beds and hadn't had their breakfast. Mindful of his mother's words, Dian sent the serving maid out again for wooden platters, bowls and spoons, and instructed her to serve everyone with generous helpings of porridge.

Anroth looked up in amazement. 'No, Dian, I need the porridge for…'

Dian interrupted. 'Sorry, Anroth, it's for Ida, - of course.'

Holding a bowl, he went over to him. Anroth shook his head but, rather than explain the purpose of the porridge, he returned to his work. Ida looked at Dian and his bowl of porridge, and wondered if this might be part of his treatment, but fell asleep before he could make his mind up.

Ollathir arrived, fresh from mucking out his pigsties. Dian promptly conscripted him to help with mealtime duties. He explained the Ceremonial Eating of the Porridge was an important part of Anroth's mystical Healing for Strangers. Ollathir took to his new responsibility with gusto, it made a change from feeding pigs.

'Now or later, my lord Anroth?' he asked, proffering a bowl to the druid.

'Not at this stage, Olly,' said Anroth. 'I'll have some later, thank you.' The druid looked inside the cauldron.

'I need much more porridge than that,' he said. 'Tell the maidservants to cook up another large potful.'

Amazing, thought Ollathir. All this sorcery and magic certainly seemed to give a man an appetite. The cauldron was by no means empty.

'Oh, by the way, Olly, have you any thoughts on the problem we talked about yesterday?' Anroth asked.

Ollathir shook his head. Sadly, his surrogate mother and sleeping partner had failed to inspire him.

By nature, Anroth was a man of solitude and quiet places. Most druids who tried to save other's lives preferred to do so undisturbed by an audience, but Anroth was different. Just as when he offered up sacrifices, he found an audience animated him.

Like the Greek actors he had watched and so admired when he lived in Rome, he was playing out a drama, or a tragedy. The bigger his audience, the better he performed. His greatest works came when the heroism of the victim, and his own artistry and ritual, combined to conjure up pure magic in the theatre of dreams. Without a shadow of a doubt, for Anroth, the most rewarding part of being a druid was caring for the sick and trying to save them.

He drew Cernunnos's golden wand from his belt and raised his arms in the air, then swayed from side to side. Ida fixed his eyes on the shiny brass raven. As Anroth moved, the pendant swung hypnotically around his neck. The wand performed mystical movements above the boy then, finally, came to hover over his leg. The crowd knitted closely around Anroth. All were united in admiration as they ate their porridge.

Anroth drank a cup of the pure water from the pitcher and said a silent prayer. He inserted the golden wand deep inside the wound and began to probe around. The crowd gasped, horrified when they realised the extent of the injury.

Dian felt his toes curl up inside his boots. He watched as the full length of the golden wand disappeared inside the boy's leg to reveal a huge cavity, almost the length of Ida's thigh. It could be him lying there. Up until then, he had dismissed thoughts of ever taking a wound.

The queen reappeared with a large supply of torn cloth-strips. She stood beside Dian and said nothing but took everything in.

The crowd clustered closer, their eyes fixed on the magician. One of the blacksmiths had taken charge of the enthralled audience. He had them eat each mouthful of porridge in unison as they willed Anroth on, doing the best they could, to help as he fought to save the Saxon. Part whispering, part hissing, the queen turned to Dian.

'Why's everybody indulging in synchronised porridge consumption?' she asked.

'I've no idea, mother,' he said. 'It must be a very important part of Anroth's healing ritual for these terrible injuries. He says he'll eat his porridge when he's finished.'

'He's never mentioned such a thing to me before,' said Cliona. Dian shook his head.

'It's very strange, mother,' he said. 'Even Anroth can get carried away with the whole druid secrecy thing.'

Ollathir arrived and, with his thumb in a bowl of the ceremonial porridge, he offered it to the queen.

'My lady?' Cliona hesitated; Dian cajoled her.

'The last thing we want is to reduce Anroth's chances of curing the boy,' he said. 'I'm no expert, but the lad's very sick. Anroth must be throwing everything he's got at it, including the porridge. We all have to do our bit. I've already had three bowls.'

'Yes, Dian, you're probably right,' she said as she dutifully took the bowl.

Anroth looked at the queen, puzzled, for he knew she didn't like porridge. Then he looked at Dian, who he realised was only doing his best to be helpful. Not saying anything, he decided to get on with the job in hand.

Ida's mind was slipping into a toxic, delusional state, which was no bad way to die. He could see a beautiful, bright star set in a warm, inviting dark-blue sky. He wanted so much to be there. He stretched out his hand like a child, and tried to catch and hold the lovely light. The star started to twinkle and moved away from him, and, around it, the blue became black. Then, beside it, he saw another twinkling star and, outside the two rounds of black, blue circles.

He was gazing into the eyes of Sirona, the Celtic goddess of healing. The blue in her eyes changed to emerald-green, and looked like inviting, limpid pools of peace and tranquillity. Her flowing, thick, red hair fell about her face. Ida stood on a beach as she floated towards him on a shimmering silver cloud. He could hear Aine singing.

Anroth heard Ida whisper, 'Bright star, beautiful bright star', and he knew his patient's mind now hovered somewhere far above the earth in the layers of thought shared by all mortals. If Ida survived, Anroth hoped he might one day be able to help him with his own vision of the future.

As he withdrew his wand, Anroth asked Nuada to pass him one of the daggers from the fire. In a single swift movement, he used the red-hot blade to reopen the entire length of Ida's old wound. Then, with the sizzling blade , he cut across the skin edges at their mid-point so he ended up with a wide, cross-shaped wound. He inserted the first and second fingers of both his hands deep into the wound, and stretched it up and down, then across.

Ida's back arched and his teeth clenched, but he made no sound. There was a horrendous smell of burning flesh, then large quantities of foul-smelling pus mixed with gobbets of black blood disgorged from the wound and ran over the table edges onto the floor. Anroth washed away the mess with spring water from the pitcher. The burnt edges of the wound oozed, but there was no significant bleeding.

Agog, the crowd clustered closer and continued to eat their sacred meal in harmony, hoping it would find favour with Sirona, the goddess of healing, and ensure the druid's success.

Anroth reinserted a couple of fingers and found even more trapped pus and old black blood. Using just the tip of his forefinger, he carefully released the walled in matter. He probed cautiously deep inside the wound; fearful he might set off the sort of torrential bleeding that even a red-hot blade would fail to staunch. Then, satisfied he'd done what he could, he washed the cavity clear with more spring water, and watched and waited.

A mixture of water and blood ran down onto the compacted clay floor and seeped into the earth below. Apart from a persistent ooze of blood from the wound, all was well. Anroth drank deeply from the pitcher and gave thanks.

He poured the honey into the gaping wound and made sure it covered all the raw and burnt surfaces, then he waited again. He washed his hands thoroughly with soapwort weed. 'When you've been using your hands to heal people, Nuada,' he said. 'Always remember to wash them well when you finish, lest the fester pass to you.'

'Would you like your porridge now, my lord Anroth?' asked Ollathir.

Anroth nodded and Ollathir handed him the cauldron, which was full to the brim. He wondered how much Anroth intended to eat.

'What's the swineherd doing here?' the queen asked, regaining her composure.

'I'm not sure, mother,' said Dian. 'I think including the Golden Child must be an important part of the mystical porridge healing ritual.'

'Well, he doesn't look very golden to me,' said Cliona. 'He looks positively putrid. Anyone would think he'd come fresh from mucking out his pigsty.'

It was true, Ollathir did have an aura about him.

'It's hard to tell, though, with so much pus draining from that lad,' said Dian.

Anroth felt someone pulling his gown and, looking down, he saw Ollathir.

'I have the solution to your problem with the Pictish pirates, my lord,' said the swineherd. 'It came to me when I was serving out all the porridge for breakfast. It occurred to me that I have something the Pictish pirates would love to eat, something that would attract them away from their ships.'

Anroth's brow furrowed, then he smiled. 'Very clever, Olly, but also very dangerous,' he said.

'Lord Anroth, my father was a noble warrior who died defending the kingdom. And however, fortune attends me, I want my father to look down on me from the Otherworld and be proud of the son he never knew.'

Anroth nodded slowly. 'Yes, it's a good plan,' he said. 'I'm proud of you too. Go and talk to Crimthain, and tell him you're to have everything you need. Just as I hope to draw the poison out of this wound, you'll draw the Pictish pirates away from their vessels! Oh, that reminds me, you wouldn't happen to have a pig's heart about you?'

'No, my lord,' said Ollathir. 'But I'll leave one in your room.'

'Thank you,' said Anroth. 'Just make sure the pig isn't still attached to it.'

Noticing the queen had been looking at him, Ollathir walked over to her. Proud to have been appointed Royal Purveyor of Porridge, he enquired if she might like some more.

'No thank you, swineherd, I have had a graceful necessity' she said, with a taut, insincere smile on her lips.

'I've played my part in the mystical porridge healing proceedings.' Dian felt a tug on his jerkin.

'What did she say?' asked Ollathir.

'She said she's full, Olly.'

'What?'

'The queen said she's full to bursting,' said Dian.

'I thought that's what I heard her say.'

Anroth explained to Ida that all had gone well. He would soon be finished and then they could fix his arms. The boy smiled and closed his eyes. The druid inspected the wound and saw the bleeding had stopped. He spooned in porridge to pack it, then covered it with a folded pad of cloth that had been heavily smeared with honey. He securely bandaged the porridge and the pad in place. Nuada looked on.

'This should draw the serpents out,' explained Anroth. 'As the wound heals and contracts, the serpents will be pushed out with the porridge, leaving only healthy flesh behind.'

The queen walked over to congratulate Anroth and to reassure the boy.

As Anroth thanked her, he noticed she was still holding her bowl.

'Cliona'.

'Yes.'

'Why are you eating porridge?' Maintaining her poise, the queen looked around.

'You don't know where Dian's gone, do you, Anroth?'

Ollathir walked over to the queen's display cabinet at the back of the great hall. Borrowing one of her exhibits, he hid it beneath his cloak.

The crowd dispersed, amazed by all they had seen. One of the young weavers ran after Ollathir. 'The ceremonial significance of porridge is interesting, isn't it, Olly?' she said.

'As we all ate in harmony, I could feel the healing power of the porridge flood into my lord Anroth's hands, helping him save the boy. Did you notice that, at the very end, he even put some into the wound?'

'That's probably a new bit Anroth just added,' said the blacksmith, who had previously persuaded the onlookers to indulge in synchronised porridge consumption.

Not long after, a large fishing boat with Ollathir and his precious cargo aboard slipped out of the bay. A brisk south-easterly filled the sails as it headed up the coast, bound for the mouth of the river that ran down from the Valley of the High Waters.

19 Somewhere More Than Love

Danu found it frustrating to try and communicate with Dancer, for everything she said, really did fall on deaf ears. She could mime simple messages that told him how much she'd enjoyed the food, but she yearned for much more.

Some of her powers as a goddess seemed to be returning and she wondered if she should try to give Dancer his hearing and speech back. Then she realised that part of his attraction was the way his vulnerability counterbalanced his ruthless capability. She feared she might destroy a precious part of what was magical about mortal love if she restored his hearing and speech, so she dismissed the idea.

When she reflected on the banquet and her numerous conversations since, she realised that talking wasn't just about what you or the other person said. Conversation was just a small part of two people enjoying each other's company. She had forgotten much of what she'd said or heard in previous conversations, but her happy memories of those occasions remained. Conversation was like the meal they'd just eaten; it was about consuming something together. It was about sharing.

She was sure Dancer wouldn't mind giving her his bit of the conversation. He'd willingly given her his fruits of the forest when he realised how hungry she was. She loved Anroth, but he didn't half hare on when she so desperately wanted to talk. Dancer wasn't like that, which only added to his attraction.

Danu decided to have a one-sided conversation, something she assumed no woman had ever done before. It didn't matter to her; he couldn't hear or speak. They could still have conversations, sharing everything but words. Words didn't matter, what mattered was the animated nature and everything else which went with conversation. Much to her delight, she found she could talk continuously to Dancer without a single pause, about anything that came into her head.

'How delightful, Dancer, sitting here in the sunshine, on this branch of the fallen tree, swinging my legs in the air, chatting away, with nothing very much to say, the other day, me and Anroth went for a lovely, long walk on the beach, far away in the distance we saw Lindisfarne, how blue that sky, how clear the air, one day, Dancer, take me there, it was very kind of you to kill Balor's spies, really it wasn't necessary because I can look after myself, apart from getting very hungry, so actually I can't look after myself, so you can look after me if you like and you can catch fish, I would love to learn how to tickle a salmon, I could always kill a wild boar with my magical spear, but that would be silly since there would be too much meat, what a dreadful waste of the magnificent animal's life and, anyway, you'd have to teach me how to butcher the beast, not only that, I don't know how to light a fire, unless I make a thunderbolt, and that can be a little bit hitty missy, and even if I did, I don't know how to cook, I think berries and nuts are lovely and it might be better if you taught me how to forage for berries and nuts in the wildwood, because it must be very good fun and because you can just eat them and don't need a fire and you don't need to cook them and I wish we could eat berries and nuts all year round, not that I don't like cooked food because I do and it would be really nice if you showed me how to light a fire and how to cook and I just loved the salmon and it was so clever when you wrapped it in leaves and mud that turned to clay, so teach me how to cook one day, and by the way, I do so hope you make clay pots because, if you can make pots, we can keep nuts and berries in them, lots and lots, and we could eat them to our hearts' content, I like eating nuts, especially hazelnuts, but eating berries and nuts is even nicer, the thing about berries is they go off, so we'll just have to make the most of the berries while we may, I hope we're not like berries, Dancer, I hope we don't go off, you look more like a nut to me, in a nice sort of way, of course, the thing about nuts is you can store them in pots for ages and, anyway, since you must be very clever, Dancer, I bet you can make little lids for our pots and then our nuts will last even longer than they would do if the pots didn't have little lids, and, by the way, I meant to say it was so refreshing when I tasted the salmon, that hint of bitterness from the burdock leaves contrasted so well with the oily sweetness of the fish, the taste was such a nice surprise, does eating salmon make men wise?'

Danu was just getting into her stride. The more she talked to Dancer, the more she thought she knew him. Then it dawned on her she had another gift apart from continuous conversation.

'I know just what you're thinking,' she said triumphantly.

Dancer gazed lovingly into her eyes. He smiled and nodded his head.

Doing her best to be helpful, she told Dancer what he was thinking.

If Dancer had not been thinking it before, he did now. Well, he would have done if he could have heard a word she was saying.

Danu grabbed his tousled, thick, black, wavy hair and bared her teeth.

'Do you know what I'm thinking, Dancer?' she said. 'I'm thinking I want to eat you, in a nice sort of way, and make you my own.'

Changing her mind, she added, 'No, I don't want to eat you, in case we're transformed into the sacred snakes of good and evil, and consume each other, starting with each other's tails and ending up as a meaningless, perfect circle, a warning against the impotence of those who strive for perfect harmony.'

Dancer was spellbound. He was no longer at the periphery of other people's vision. All her attention and her bright, laughing eyes were centred on him. She was exciting, excited and animated. She'd laugh and gesticulate with her hands, her vitality bathing him with everything that came into her head.

Beside those waters into which the waterfall fell and beneath those towering trees, they found sanctuary together. Dancer assumed the mantle of a statue set in stone, drinking it all in. Despite all the outpourings from Danu's heart, all those confidences casually shared, he remained impassive and responded with silence. Was this why mortal man made their deities in stone? The blurred edges of reality were swiftly departing from them both.

If Dancer was an unlikely statue, then Danu was an even more unlikely child of man, for she was the greatest goddess of them all. She was worshipped throughout the Celtic world and even, it was said, as far away as the lands of the Scythians. She'd been worshipped in India before her influence first flowed into the Celtic nations. The

Celts worshipped more than four hundred deities, and countless warriors and heroes who had joined them.

Danu was the mother of many, the lover of more; of the Dagda, of Ogma, Lir, Goibniu, Lugh and countless others. She was the matriarch of the tribe of the Tuatha da Danann, the Irish Celts.

She was an earth and river goddess who'd given her name to the mighty Danube and other rivers too numerous to mention. Yet for all her renown, she remained a shadowy figure. In the magical and mystical tales told by the Celtic seers and storytellers, she was rarely mentioned. Like a queen in a hive of honeybees, she was condemned never to spread her wings and fly.

Her rivers and sacred waters were filled with rich treasures: golden torques, beautiful jewellery, richly embossed swords, cauldrons, helmets and shields, proffered in veneration by generations of Celts.

Her sanctuaries, were cold and sombre places; her stone images so still, as in a trance, for who has ever seen a statue dance? Her eyes forever closed, behind a veil of weathered stone, an aging goddess all alone.

From time to time, Dancer's neck became stiff, for, as they sat side by side, he had to keep his head turned sideways to look into her eyes. When his head started to stray, she held it firmly in her hands.

'You have to look at me,' she pleaded. 'Listen to me with your eyes.'

Dancer was happy beyond words. In his life, women had kissed him far more often than he had ever deserved, he had no complaints, for a kiss bestowed out of sympathy for his afflictions was as beautiful as any other. His relationships with women were based on touch and all too fleeting. Whilst he enjoyed their company, he knew they never took him seriously. They actively sought out his company, knowing the covert affairs they shared were safe. Those without the power of speech are seldom indiscreet.

Now the opposite was true. Danu was devoting herself to him as a man, not as a beneficiary of female desire. It felt all wrong. He worried she was too good, too beautiful and too perfect to bother with him. He didn't deserve her affection, this outpouring of love.

Danu had never realised how satisfying it was to sit down and have a decent conversation with a man, someone who showed an interest in what she was saying. Dancer was a wonderful listener, even if he couldn't hear a word she was saying.

'You know, you're the sort of man I could talk to all day,' she said. 'I can even talk to you about love because I know you haven't a clue what I'm talking about. I know about the goddess spot, even if I don't know where the goddess spot is. You might be able to find it for me, Dancer.'

Dancer stood up, lifted her from her seat and casually kissed her on the lips. They walked towards the waterfall.

'That's enough about me,' she said. 'What about you? Can you make me laugh? Or shall we just continue walking hand in hand? I like walking hand in hand.'

She pointed towards the river and then to the waterfall where it cascaded down deep into the river below. 'That's me,' she said. 'I'm the river of life. You're the waterfall, Dancer. That's you, plunging down into me, incapable of leaving me!'

Dancer scratched his head. Pulling all his clothes off, he pointed to the top of the waterfall, then dived into the pool and climbed out on the other side.

High above the rocky backdrop to the pool was a sloping plateau, where silver birches bent and swayed in the evening breeze. It was here that the river gave birth to the waterfall, where its waters cascaded over the cliff before returning to the river far below.

Danu lay back on the riverbank and watched Dancer climb the wet rock face. The waterfall plummeted and pulsated down beside him. Soon he was standing on the edge of the plateau above. He danced in circles until she started laughing. Then he stood as still as a statue of a nameless god and looked down on her.

Of all the trees of the forest, Dancer treasured the silver birch the most. It was a tree as deaf as he was, yet it danced in the wildwood like no other. Like the woodwose, the silver birch was a wind dancer. A tree of love, it lived but forty seasons. Its life was as brief as that of man. And, like Dancer, it forever reached up and searched for the light.

Dancer, sometimes full of sorrow, pondered with a sigh why every sound he used to know had somehow said goodbye: birdsong long before the dawn; swaying, singing barleycorn; he'd never know the cockerel's crow, endearments whispered in his ear, words he could no longer hear; someone snoring soft, then loud; the chatter of the passing crowd; thunder rolling around the sky; the curlew's lonely, plaintive cry; the oystercatcher's strident call; urine splashing on a wall; the banging of a swinging door; waves breaking on the shore; sails flapping; boats beaching; foxes barking; vixens screeching; in the dark something screaming; maybe he was only dreaming.

Mud squelching; men belching; horns blow; champions bellow; the wounded groaning; women moaning; mumbled words; a dying wish; the sudden splash of jumping fish; the dismal din of brutal battle; sheep bleating; farting cattle; babies crying; mothers sighing; children playing; ponies neighing; the clattering hoof; a howling wolf.

Hounds hunting; pigs grunting; the crunch of footfall in the snow; the sound of songs he used to know; tunes he once held in his head; alas, those songs now long since dead; goldcrests singing in the trees; the gentle hum of busy bees. Dancer heard none of these.

Animated by the wind, Dancer and the silver birch slowly started to move together in their silent world. That late-summer afternoon, the woodwose and wind dancer of the wildwood danced for the love of Danu. As the silver birches swayed around him, he shed his godhead and lost his trance. Dancer started to dance. Borne upon the breeze, his arms as branches rose and fell. Danu watched, under his spell, she saw him sway, move towards her then move away.

His neck twisted and turned and his quivering body pulsated as it responded to the silent throb of a fitful drum. Dancer and the silver birch danced as one. All about him, its leaves fluttered as they spun. His body unfurled, turned to run. Blown by the breeze, he danced to the flutter of the trembling leaves. Mist and spray blew up from the waterfall. Caught in the sunbeams, he was enveloped by a rainbow. And, as Danu watched, he seemed to flutter into the air, seemingly transformed into a multicoloured butterfly.

Danu was captivated. There was something magical about Dancer, despite his imperfections. Could this be love?

She remembered Anroth's advice - 'If ever you're attracted to a man who's a confusion of imperfections, you've found love.'

Danu stretched out her hand to try and catch him and, as she did so, the multicoloured God dived from above and sank like a stone into the pool below. A plume of white spurted upwards and spray blew across Danu's face. She groaned and laid back to watch the branches above her move up and down. High in the sky she saw the dance of the marsh harrier as it tumbled in circles around its dowdy mate.

Without warning, Dancer appeared beside her, shivering and trembling like a leaf. She stretched out her arm. As he came closer, she pulled him down and wrapped her cloak around them both, to share her warmth with his needful body.

Dancer thought it would be impetuous to be too forward with a goddess. Particularly when he was naked and lying beside her. He had intended just to snuggle in and curl up with his back to her but, feeling adventurous, he reached down, took her hand and kissed it, then pressed it to his chest.

She pulled herself closer, but left her hand where he'd laid it. For a long time, they rested contentedly, Danu in human form was adorable. Then he remembered the woman lying beside him was thousands of years old, a goddess of alarming power, the mother of many, the lover of more.

Prudence prevailed and he adopted the hedgehog position. This was not what Danu had in mind, her hand started to wander up and down, moving lower. Dancer reconsidered his plans and, forgetting about the hedgehog, rolled over. Danu's hair had fallen away from her neck, softly he stroked behind her ear. She turned towards him and smiled.

He wanted just to hold the moment forever, but then came the stillness and anticipation of a shared journey. He looked at her graceful hand as she held his against her cheek. She brought it around to her mouth and kissed his fingers, nibbled the tips then moved them to the other side of her neck.

His fingers pulsed up into her raven-black hair and his fingertips separated then came together again. As he kissed her on the lips, his hand moved down to caress her breast. Then, lying back, he let his hand trail to the other. Insistent, she pulled his hand back to the frustrated nipple he'd left behind.

He came closer and softly squeezed it with his fingertips, then sucked the other nipple. The slower his incursions, the more she made them welcome. Where is the merit in undue haste? Robbers ride roughshod, intent on galloping headlong to journey's end. But those who find a fuller meaning will hesitate and pause along the way.

His hand meandered down her stomach, passing by her valley of fruitfulness.

Like the tendrils of the sea anemone, his fingertips stroked her kneecaps, opening and closing, then opened again before his hand slowly retreated back up her legs, inflaming smouldering fires, rekindling old desires. Something stirred, so soon to flower, and a rosebud bloomed within the bower.

Aroused, Danu guided his fingers, but Dancer failed to discover the elusive Goddess spot she searched for. Frustrated, her hands moved to his head and her fingers massaged his wet, wavy hair. With each movement, she pulled his head across and pushed it down her stomach. She opened her legs further, and guided his head further down, then kept it there. Later she let out a sigh. He'd found the spot the gods deny.

'You may be dumb, Dancer,' she purred. 'But you're certainly not tongue-tied.'

She pulled him up beside her and made him welcome. Her right leg moved out beneath his body and her knees came up as he slipped between them.

No longer animated by the passing breeze, Dancer's body moved to a different rhythm as he deliberately slowed down the urgency of Danu's dance. And, for the first time in her long life, Danu discovered that initial magical plateau of sublime sexual arousal. Neither of them wished to bring it to its conclusion, believing the other should choose when to create the crescendo.

Together they climbed a golden staircase of strange, inviting pulsations, which took them to a glowing, limitless space. As they discovered those multicoloured layers of human thought and understanding that surround the world, their separate minds melded into one. Spinning into the crescendo, their two loves diminished to a singular point.

Less proved more, their love was much greater than before. Enlightenment briefly touched them, then passed them by. They were consumed and lost in the Mindglow.

'Oh, Dancer,' she whispered into ears that couldn't hear. 'That was earthly, so utterly earthly!'

The boundaries of Danu's mind dissolved, Dancer succumbed, subsumed within the goddess. A loud love growl, a groan of gratification and surrender, ebbed out of him.

'Into this world,' sighed Danu as she slowly released him. And from where they had ended, back to where they began, she had found him a very gentle man. Reaching out together, they had discovered love's elusive promise, but had failed to notice the abyss below.

Danu removed her golden torque and slipped it around Dancer's neck, a token of her love.

Looking upwards, Dancer noticed two tall blades of grass, bridged by a spider's web. Hanging on its silken threads was the empty shell of a butterfly. The once-bright colours of its wings had faded away to nothing, though they still fluttered in the passing breeze, kindred spirits, like Dancer drained of everything.

He would have done anything to prolong forever, that exquisite feeling of sublime helpless submission, but it ebbed away. All too soon, reanimated, his forceful inner nature, welled up within.

20 The Gift Of Hands

Ida had fallen asleep with his head resting comfortably against Aine.

'Now, Nuada, let me show you how to become a bone-setter,' said Anroth. 'We start by talking to the boy and warning him what to expect.'

The druid put his knuckles on Ida's cheekbone and turned it one way then the other, gradually increasing the pressure until the boy opened his eyes. He explained how they were going to mend the broken wrists. Ida nodded as Anroth introduced Nuada.

Before they started, Anroth checked they had everything they needed to hand, the two wooden slats, the clay, the wool and what was left of the cloth-strips.

'Dian, take half of that wool and all of the clay,' said Anroth. 'Then work the clay into the wool until it's firm but still pliable. When you've done that, divide it in two. I want two thick slabs that can reach from the boy's elbow right down to his knuckles. Each slab needs to be as wide as his hand.'

Dian began thumping and bashing the clay into the wool on the available table right next to Ida's head. Aine looked on and gave him advice. Ignoring all the lumps of black blood, congealed pus, porridge and honey stuck to her banqueting table, the queen protested.

'No, Dian, not on our good table, you're making an awful mess. Go and do that in the kitchen. Take Aine to help you. It looks like kneading bread to me.'

'Cliona, you don't by any chance have a couple of forearm bones, do you?' asked Anroth.

The queen went off to rummage around in the severed head cabinet and returned triumphant. 'I knew we had some somewhere,' she said, handing the bones to Nuada. 'These are your Uncle Segomo's. He was my favourite brother and a great warrior, famed for the strength in his right arm.'

Nuada studied the bones carefully.

Disturbed by Dian's merciless attack on the clay and wool, beside his ear, Ida was restless, tossing and turning. Demons hovered in the shadows of his mind. Cliona had taken over from Aine and was standing behind Ida, running her fingers through his thick blonde hair.

Like the goddess whose name she shared, the queen had been born with a gift: her voice had remedial powers. She could create the divine sounds of songbirds, soothing the troubled minds of those in distress. Like a nightingale she sang to Ida and filled his mind with joy, releasing him from his demons.

'Now then,' said Anroth. 'The first thing to remember about broken bones is that, whatever you do, you avoid making the injury worse than it already is. It's a great deal easier to maim or kill a man you're trying to heal, than it is to kill him in battle.

'The second thing is, learn as much as you can by looking at the injury and feeling the bones. Unless the skin is broken, you'll never be able to see the breaks in an injured man's bones. So, look at Ida's wrist and try to imagine what it looks like inside. Only then will you discover the magic of turning a broken bone back into a whole one. If you succeed, it will be even stronger than it was before the injury.

'The third thing is that, before you start, you must have everything you need set out before you. Remember, you may have only one chance of success. Tell me, Nuada, what's there to see? What's there to feel?'

Nuada looked at the boy's left wrist. The skin wasn't broken, but the hand and wrist were bent backwards on the forearm and pushed over to the thumb side. On the little finger side of the wrist, the rounded end of a forearm bone jutted out beneath the skin and Nuada felt around its end, just as he'd seen Anroth do in the past.

Ida opened his eyes. He watched as Nuada traced the bone along its length as far as the elbow. Nuada smiled at the boy and indicated he was going to mend the wrists. The boy nodded and wondered if Nuada might be Anroth's son. He had the same gentle, grey-blue eyes.

Nuada found some tenderness at the wrist end of the bone, but realised the bone itself was intact. It was the same size and shape as the bigger of Uncle Segomo's two bones. He explained to Anroth what he'd learnt.

'Very good, Nuada,' said the druid. 'But if we're really going to help this boy, we need to understand more about the way the arm and the wrist work together. Pass me Uncle Segomo's other bone.'

'I have Uncle Segomo's wrist bones as well, if that would help,' said Cliona.

Anroth looked up as the queen started to undo her green-and-gold necklace. 'That's really kind, Cliona,' he said. 'But we're fine.'

Nuada looked across admiringly. 'Gosh, mother, you're really good with bones.'

She smiled appreciatively. 'Indeed, I get so attached to them.'

'Consider this, Nuada,' said Anroth. 'To understand how these bones work together, you need to compare them with animal bones.

Animals are superior to us in many ways. The deer more fleet of foot, the swine more adaptable in what they can eat, the bull stronger, the fox more agile and cunning, but none can do with their front legs what we can do with our forearms. What do we have those animals don't possess? What will Ida lose if we don't set these bones properly?'

Nuada looked puzzled.

'If I were just to tell you, Nuada, you might forget,' said Anroth. 'But if you work it out for yourself, you'll always remember.'

Nuada bent and extended his arm, at the elbow, as animal might. Then he smiled and rotated his lower arm. 'I can twist it,' he said. 'I can make the palm of my hand face the surface of this table or I can turn it around completely and have it facing the rafters above. No animal I know, can do that.'

Nuada demonstrated what he meant, using Uncle Segomo's bones. He placed the ends of each together then twisted them through a half circle and back again. Then he felt the bones in his own arm and worked out what effect it had when he twisted his arm. 'Look, Snout, I've discovered how the bones move!' he said.

Anroth said nothing.

Nuada re-examined Ida's arms and continued.

'Because of the fractures, Ida's lost the ability to rotate his arms. If I can't realign the bones properly, when the wrist ends fuse together, he'll lose the ability to twist and rotate his forearms forever.'

'I've two final, important questions,' said Anroth. 'Which bone is broken and where's the break?'

Nuada picked up Uncle Segomo's bones. 'Well, the bone on the little finger side is intact,' he said. 'So, it can only be the bone on the thumb side. The bit that's broken off is at the large end. It's been forced backwards. We'll have to pull that big chunk of bone back to where it was if his wrist's ever going to work properly again.'

'Cliona,' said Anroth. 'Your son may be a fine warrior, but he's got the makings of a druid too!'

Aine and Dian returned from the kitchen, each carrying one of the clay-and-wool slabs. They laid these down on the table. Anroth inspected them and pushed a finger into the thickened, reinforced clay.

'Excellent, these are just the consistency I'm looking for,' he said. 'Right, Nuada, you've worked out the problem. Now what's the solution? To understand this, you need to work out how the injury occurred in the first place. Imagine you're standing in the courtyard, just outside the kitchen door, then you get knocked over the cliff edge. What would you instinctively do?'

'I'd throw my arms out to break the fall,' said Nuada.

'Exactly,' said Anroth. 'That's what Ida did. Breaking the fall may have saved his life, but it broke his wrists in the process. This explains why the broken bones have been crushed backwards and pushed over to the thumb side.'

Nuada paused and looked down at Ida's broken wrists. He rubbed his chin. 'Ah!' he said. 'What I need to do is pull the wrist and the hand away from the forearm so I can create a gap where the end bit has broken off and been forced backwards. Then I should be able to pull the wrist bit back to where it used to be. I might need to push it over to the little finger side to get it straight.'

'You've worked out the theory,' said Anroth. 'Now let's see what you're like in practice.' Dian imitated his elder brother and rubbed his chin thoughtfully. He was eager to get involved.

"This all this sounds as though it's going to hurt a lot, Snout,' he said in what he hoped was a sympathetic voice.

Anroth nodded. 'Yes, Dian, it's worse for some than others. And there are two wrists to fix.'

'Would you like me to give him something for the pain, Snout?'

'Oh, Dian!' exclaimed Cliona, clasping her hands together in excitement. 'How kind and thoughtful. Dian, I had no idea Snout had been teaching you the secrets of alchemy and sleeping draughts. Am I seeing a new, caring side to you?'

'Snout hasn't been teaching me anything, mother,' said Dian. 'I just thought that, since that lad is going to be experience a lot of pain, I could help by giving him a clout on the jaw and knock him out.'

Anroth looked up. "That's very considerate of you, Dian,' he said. 'I'll ask him, but I think he's already sustained quite enough injuries for one day. You seem to be forgetting that all this started with Aine's decisive, jaw-dropping contribution to the proceedings.'

Anroth spoke briefly to the Saxon. Ida looked at Dian towering above him and shook his head, declining the offer of a transient oblivion, with or without a broken jaw.

'You can still help, Dian,' said Anroth. 'It's important that, when we straighten the bones, the elbow is held rock-steady. We don't want the arm moving around. Get your hands around his upper arm and hold the elbow firmly against the table.'

Dian nodded.

'Right, Nuada, let's begin,' said Anroth. 'Your mental approach should be the same as that of the warrior, when you must make a series of decisive moves. Once you start, make sure you don't vacillate. You must take matters to their conclusion, no matter how much the boy suffers. Hesitation only adds to the suffering. Now do exactly as I say for the first wrist.'

Anroth ran the tip of Cernunnos's golden wand up and down Nuada's arms. The prince felt its magical, healing powers flow into his hands.

'Grip his left hand with your left hand,' said Anroth. 'Now grip the back of his left arm well above the wrist with your right hand. Make sure you have a secure and comfortable grip.'

Ida remained calm and watched everything. Aine had taken over again from Cliona, standing behind him, her hands gripping his shoulders, her thumbs massaging his muscles. Nuada looked at Ida, smiled and nodded, Ida nodded back and closed his eyes.

'Good, keep the arm steady, Dian,' said Anroth. 'Now, Nuada, increase the power with your left hand. Pull the lower end away from your right hand and a bit further backwards to start with. If it's a bit stuck, then a slight side-to-side rocking movement may help.'

Nuada did as he was told and, as if by magic, there was a satisfying crunch as the ends of the bones separated. Ida grimaced but remained silent.

'Now pull that lower end forward until it slips back into its normal position,' said Anroth. 'Yes, a bit more, that's it. Now, with your right thumb, push the broken end inwards, towards the little finger side.'

Nuada felt another crunch as the broken bit finally slipped back into place. 'Unbelievable!' he said, barely able to take in what he'd done.

'Very good,' said Anroth. 'Now don't move a thing. All our efforts will be in vain unless we can keep the arm stable in this position. Dian, bring one of those clay slabs over and lay it over the back of his hand and arm.'

When this was in position, Anroth moulded the clay around the back of Ida's forearm, wrist and hand, and the clay took on the shape of the manipulated contours. Then he gave the slab to Aine. 'Put this beside the fire,' he said. 'I want it slowly baked but not burnt. Turn it every hour or two and, when it's hard enough, I'll fit it.'

Using the long slat of wood, the wool and the cloth-strips, Anroth and Nuada temporarily stabilised and immobilised the fracture, and used wads of wool to ensure the hand stayed wedged and angled over to the little finger side. Finally, Anroth asked Ida to move his fingers, which he did with evident satisfaction.

'Well done, Nuada,' said the druid. 'This time, you're on your own. I'm going to watch.'

Nuada reversed his hands and repeated the sequence on the other side. He was a natural. His hands moved like quicksilver. Soon the arm was safely secured and another slab was left to harden by the fire.

'That, Snout, is the most satisfying thing I've ever done in my life,' he said.

'You did well,' said Anroth. 'You have two natural qualities all good bone-setters and healers require: confidence and speed. But I must warn you that, all too often, failure is the outcome of our endeavours.'

'Be that as it may, Snout,' said Nuada. 'There's more satisfaction in healing an enemy than killing him.' Dian laughed and shook his head.

'Either that brother of mine is very clever or he's an idiot,' he said. 'Where does the lad get his ideas from? Aine, if you come across any more Saxons while I'm gone, can you knock them off the cliff and hang on to them until I get back?'

Aine shook her head and laughed, then punched him on the arm.

'I'll do my best,' she said. 'But don't expect me to knock them off the cliff and hang on to them at the same time.'

'Don't worry if you're unable to break his arms, Aine, I can do that on my return,' he said mischievously as he rubbed his hands together. 'I fancy this arm mending business.'

Just then, one of Dian's warriors entered the great hall to tell his master the additional forces from the south had arrived.

Anroth embraced the wayward prince. 'Enough of this nonsense, Dian,' he said. ''Thank you for your help, but it's time to take your troops north. Have a safe journey and be sure to tell your father about the Saxon.'

Anroth, turned towards Nuada.

'Remember, the warrior and the healer with hands have much in common. Both need courage and decisiveness but, above all, they require monumental self-confidence coupled with monumental self-criticism. None of us are so skilled that we should ever fall foul of arrogance.'

21 Changed Circumstances

Once the tables had been cleaned, the floor swept and fresh rushes laid, Nuada called a meeting. The wider implications of Ida's visit disturbed him. Sirona and Luchtain had returned, neither had seen any Saxons.

'Why was there just one boat?' asked Nuada.

'Could it be the advanced vessel of a much larger fleet, moving up from the south?' said Crimthain.

'Well,' said Cliona. 'If Ida is the son of a powerful warlord, as I believe, why did he come here? That vessel didn't sail all the way across the North Sea on its own, it is part of a far, far bigger fleet, and they are somewhere close by.'

'Under normal circumstances, he'd be a valuable asset we could sell for a fine ransom, but now that most of our soldiers have ridden north, he's a major liability. If his father's anything like Midar, he and his men will descend on us with force.'

'If they only have a few ships, we've more than enough men to destroy them,' said Crimthain. 'And if we trade the boy for a bounty they might leave.' Cliona pointed out.

'He's in no fit state to move, and I remember times like this, in my father's kingdom, Rheged. There, we had Irish sea raiders, across the Irish sea. If we captured a warlord's son, from just one solitary ship, we knew there would be many more ships hanging over the horizon.'

Sirona nodded. 'A Saxon raiding party might be just a few of ships, but if they're intent on conquest, we can expect at least ten. And they won't necessarily land in the same place at the same time. Even if we see just a few ships sail in, it won't be that reassuring.'

'Giving them Ida is asking for trouble,' said Luchtain. 'Saxon raiding parties do their bargaining with the blade of an axe. But if Ida was leading a raiding party, why was he so far away from his ship and the rest of his men?'

"Thank you, Sirona, and Luchtain,' said Nuada. 'So, we're all agreed? Even if we've only seen one ship so far, it would be prudent to assume more are on their way and that we'll have a fight on our hands.'

'I can station men along the headlands,' said Crimthain. 'But we're already thinly stretched. If the Saxons land further down the coast, there's a risk we'll lose those men before the battle starts.'

'Yes, all our men need to stay close to the stronghold,' said Cliona. 'It's too late to get Midar and his troops back and delaying the raid on Gododdin would result in an even more disastrous state of affairs, giving Balor's allies time to join him. For the next few days, we're on our own.'

Nuada looked across the table. 'Anroth?'

'My feeling is that, for whatever reason, the boy and his crew got separated from the main raiding party,' said the druid. "Those gusting south-westerly winds that flatten the sea can be deceptive. Very quickly, you can get blown off course much further than you realise. Like a storm-tossed gull, the boy may well have had no idea of how far north he'd been blown.'

'Given the severity of his leg wound, he could have become confused or delirious. He didn't expect to be caught out and cornered by Aine so early in the morning. It's reasonable to assume that, by now, the rest of his crew will have linked up with the main raiding party.'

Aine arrived with an amphora of wine and Cliona rose to help her serve it.

'We weren't the intended target,' continued Anroth. ''They probably planned to attack the Kingdom of Deira. I suspect that, by the time news reached them of Ida's capture, the rest of the raiding party had landed and were already fighting.

'Cliona is right. This boy is, without doubt, the son of a powerful warlord. No father would deliberately send him out on a fool's errand. And, if the boy had more experience, he'd never have risked coming so close to the stronghold. But, bearing in mind his status, the Saxons may well have abandoned the attack in the south to sail towards us. Now, if the father knows where the boy is, he'll bring all the men he can muster.'

'If he has abandoned his ambitions in Deira, for the time being, many more warriors will follow later. He'll be in no mood to bargain as, even with just a few ships, he's capable of doing an enormous amount of damage unless we can defend everything we have outside the great hall.'

Crimthain shook his head. 'We've no defensive outer ditches or ramparts,' he reminded them. 'When we built this place, an attack from the sea was never foreseen.'

''That's true,' said Anroth. 'And, in those days, none of our enemies could get close enough to the stronghold to attack from the land. Crimthain, we've got four boats left after Ollathir's departure. Get your men to launch these and make ready to sail.

Cliona, gather all we have of value and as much food as you can. Fill the boats and move them further up the coast, away from where the Saxons are likely to land.'

The queen nodded.

'All those remaining who can't bear arms must make haste and leave for the safety of our lands in the west,' continued Anroth. 'They must take as many animals and as much food as they can herd and carry. We can't spare any of our remaining ponies for pack animals.

At the first sign of Saxon ships on the horizon, two boats must set sail and head for the estuary below the Valley of the High Waters. We should be able to link up with Midar from there. If it becomes obvious that the stronghold will be overwhelmed and we're forced to retreat, then we'll need the other two boats to help evacuate those who can fight their way out.'

'If we're forced to abandon the stronghold,' Luchtain interrupted, 'we'll need a rear-guard action until we've got the other boats away,' he said. 'We still have a few ponies left. A few of us using slingshots and bows should do enough damage to slow the Saxons down and keep them at a distance. We could then make our escape on the remaining ponies.'

Crimthain nodded in agreement. 'Yes, that's an important point, to defend the great hall to the last man would only end with wasted warriors – men Midar will need for the counterattack. I'll get some of the older men from the settlement who are still sound with sling and spear to help with the rearguard action. They'll be able to mount a strong defence. But, if things go badly, they'll be slaughtered in the hand-to-hand fighting. Bear in mind that our finest warriors are with Midar.'

'Two other points,' said Sirona. 'We don't need to use warriors as lookouts up and down the coast. There are plenty of older children with keen eyesight who can help with that. If you let us take some of the ponies with us, I'll lead a party south and Luchtain can take one north. Between us, we'll be able to give fair warning of any Saxon ships. Then, once the Saxons are spotted, the children can escape through the woods and catch up with those fleeing west. We can leave the ponies tethered in the woods near where we plan to fight the rear-guard action.'

Anroth looked at Sirona as she spoke with such confidence and authority, and remembered the day she'd arrived, a shy young girl. He was proud of her and pleased her many skills were coming to fruition.

'Secondly, when battle commences, we must have people concealed outside in the woods,' continued Sirona. 'If things aren't going our way, it'll be impossible for those inside the stronghold to know when best to evacuate. Only those outside will be able to tell.'

'Anroth, you're not staying inside. If you have to fight your way out, you'll never make it. Think how much damage you and I can do from the woods with our bows and arrows.'

The queen nodded approvingly. 'Sirona makes some very good points, all of which I agree with,' she said. 'She's right about you, Anroth.'

'Alright, Cliona,' said the druid. 'But what applies to me applies to you, too. The last thing we need is for you to be killed or taken hostage. You're coming with me.'

'I'm sure we all accept Sirona's suggestions,' said Nuada. 'But they do leave us with one problem. When we're barricaded inside the stronghold, how will we know when breakout and retreat is our only option?'

'We'll take a battle horn with us,' said Anroth. 'If you hear it bellow, it'll be time to fight your way out.'

'But none of you can play the battle horn,' said Nuada.

The queen rose and picked up a horn that hung on the wall, then she blew it until its bellow filled the room. For the first time during the meeting, Nuada laughed.

'Mother!' he said. 'All these years you've complained about us trying to play the Carnyx and you never let on you could play it! Just wait till I tell Goibniu and Dian.'

Anroth wagged his finger knowingly. 'There are a lot of things you don't know about your mother.'

'One other thing,' said Nuada. 'I'm setting all our slaves free. Crimthain, give them weapons. They're welcome to stay and fight with us or, if they prefer, I'll grant them safe passage either to our lands in the west or wherever else they choose to go.'

That evening, Nuada and Anroth went to visit Ida. By now the clay-and-wool splints by the fire had dried and hardened, and Anroth fitted the first slab to the back of the Saxon's arm while Nuada watched. Then Nuada fitted the second. They sat with him for a while as Aine fed him. And, before they left, Nuada put his hand on the boy's shoulder and smiled. Ida smiled back.

22 The Watchtower

In the evening, Nuada walked with Anroth to the deserted watchtower. The sentries had moved out to form part of a defensive perimeter.

'I liked the way you handled the meeting, Nuada,' said the druid.

'As you've pointed out to me in the past, those who wish to be listened to should start by listening to those they want to do the listening,' said Nuada. 'I was surprised how useful Sirona and Luchtain's ideas were.'

''This day has always been coming,' said Anroth. 'I've spent many years training them to behave like druids, but to think like warriors. And now, with Crimthain's help, they'll have to fight like them, too.'

'Anroth, you look weary.'

'I am,' said the druid. 'But it's a weariness more of the mind than the body.'

'Since his death, no one has said a word about Keeva,' said Nuada.

'Indeed, there's been a conspiracy of silence,' said Anroth. 'His sacrifice has marked us all. I must take some of the blame. I used to worry that my novices might be attracted to black druidism, but none were. It never occurred to me one of them would choose ritual suicide.'

'You can't blame yourself.'

'Never look to the followers, Nuada,' said Anroth. 'When religions fail, look to their leaders and teachers. Without exception, all religions have a sinister underbelly of evil and, the longer the religion prospers, the larger that underbelly grows. Evil grows out of arrogance and greed, and thrives on misplaced ambition.'

'It must have been hugely distressing for you to slit Keeva's throat and watch the blood spurt out,' said Nuada. 'Did you find it difficult?'

The words had barely left of his mouth before Nuada bitterly regretted the stupidity of his question.

'No,' said Anroth. 'Once we'd tried everything to dissuade him from invoking that grotesque druidic rite, it was no different from any other sacrifice. I've slit a thousand throats and more. It requires no emotion to perform something so routine.'

'But you've never slit a man's throat?'

'In the old days, when I worked for my father, it was sometimes unavoidable,' said Anroth. 'But I've never been involved in ritual human sacrifice since I became a druid. Had we denied Keeva the ceremony, he'd have left life dangling from a tree, a slow, depressing way to die. Brutal as it was for all of us, the ceremony was cleaner and kinder than leaving him all alone, dancing his death throes at the end of a rope.'

Nuada nodded.

'The last thing he felt before dying was the love of those around him who, in turn, he'd loved so much and served so well,' continued Anroth. 'We were there for him, to help him cross the threshold into the Otherworld.'

'I'm sorry,' said Nuada. 'I should never have said something so stupid. We've enough to think about.'

'Well, Nuada, if you can't mention it, then nobody can,' said Anroth. 'It helps me to put my feelings into words. That said, his ghost walks beside me.'

'I've been thinking, Anroth, are we seeing the whole story? Apart from his devotion to druidism, there was another major influence in his life. Like you, he was enormously attracted to Jesus, the person. He was drawn to his love of nature, and all the kind and loving things he said and did.

'Some of Keeva's family were Christians, so he knew more about it than me. He believed Jesus very deliberately planned his death, sacrificing his life to save us all. Keeva's death may have had nothing to do with you or his druidic beliefs, however he justified it to us, at the time. The influence of Jesus might well explain what led him down the lonely road we found him on.'

Anroth nodded, finding some solace in the suggestion.

'I'm not sure mother agreed with me releasing the slaves,' said Nuada, changing the subject.

'She might have been surprised, but I doubt she disapproved,' said Anroth. 'Aine was given to her as a slave. Your mother was quick to return her freedom, sometimes, when you hear them talking, they sound like sisters. She adores Aine and Aine adores her. Anyway, Nuada, it was an intelligent decision. All the slaves have stayed. They'll fight hard to defend their new-found freedom.'

'I was amazed when mother revealed she could blow the Carnyx,' said Nuada. 'How little we know about our parents' lives!'

'Well, Nuada, parents rarely reveal much about their past to their children,' said Anroth. 'Children rarely ask. They only start to wonder when their parents are dead.'

'There's something I've always wanted to ask you, but never dared,' said Nuada. 'Why is there such a strong bond between you and Dancer?'

'Given another life, I could so easily have been him and he could have been me – as, indeed, could you,' said

Anroth. 'Many years ago, I trained him as a druid. He had an agile, creative mind. He loved to engage in debate with his brother novices.'

'But, Anroth, he's deaf and dumb.'

'He didn't used to be, until he became preoccupied with just one particular aspect of druidism: the pursuit of wisdom. Dancer lost interest in everything else. It didn't trouble me, for he was better informed than the rest of my novices on most matters.

'Increasingly, he sought enlightenment by attempting to become one with nature. Taking nothing with him, he'd wander off into the woods for days on end, where he'd fast for long periods, stand still or just move silently among the trees. I've no doubt he developed an affinity with the living, breathing wildwood that few possess.'

Anroth had all of Nuada's attention.

'He seemed to be travelling on a spiritual journey back to the mystical origins of the Celtic nations and the faraway lands of India,' continued Anroth. 'I pointed out to him that enlightenment, the ability to release one's mind into those rivers of sublime consciousness in the sky above, should not be confused with wisdom. Enlightenment is a disembodied awareness of our own mind as a part of all consciousness. It's part of a personal journey few are equipped to make.'

'Have you ever searched for enlightenment?' asked Nuada.

'No, Nuada, it's a private indulgence,' said Anroth. 'It gives you no guidance on how best to advise others or pass judgement, which is what wisdom allows you to do. Wisdom requires many things – above all common sense, experience and an open mind.

'I'd taken Dancer as far as I could, so I sent him to the large druidic school in Rheged to see what they could make of him. In spite of his undoubted ability, he was immature and innocent of mind. There's an endearing, childlike quality about him that he retains even to this day.'

Nuada's eyes widened.

'I'm not too sure about that last bit,' he said. 'When I think of the dead bodies we find littered around the forest, I can't help but feel the Picts would disagree about his endearing qualities.'

'Well, be that as it may, it's not his fault,' said Anroth. 'He's misunderstood. There are good reasons for his behaviour, but let me return to my tale.'

'Shortly after he went to Rheged, he met Birog who was training to be a druidess. Even in those days, she'd secretly embraced the dark, sinister side of druidism. What happened next, no one knows. But Dancer and Birog became lovers. She may have persuaded him that enlightenment could be attained through her body.'

'It's not as fanciful as it sounds. But it's a very dangerous game to play with a creature such a Birog. A man's mind is at its most compliant and susceptible to suggestion at the moment of orgasm.

'Dancer left Rheged,' continued the druid. 'I can only assume he rejected her. Not long afterwards, Birog's tutors discovered she'd chosen the ways of the black druids and dismissed her. Birog blamed Dancer. Her fury knew no bounds. She still sends assassins to kill him.' Nuada raised his eyes.

'Dancer returned and I was enormously impressed with how much he'd learnt in Rheged. The knowledge he'd acquired was astounding. I couldn't believe how much they'd taught him. He'd become proficient in all things apart from creating a sacrificial fire.

I was worried that Dancer's mind, overloaded as it was with so much information, might fracture in two. Splintered minds, like Keeva's, are often associated with strange confusions of religious belief. Fortunately, Dancer remained firmly in touch with reality. The form of existence he sought involved becoming as one with all living things. He was enchanted by the trees and the creatures of the wildwood.'

'But, Snout, where does Dancer fit in with Danu in this unsettling, tortuous tale?' asked Nuada. 'Why not send one of my brothers or me to accompany her?'

'I fear I've made a bad mistake with Danu,' said Anroth. 'The other day, I found mistletoe growing out of season, which fulfils an old prophecy, warning of the arrival of a stranger coming from the east, and the fall of the house of Midar. The stranger would also provide us with a means of salvation.'

'At the time, I assumed the prophecy related to Danu, who had arrived that morning. But, today, when we were trying to save Ida, I realised Danu wasn't part of the prophecy, Ida was. I may have sent her on a fool's errand from which she might never return.'

Nuada grimaced.

'To return to Dancer,' said Anroth. 'He didn't stay long before he set out for Gaul. Travelling widely, he moved from one introduction to another. You can always count on the hospitality of the Celts when you're far from home. Some years later, he returned.'

'Had he found enlightenment?'

'He didn't say, but I very much doubt it,' said Anroth. 'He'd heard that somewhere up in the northwest of Ireland, the fabled Fintan, the ancient salmon of infinite wisdom, was living in a river that ran into the western sea. This mystical fish resided in a pool beneath a hazelnut tree and fed from the nuts as they fell. Many had tried to catch the fish and failed. It was said that whoever caught this Fintan, and consumed it, would attain infinite wisdom.

'I warned him the story was no more than a cruel delusion,' continued Anroth. 'I pointed out that the man who finally caught such a fish, after so many had failed, must already be wise. And though he'd become renowned for his wisdom because he'd caught and eaten the fish, the wisdom would already be within him before he ever sat down by that hazelnut tree. I told Dancer he'd never be that man.'

Nuada nodded.

'We argued and I pointed out the futility of trying to acquire wisdom in such a manner. I also warned him that if he ever ate the sacred fish but hadn't caught it himself, he'd bring down the fury and wrath of the gods on his head. Dancer would have none of it. We parted as friends, and he left to search for Fintan.

'When he came home, he'd been struck deaf and dumb. He returned to a life of solitude in the wildwood he loved so much. I worried he was changing. Sometimes, when I walked through the wildwood in the moonlight, I'd find him fast asleep, standing upright among the trees but not supported by them.'

'There are legends from days gone by, about trees that gradually transform those who worship them into their own likeness. One morning Dancer may wake and find himself rooted to the ground, his body adorned by branches, able to speak only through the rustle of leaves.'

'Snout, this is a dreadful end to your tale,' said Nuada. 'How did he become deaf and dumb?'

'Well, the story goes that, after many months of fruitless searching for the salmon of infinite wisdom, Dancer came to a beautiful valley,' said Anroth.

'As he wandered down to the river, in the distance, he saw a pool overhung by a hazelnut tree and an old man fishing beneath the tree. The old man's line tightened and, suddenly, the biggest salmon Dancer had ever seen leapt into the air. He watched the battle rage to and fro and, as he drew closer, he realised the salmon was winning. The old man was all but done for.

Jumping into the river, Dancer grasped the fish's tail, dragged it ashore and dispatched it. And, in gratitude, the old man insisted Dancer share his meal. Though Dancer had saved the old man and helped catch Fintan, the gods struck him deaf and dumb for daring to eat some of the mystical fish.'

'But, Snout, that wasn't fair,' said Nuada. 'The old man would never have landed the fish without Dancer. He deserved a share of the meal.'

'There's little about life that's fair, Nuada,' said Anroth. 'No one has ever suggested the gods and goddesses are.'

'Now I know why you sent Danu on her own,' said Nuada. 'You hoped she'd meet Dancer and come to love him, thus releasing him from the curse.' He saw Anroth's eyes fill with tears.

'What would you have me do?' the druid asked. 'Stand idly by and wait till the wildwood claimed him? Without love, Nuada, we change into things we were never meant to be.

Dancer needs to feel the love of a woman to protect him from himself, lest we lose him forever. The return of his hearing and voice, would be no more than a pleasant additional windfall.'

He sighed. 'Whether she chooses to help him or not, one thing is certain,' he added. 'She'll need him much more than he'll need her.'

There was an awkward pause.

'You never talk about it,' said Nuada. 'But he's your son, isn't he?'

Anroth nodded. 'I'm not ashamed of him, I'm very proud of Dancer.' He hesitated. 'Fathers don't always talk about their sons, Nuada.'

'Before I knew you, did you have any other children?' asked Nuada. His voice was soft and slow, almost to the point of disinterest, but inside his heart pounded.

Anroth faltered. There was something the old man desperately wanted to share with the prince. 'Not before I knew you, Nuada,' he said eventually. 'My wife died in childbirth and, of course, my child died with her.'

Nuada put his arms round Anroth's shoulders. 'Thank you for today,' he said. 'You gave me the greatest gift I've ever received. I felt the magic flowing down my arms into my hands. I hope I always retain it.'

Anroth gripped Nuada's bronzed forearms. 'As long as you have these, you'll never lose the magic,' he said.

'If Dancer could speak and hear, what would you want for him?' asked Nuada.

'To complete his training as a druid and for me to ordain him,' said Anroth. 'My life couldn't have been more fulfilling. I wish I could watch him following in my footsteps.'

'But if you had a son who could hear and speak, what then?'

'I'd help them do whatever they wanted.'

'No!' said Nuada. 'Tell me what you would want him to do.'

'The same as I wish for Dancer.'

'Is it too late to train me as a druid?' asked Nuada.

The old man's face lit up in surprise.

'No, I will teach you,' he said.

Nuada hesitated. 'I can still be a warrior, can't I?'

'Indeed, you wouldn't be the first to be both. Did I ever tell you about the High Druid and warrior Divitiacus of the Aedui tribe, who once led his army to fight beside Julius Caesar?'

Nuada gave a mock yawn, which Anroth pretended not to notice. 'He was highly regarded by Cicero,' he continued. 'He addressed the Roman senate, and debated philosophy, astronomy and even divination.'

'Snout, this is sounding like a history lesson from my childhood,' said Nuada. 'Can we get back to the present? Was what we did today something of your own invention?'

'Not entirely,' said Anroth. 'Many years ago, I watched an old druid try to do something similar. You know, Nuada, there's a side to healing that's easily forgotten. The druid is forever looking into the future. But it's not just a matter of predicting it; it's even more important to change it.'

'All life spins on the point of a needle, in balance between harmony and discord. Take the way we helped Ida. The next time you see something like that, don't be afraid to do things differently if you can think of a better way. Move our world in the direction of harmony and away from discord.'

'I'd prefer to fight the battle we fought today than the one we expect tomorrow,' said Nuada.

'Have I ever talked to you about the magical, multicoloured layers of thought that drift in the sky above us?' asked Anroth.

Nuada laughed. 'First history, now mysticism,' he said. 'What are you going to come out with next, Snout?'

'Have you ever wondered where your thoughts go, once they leave your mind?' asked Anroth. 'They must go somewhere because, as often as not, they return to you the same way they left you. What if they become thoughts that others may chance upon and share, a common property that drifts above us in the air?'

'Imagine a layer of thought that embraces the whole world. It happened to me today. When I fought desperately to save Ida's life, I imagined myself beside a sacred river. Ida sat beside me. We turned and beheld two rivers, his and mine, flowing together as one. Share the vision with me, Nuada.'

Anroth raised his hand.

'Imagine that layer of thought in the sky high above,' he said. 'I see a mosaic of many colours – our hopes, dreams, our plans for the future, the sunshine and the rain that all our minds must share. When the sun shines through the rain, you'll see a rainbow. What if the rainbow was a channel of our thoughts?'

'Just imagine the rainbow bursting out from the multicoloured chimera of consciousness and that those at one end are thinking in harmony with those at the other. If it were not so, then why do we sometimes find ourselves thinking the same thoughts without speaking to each other? How would it be if our minds and the Saxons could find harmony? You and Ida could face the future as friends.'

Nuada smiled. 'And how might I find such a place?' he asked.

'Who knows, Nuada, there may be many doors. It would depend on your state of mind and what you wished to find.'

'Snout, your imagery is dazzlingly plausible,' said Nuada. 'If I meditated on the matter, I could come to believe it. I fear, however, you've dreamt one dream too far.'

Anroth looked up at the night sky. He said,

'I hope that somewhere up there, - my dreams of a peaceful future have found Ida's feverish mind.'

23 Ominnios

Despite her very best endeavours, the Black Druidess Birog, only ever succeeded in giving birth to one child, the weedy weakling Cu Roi.

That was bad enough, but what particularly peeved her was the realisation that the only occasion she'd ever achieved orgasm in her life was during her chaotic dalliance with Dancer.

It was hardly a surprise. What she could never understand, was because of her obsessive desire to always be in charge, and control, she was incapable of ever letting go, and sharing her emotions with another.

Predictably, she blamed her husband, Bres, and tried to make him feel guilty. Coercing and controlling him, screeching at him, proved scant consolation. After every doomed excursion in the bedchamber, under her breath, she cursed Dancer becoming increasingly obsessed with his destruction.

Bres never understood that Birog had never loved him. He received a litany of vicious verbal insults from her and, Birog, inflicted on him more brutal physical injuries in private, than ever he received fighting on the battle field.

Concerned about her son's less-than-impressive looks, Birog made the great mistake of gazing into his future by looking deep within the Black Obsidian. She was shocked when she saw the mirrored image of what he'd look like when he had grown to adulthood.

Cu Roi's obsequious, snivelling, shifty nature was due in part to his unfortunate upbringing. He grew up loving simple things, such as pulling butterflies from their wings, squashing the shells of big, fat snails and separating puppy dogs from their tails. He was a 'sickly' child, but only to attract attention, a product of his own manipulative invention.

Birog's sister-in-law, Balor's queen, had no such fertility problems. She gave birth to a daughter, Eithne, then three sons. Eithne, like the oldest two boys, was as devious and cruel as Birog and Balor.

The Queen's youngest child, who was gentle and kind like his mother, died unexpectedly. Birog regarded the queen, as surplus to the requirements of the kingdom. Left to her own devices, the queen could well have been a disruptive influence for good. It was no surprise, when she died, not long after the death of her youngest son, bitten by a small, black snake.

However, her memory lived on. When Balor was taken in drunkenness, Birog would shape shift into her dead sister-in-law's body, taking her brother to bed. Mixing their venom and bodily juices, and thus did she rule the kingdom.

With the death of the queen, Birog took Eithne and her two remaining brothers under her own dark wing. At a stroke, Cu Roi acquired a stepsister and two stepbrothers, becoming an outcast in his own family.

After the cattle raid, when Birog had discovered the loss of the Black Obsidian, she moved fast. At first, it had seemed exciting to Cu Roi to be part of his mother's plans to retrieve her precious spellbinder. And when she'd suggested she shape-shift him into the hound Ominnios, he'd eagerly accepted. The heavy silver torque around his neck, gave him the sense of dignity he craved.

Bending the ends inwards, Birog warned him she could always make it tighter if he misbehaved. As he prowled around Gododdin, all who saw him looked on with a mixture of admiration and fear.

On the journey to Bamburgh, he'd made the most of his new body and indulged in a killing spree. At first, it had been just a few sheep, then some cattle and a stag, wanton destruction simply for the sake of it. He'd even managed a couple of swans and a duck after he'd launched himself headlong into a lake.

Irritated, Birog, reprimanded him for showing off. The best bit of all, had come in the great hall, when mother came to call. It didn't get any better than slaughtering one's own kind, and he'd relished ripping the guard's throat out. His lifelong compulsion to pull the wings off butterflies paled into insignificance.

Still imprisoned in the body of the beast, Ominnios had followed Danu north. By now, he was getting very fed up, and missed life's little luxuries and distractions. Constantly walking on all fours humiliated him, just as his mother had intended. And he was tired of eating raw meat and chewing through mouthfuls of feathers.

He loved his mother dearly, much more than he'd ever respected the virtues of his father, no one could create pure, unadulterated evil like her. He was the first to admit she had a vindictive streak. If she took a dislike to someone, she was never to be found guilty of the frailty of forgiveness.

She'd once had an old and crotchety maidservant whose croaking voice had annoyed her. To teach the woman a lesson, she'd turned her into a crane. But the bird's harsh, strident voice had irritated Birog even more, so she'd slowly skinned the wretched bird alive then wrung her neck.

Cu Roi and his mother had eaten her for supper and a fine feast she'd proved to be. From the crane skin, she'd fashioned a bag to keep the Black Obsidian in.

After Birog's raid on the stronghold as the Lama, she'd changed back to human form. Clutching Anroth's cauldron and mounted on a pony, she had galloped north. Cu Roi in the body of Ominnios, had bounded after her. As he ran along beside her, she'd briefly given him back the power of speech.

'Mother, dear mother, please change me back to human form,' he'd pleaded. 'I don't want to be a hound anymore.'

'You'll stay as a hound until you've discovered Midar's plans, and killed Dancer and anyone foolish enough to venture north with him!' she'd said.

'But Dancer might kill me, mother! I'm frightened of him.'

'I was rather hoping he'd have done so by now. Why do you think I changed you into a hound with a nice, bright, shiny collar? If you really want to please me, get yourself killed. Then I can give you a hero's funeral.'

'Please take me home,' he'd said. 'I won't pull the wings off butterflies anymore.'

'Why not? It's one of your more endearing little habits. Now stop following me!'

'But I'm not well, I feel sick, I think I'm going to vomit. 'When I've been sick, I always feel hungry.'

Birog was exasperated. 'You're a hound, aren't you?' she said. 'Do what any other decent dog does and eat your own vomit.'

Over the years, Cu Roi had developed the unerring ability to distract his mother at the most inconvenient of times, clinging to her like a whelk. Like all demanding children, he never knew when to stop. He lacked the good judgment to drop back and let his mother escape.

This time, he'd done it once too often.

Infuriated by Cu Roi's insistent bleating, Birog finally admitted to herself what she'd always known. Her son's whole life had been one long private and public inconvenience, an irrelevance she had no further use for. Henceforward she would channel all her talents, and what questionable love and affection she possessed, into her stepchildren.

Birog had never really believed in love of any form. She regarded men as nothing more than appendages of her own body and mind. There was certainly no obligation for a woman to love a husband; he was nothing more than a possession, a commodity, there to be used. Why then would she love a wastrel son, just because she'd had the misfortune to give birth to him?

She relieved Cu Roi of his powers of speech. Any further bleatings became barks.

Seething with fury, she called out to him.

'I want you out of my life. You're twenty-four years old. It's high time you got married. If you don't find someone yourself, I'll marry you off to your stepsister Eithne. Enjoy your life while you can. I can't see you living long, given Eithne's delightful, spiteful nature.'

By now, Cu Roi was yelping in fear.

'Every royal household worthy of the name needs some incest and an occasional murder in the family,' Birog said.

'Eithne deserves the pleasure of murdering one of her nearest and most deranged relatives. After all, I murdered her mother and youngest brother.'

Rejected and dejected, yet hoping his mother might still forgive him, Cu Roi had dutifully trekked north and shadowed Danu until she'd met Dancer. But, after Snibo's attack, he'd retreated a safe distance from their camp. The miserable beast feared for his future and knew that, unless he could kill Danu, Dancer or both, his days back in Gododdin would be numbered. Frustrated, he'd drifted off to sleep, knowing that when he awoke it would be time for a kill.

Dancer sat by the fire thinking. There could only be one reason that his path had crossed with Danu's. Like him, she must be intent on killing Birog. All this had Anroth's touch about it. He was sure the druid had hoped he would help Danu. He hadn't needed to ask. But they were playing a deadly game, gambling their lives against Birog's malign power.

He had taken Danu on a voyage of discovery, she had taken him to another world, far past the final point of breathtaking weakness, over the edge of loves reality. Miraculously, his mind was now crystal-clear. The lethal side of his nature had returned. The virtuous snake had shed its skin, revealing the cold, grey warrior within.

He hadn't always been that way. Birog's numerous attempts to kill him had left him mistrustful and merciless. Danu had put him back in touch with his youthful, optimistic past, which he'd all but forgotten.

He wondered if his old self was still there to rediscover after so many years of neglect, though this was hardly the time to speculate on future uncertainties. Before long, Cu Roi, in the body of Ominnios, would have to make a move. It was time for Danu to be blooded before she faced Birog. Only Danu could be certain of delivering the fatal blow. Seeing Cu Roi's dead body might just give her the edge.

His eyes never far from his guardian, Dancer looked up at the trees. Snibo was perched nearby, and his head bobbed up and down as he peered into the undergrowth behind his master. He flew off and landed on a tree above where he'd been looking. Dancer noticed a flash of silver and something furry, half-hidden by the undergrowth below.

He stood up, stretched and knelt down beside Danu. He smoothed her cloak and blew her kisses until she awoke. She looked up, smiling, and idly ran her fingers through his hair.

He placed her spear beside her hand, and squeezed her fingers around the shaft. As she watched him, he flicked his eyes in the direction of the threat in the undergrowth. She nodded. He lay down beside her and half-closed his eyes, ready for the beast's impending attack.

Ominnios watched, panting, his tongue lolling out of his mouth. His thick fur, made him uncomfortably hot, all he wanted was to go back to Balores, to return to human form, and wash his face in a cold, refreshing bowl of water.

At last, he saw his chance to move in for the kill. They both seemed to be sleeping. It would only take a moment to rip their throats out. Any common hunting dog capable of Ominnios's ferocity would have wasted no time, but he was no ordinary hound, informed as he was by Cu Roi's thoughts. He had the mind of a coward and continued to lie there, petrified, unable to move.

Dancer was exhausted, he had hardly slept in days. But now Ominnios was about to attack, he knew how important it was to stay awake. If he'd been on his own, all would have been well. But, as he looked at Danu, still bathed in the beauty of the Mindglow he was seduced by the illusion of safety it provided. For the briefest of moments, he relaxed, and with that relaxation came deep sleep. The abyss beneath them opened up.

Snibo looked down from above. He assumed Dancer was feigning sleep, and that he was still alert and ready for the attack. Worried Ominnios was never going to make a move, he decided to provoke him into action.

He shuffled along a branch until he was directly above the hound then, with his tail feathers splayed out and his bottom up in the air, he splurged out a large dollop of white. With a splat, it landed on Ominnios below, a direct hit. Ominnios was furious. Snibo's sloppy, white excretion had splattered all over his forehead and now ran down into his eyes. They stung and watered. And then, just in case Ominnios wasn't suitably enraged, Snibo squatted down and unleashed another sloppy, white torrent onto the hound's nose.

Ominnios gave a deep-throated growl. Danu heard branches break and, when she looked up, she saw the beast charging from the undergrowth, teeth bared. Holding her spear out of sight, she waited until Ominnios launched himself in the air, then she threw it. But, in all the excitement, she had timed her throw too late and she forgot to call out the magic word, 'Ibar', that ensured the spear always ran true.

The spear hit the hound in the flank, ripping through his flesh. Ominnios landed on the far side of the clearing. He rolled over, crouching low.

Snarling like a thing possessed, he slowly got to his feet.

Danu called out, 'Athibar.' The spear returned to her hand.

The hound licked his bleeding wound and, as he looked around, his eyes came to rest on the still-sleeping Dancer. Realising Ominnios would now set about her lover, Danu tried to distract the beast. She shouted at the brute and goaded him to attack her, then she backed up against a tree.

He turned on her. She wedged the base of the spear against the trunk of the tree and steadied herself. Ominnios rose in the air and went for her throat, but she angled the spearhead beneath the beast's jaw. The long, serrated blades slashed through his neck and blood spurted from the jagged wound as the point of the spear embedded itself deep in the base of his skull.

Impaled upon the spear, the hound continued to rear up until his head collided with the trunk of the tree above Danu. Crushed against the tree and repulsed by the stench of his sweaty coat, she was shrouded within the creature's shuddering, furry body.

His long forelegs hung over her shoulders, which made it impossible to push him away. She gasped, unable to draw breath, and started to suffocate. The hideous, heaving body of the beast caressed her face, holding her in its dying embrace.

Dancer awoke, Snibo was pulling his ear. All he could see was one of Danu's legs, weakly kicking beneath Ominnios's quivering body. He ran across the clearing and dragged the beast off her, just as Danu began to lose consciousness.

Crestfallen he had failed her; he tossed the hound's crumpled carcass to the ground. She held him close and gave him a reassuring embrace, as she recovered her breath. At least the beast was dead.

Danu went down to the river, like the Washer at the Ford, and washed away the blood of the newly dead. As she did so, she remembered Anroth's stark warning when they were on the beach.

'I just wonder, is the Mindglow really a gift and a blessing? We live in a treacherous brutal world. Too much love may be bad for your health. How can you protect yourself against evil if all you can feel is love?'

Dancer's love and trust had almost cost them their lives. It was a warning she would fail to heed with tragic consequences.

24 Making Ready For The Day

Danu looked at Dancer, he seemed worn out, did he ever really sleep? Surely, they were safe enough now?

Lying back against a tree, she drew his head onto her lap, cupped his face in her hands and kissed him softly. Not the kisses a goddess gave, as a prelude to loveless conjugation, but kisses that talked to Dancer and fed him things he was desperate to feel until he fell fast asleep. Never had crossing the boundary been more magical.

Snibo flew down and waddled along, then pulled and played with the gold-and-garnet ring on her finger. Danu had been accepted into his select little group of friends. She talked to him and he, in turn, chuntered back to her.

'Well done, Snibo,' she said. 'You saved the day. Thanks to you, our work is now half-done.' Truth be told, it had barely begun.

So much had happened. She remembered falling into the river and Dancer stretching out his hand. As he'd pulled her out, for the briefest of moments, they'd become as one. That was how it had started. It had felt quite natural to be a part of him.

She thought back to the night that Lugh had wrestled the Lama, ending up all covered in slime and rotting skin. He had gone down to the sea to wash it off, and she'd watched over him.

She remembered him rising from the waters, his body bathed in moonlight, his powerfully built form silhouetted against the shimmering, undulating waves. She'd been full of admiration for his strength and unassuming nature, and couldn't believe a man could be so physically perfect, perplexed she wasn't attracted to him. Then she'd realised his godlike features were, for her, a defect. Lugh, the embodiment of perfection in a man, too beautiful by far; a god awaiting the death of his mortal frame.

Danu mused on the differences between the gods' and mankind's manner of loving. She'd expected the love between humans to be enduring, but probably weaker and boring compared with that of the gods. Celestial love had the element of the frantic about it, she had never understood why because it was meaningless.

It involved finding an unoccupied cloud, making sure it was thick enough to prevent you falling through it, then briefly bouncing up and down. Compared to human love it was uncomplicated, potent, but frustratingly brief.

The love of man was much more confusing. She realised that making love was only the final part of a variety of changes that created a shared awareness. At what stage making love became inevitable was hard to tell.

The image of Dancer's wet body climbing the waterfall and dancing in the mists of the rainbow had aroused her, that image created need. Unlike with the gods, where physicality was everything, the greater the variety of expression Dancer was able to find, the more powerful her response would be.

By the time he'd dived from the waterfall and a plume of white spray had spurted upwards from the pool, she knew they'd make love. Had Danu been able to ask Dancer when he'd realised it would happen, he'd have probably said it occurred to him when he licked the end of his wand and put it inside her hand. She'd felt something moving within, new life. They had created something beautiful. Release came when she opened her hand and set the butterfly free. He'd made her dream come true.

Snibo stopped playing with the ring, cocked his head and looked around. Danu looked across to the bushes from where Ominnios had launched his attack. Was there something moving?

A moment later, Snibo stopped again, extended his neck and looked across to the other side of the clearing. A tingling sensation shot up her spine. They were not alone.

Her heart raced.

Where was her spear?

She realised it was still embedded in Ominnios. She shook Dancer and tried to struggle to her feet.

She felt a large hand on her shoulder and froze, unable to turn as a bronzed muscular arm came round the other side of the tree.

'You two need to be more careful. I could have been anybody.'

Goibniu appeared, helping Danu up. He smiled, as he gave her a bear hug, then did the same to Dancer.

Dian emerged from the far side of the clearing. For big men, they were remarkably skilled at moving silently. Dian whistled and two outriders arrived, leading their ponies.

'Thought you might need some help,' said Dian. 'Have you got anything to eat?'

Goibniu unwrapped his cloak and revealed the golden shield. 'My mother wanted you to have this, Danu,' he said.

'It's beautiful,' said Danu. 'Did you make it?'

'Yes,' said Goibniu, handing, Dancer, Nuada's sword.

Recognising it, Dancer was overjoyed with the gift, as he looked at it admiringly,

Goibniu walked across to Ominnios, rolled the body over with his foot, then yanked out Danu's spear and returned it to her. She explained what had happened.

Goibniu shook his head. 'If you're going to kill Birog, you're going to need to take a great deal more care when you aim'.

'I forgot to call out the magic word "Ibar", so that the spear always runs true,' she explained.

'I almost feel sorry for Ominnios, ending up like this. Mind you, by all accounts, he was always an armful short of a bushel of barley.'

Above them, Snibo began to squawk and flap his wings. A large, rusty-red snout pushed through the bushes, closely followed by two bright-red ears and the head of its owner Bebhionn. Sitting on her back was Ollathir.

'Greetings friends,' he said. 'I bring you invaluable reinforcements.'

'Ah, good, supper has arrived,' said Dian.

'Don't upset Bebhionn,' warned Danu. 'She's not what you think she is.'

'And don't upset Ollathir,' said Goibniu. 'He might wallop you on the kneecaps with that mighty club of his.

Good to see you, Olly, you're most welcome. I mean no offence but these reinforcements. You're not exactly Hannibal arriving with his elephants, are you?'

'Indeed, I'm not,' said Ollathir. 'But don't mock me, for I've solved the problem of how best to lure the Pictish pirates away from their ships. It came to me when I was assisting my lord Anroth dispense the sacred porridge.'

Danu went down to the river.

In the cool of evening, she crawled slowly through the lush, green grass of the water meadow until she reached the edge of the bank. Looking into the pool, she saw a fine salmon, its tail wafting slowly, staying stationary in the slack water beneath her.

Introducing her hand to the river, she tickled the fish, until she was able to get it out onto the grass beside her. Then she dispatched and cleaned it, wrapped it in burdock leaves and coated it with mud.

Dian, who had built up the fire, buried the fish in the embers. His warriors rested in the woods to the south while his scouts were already spying on the Pictish fleet.

Goibniu sent the outriders to his father to let him know of Ominnios's death. After supper, they considered their assault in more detail. Goibniu explained that Balor's stronghold was on the north bank of a wide river, situated some distance inland from the estuary where the pirates were moored. He drew pictures in the dirt for Dancer's benefit.

When they had finished, Dancer stood up and motioned for them to follow him. They came to a large clearing where the fabled herd of the wild white cattle were gathered, stretching out as far as the eye could see. Standing on a mound in the middle was, the mighty bull Chillingo.

'Oh dear,' whispered Dian. 'Now what?'

'Amazing,' replied Goibniu. 'Dancer's brought some of his friends along.'

Dancer noticed they hung back, fearful of the murderous reputation of the cattle, so he took Danu by the hand and urged the others to join him as he walked towards Chillingo.

Ollathir tugged at Goibniu's tunic and held up his arms. 'I can't see,' he said.

Goibniu grabbed the little man's wrists and swung him up to sit astride his shoulders.

'Oh look, there's Chillingo,' said Ollathir. 'I've always fancied having a snuffle and a snort with him.'

'Shut up and hang on,' growled Goibniu.

Grabbing Goibniu's thick curly hair with one hand and raising his other arm in the air, Ollathir called out to Chillingo, punctuating his greeting with snorts and snuffles.

The mighty bull turned towards them and lowered his head. His flanks were deeply scarred by the many battles he'd fought to retain his supremacy. There were swellings on the sides of his stomach where the horns of pretenders to his throne had torn into the muscles, leaving the walls weak and ruptured.

As Dancer and Danu approached, he bent down on his front legs. Taking hold of his long, sharp horns, Danu swung herself onto his back. Chillingo raised himself to his full height, threw back his head and bellowed. The whole herd turned towards their king and bowed their heads in Danu's honour.

Ollathir scrambled off Goibniu's back, ran over to the legendary bull and grabbed his muzzle. He rubbed his little nose into the bull's. Sticking his nostrils directly up against Chillingo's, he blew, snuffled and snorted into them.

A succession of grunts and snorts passed between them for a considerable time and, when their discussion concluded, Ollathir grabbed the beast's ears. Chillingo casually tossed his head upwards, and the swineherd somersaulted backwards over the beast's shoulders to land in front of Danu.

Patting Chillingo between his horns, Ollathir turned to Danu.

'He likes my plan,' he said. ''They're all going to help you tomorrow, Danu. He says he'll help me as well, not that I'll need it, of course, but one doesn't like to offend one's friends, does one?' The great white bull bellowed once more and the herd gave voice in unison.

Once they'd returned to camp, Goibniu clarified their plans.

'Dancer and I will take Cu Roi's body with us and cross the river above the stronghold of Balores,' he said. 'Midar and his men will be waiting in the woods to the west. Once he sees Danu make her move against Birog, Midar will sweep in.

Danu, riding Chillingo at the head of his herd, will approach from the south side of the river and distract the sentries. Once they see her moving towards them, over the brow of the southern hills, Dancer and I will scale the back of Balores and dragging Ominnios's body with us.

'When you see us on the roof, Danu, that's your signal to lead the charge. 'Dancer will wait until you reach the river before he hurls Cu Roi's body down. I just hope Dancer will be able to recognise Birog in whatever form she's shape-shifted into. The worry is that, unless the body lands right in front of her, she may not change back into human form.'

'Dancer will find her,' said Danu reassuringly. 'It's surprising what he knows.'

Dian returned to his warriors and Ollathir followed on his rusty-red friend. The others broke camp while the moon was still in its ascendency. Dancer and Goibniu struck out northwest, and Danu returned to the white cattle.

Bearing her golden shield and spear, she mounted Chillingo. The beast bellowed and started to lead his mighty herd north.

25 The Lonely White Stag

Leaning on the balustrade, Nuada looked out from the watchtower and searched the moonlit sea.

'The Saxons won't risk a night landing, we can rest easy.' he said, sitting down beside Anroth, who nodded.

'It's odd, the things that circle through your mind on nights like these,' continued Nuada. 'The moon sheds light into ones thoughts. I see Aine, standing alone and singing in the great hall. I've never told anyone this before, but I feel closer to her than I do to my real mother. That can't be right, can it?'

'The two loves you feel aren't in conflict,' said Anroth. ''They're different, just as your mother might love men in different ways. One doesn't necessarily diminish the other. You love Cliona more than you realise. I'd worry more if you didn't love Midar. There's more harm in loving a mother too much and a father not enough.

'Aine answers your need for simple, reassuring, childlike love, I'm pleased you still possess it. As a baby you gave her back the dignity of motherhood, which had been so cruelly stolen away from her. All she wants is to hug you sometimes, to share with you, the mother's love she feels.'

Nuada looked at him.

'I feel closer to you,' he said, then hesitated. 'I feel more like you than Midar.'

Anroth realised he had no need to speak, that letting the moment pass, would answer the question Nuada never quite managed to ask.

'Snout, remember the song that Aine sang on the night of the banquet?' he said, 'it changed Danu. Can you tell me about it?'

''That's because the song was all about Danu's mythical past as the mother goddess of the Irish,' said Anroth. 'Aine was born in the land of the Kerrymen and she'd have heard the song at her mother's knee. She couldn't have recognised Danu or known she was singing about her. The song, like Aine's life, was about unfulfilled love. Love briefly found then lost.

''The story goes that the goddess, weary of war, was wandering in the county of Kerry and laid down to rest,' continued Anroth. 'She cried a thousand tears and more. And where they fell, they formed a sacred well. It flowed into a lake of tears. When she fell asleep, her beautiful body was so in harmony with nature they became as one. Her breasts rose majestically out of the landscape, two lush, verdant hills. If you journey to Kerry today, you can see them still. They're named the Paps of Anu in her honour.

'As the goddess slept, a prince and princess rode by. Seeing the lake of tears, the lovers rested beside its banks. Soon they were swimming, laughing and splashing in the water. Danu awoke and grew angry. They had brought happiness and love to her self-indulgent vale of tears. Watching them made her jealous of the mortal love they shared, a love that would always be denied to a goddess.'

''When they emerged from the waters, Danu turned the prince into a magnificent white stag and the princess into a gentle white hind. Ashamed of her nakedness, transformed into the body of the beast, the princess ran from the prince.'

'The prince ran after her as she climbed and circled all around the Paps of Anu. But, however fast the prince ran, the princess remained enticingly in the distance. She passed between the Paps of Anu, over a high plain and into some bushes; then she carried on down a long ridge above a valley with another ridge on the opposite side. Little did the white hind and the lovelorn stag know, but they were running the length and the breadth of Danu's body. The two ridges were her legs.

'Finally, the white hind ran to the top of the valley and, beneath some bushes, she saw the entrance to an inviting cave. She took refuge inside it. She'd entered a portal to the Otherworld and became immortal, losing the power of mortal love and becoming trapped forever.

'When he saw the white hind enter the cave, the great white stag rejoiced, for he thought they'd soon be reunited. But, as he drew closer, what had seemed to be a welcoming entrance had vanished. All he found were briars. Danu had stolen their love.

Even today, all these centuries later, if you look up at the Paps of Anu when the swirling mists blow in from the western seas, you may still sometimes see that lonely, white stag, searching in the mists for his lost love.'

'A moving but confusing tale,' said Nuada.

'Indeed, no one does grief and anguish quite like the old Irish storytellers,' said Anroth. 'They specialise in haunting parables of clouded uncertainty. I fancy it tells us more about those who wove the words than it does about Danu.'

'Snout, I could listen to you all night,' said Nuada. 'But we need to give further thought to the Saxons.'

'Tomorrow will be soon enough,' said Anroth. 'Let's just sit and talk. Think about it, how many more times in our lives will we be together and have the opportunity to pass the time this way?'

There was an urgent, disturbing intensity in the old man's voice.

'Don't go all morose on me, Snout,' said Nuada. 'You're a tough old bird. You'll live to fight another day.'

Anroth wasn't scared of dying, grateful he'd lived a longer life than many. Fearing he may have left it too late, he regretted never taking the time to tell his son more about his life.

'You've only ever known me as a druid, Nuada. When I was young, I worked for my father, a prosperous merchant who ran ships out of the western ports of Rheged. His ships traded across to Ireland, sometimes even to Spain, to Gaul and further. To find new markets, I persuaded my father to send me to Rome. I loved it there, for it was the centre of the whole world.'

'Was it a hazardous journey?' asked Nuada.

'It could be,' said Anroth. 'You had to change ships a few times, but the ports of Gaul and Spain had many vessels plying their trade in both directions. It was back in 513 when I went to Rome, a long time ago. By then, that merciless empire was long since dead. Theodoric the Ostrogoth had ruled Rome for twenty years, bringing with him stability and peace.'

Anroth paused. 'No kingdom, no empire lasts forever, Nuada. A man may die in a moment, but civilisations like Rome often die slowly over centuries. The ending of their days is as predictable as their birth is unexplained.'

'Mind these words well. Those living through and witnessing their society in its terminal decline can never bring themselves to believe that someone is carving their gravestone, that their civilisation is in its death throes. What happened to the Romans may be closer to us than you think.'

'One day, Snout,' said Nuada. 'But not now, not in the near future.'

'Rome, the eternal city, was like no other,' said Anroth. 'Some cities, like Carthage, die with the society that gave it birth, only for Rome to raze it to the ground, then, to be buried beneath the detritus of time. But Rome would never die. Because it was the centre of the universe, a trading city buoyed up by merchants from the Levant, North Africa, Gaul and those from the west like me, who passed through the Pillars of Hercules. As I walked those noisy, crowded streets I felt welcomed home by a place I'd never known. Many of the old communities, like the Greeks, still survived there. I was interested in everything and much influenced by the traditions of the Stoic philosophers.

'Christianity intrigued me. More than anything, I wished I'd been alive in Jesus' time, so I'd have had the opportunity to have walked and talked with him. Centuries after his death, the Bishop of Rome claimed supremacy and authority over every other bishop, aping the power of the old Roman Emperors.'

'So much authority in the hands of one man was a disastrous error, an invitation to the greedy and corrupt. Becoming the Bishop of Rome became an irresistible prize for those obsessed with wealth and power.'

Nuada was losing interest. Bored by the old man's religious ramblings, his mind was drifting elsewhere, but he could not bring himself to interrupt.

'They created a new Roman Empire,' Anroth droned on, 'one that could prolong Rome's authority and influence for many centuries to come. It wasn't a military empire, but one far more invasive, capable of subjugating the common man and humbling kings.'

'The Bishop of Rome became an emperor in all but name. His bishops were the equivalent of the Roman senate. In time they developed a ruthless appetite to crush anyone whose interpretation of Jesus' message was at variance with their own imperfect opinions.'

Nuada stood up and stretched, scanning the horizon for an enemy that wasn't there. His mind smouldered, soon to be ignited by the impending warp spasm of brutal war, aching for combat, long before it began.

Blissfully unaware of Nuada's increasing agitation, Anroth continued.

'Why is it, Nuada, that religious leaders never have the humility to accept the many meanings of a prophet's message? Like the druids, Jesus taught in an enigmatic way, often in riddles, inviting many interpretations. My enthusiasm for Christianity evaporated in Rome.'

'If Jesus was reborn today, Nuada, he'd be an unwelcome embarrassment.' Nuada's mind jolted back into a semblance of normality.

'Do you think they'd put him to death?'

'Well, they certainly wouldn't make him Pope,' said Anroth. 'They seem to have spent their days inventing pompous ceremonies, adding sacraments, saints, feast days and relics. Jesus made no mention such dubious distractions.'

'Saints?' said Nuada.

'They are a bit like our lesser gods, and dead warrior heroes, but not quite as good,' explained Anroth.

Despite the druid's instinctive rejection of Christianity as a religion, he'd continued to love and worship Jesus for the rest of his life.

'Paradise is to be found in this world,' continued Anroth. 'It's not just a distant hope for the dead. Whatever follows can never compare with the happiness that catches us by surprise, those magic moments of our day-to-day lives. Cherish the joy that comes your way, Nuada, cherish those memories and the precious moments we found today.'

'Do you regret leaving Rome?' asked Nuada.

'I wouldn't trade where we are tonight for Rome,' said Anroth. 'It was an important part of my life, but it was never going to be my life. I may be a druid but, because of Rome, I walk in Jesus' footsteps and those of the Stoics. The inspiring fundamentals of religion are never far apart.'

'Do you remember, when we were young?' asked Nuada. 'We slept under the stars and, come the morning, you taught us to recognise the birds by the songs they sang. You showed us those magical little places, with mossy banks and waterfalls. You introduced us to so much beauty that would otherwise have gone unseen.'

Anroth's face lit up.

'You taught us just to stand still, to revere the earth as a holy place and to savour the splendour,' continued Nuada. 'You reminded us how privileged we were; for the flowers and the landscape they adorned were but a brief, passing moment. All too soon, those flowers would die. No mortal would share their life, save for my brothers, you and I.'

'I'm glad you remember,' said Anroth. 'I suppose they have a greater purpose than just to be stumbled upon by the fortunate wayfarer. To these old eyes, they're part of paradise, where the living and the dead may intermingle.'

Nuada turned, looking intensely at his father.

'Anroth, how best should I fight tomorrow?'

'Remember, you won't have your brothers fighting beside you. Do what Crimthain tells you to do. There's a fine line between heroics and stupidity.'

'I'm glad Crimthain is with us,' said Nuada. 'He's been around all my life, yet I barely know him.'

'My father employed many mercenaries,' said Anroth. 'He used Crimthain on difficult missions as a scout, a spy and an assassin, for he was a man who could merge into the background. When your mother and I first journeyed here from Rheged, my father sent Crimthain as our bodyguard.'

'Midar invited him to stay on. At the time, Midar was expanding his influence beyond the borders of old Northumbria and I became his emissary, involved in negotiations and treaties with our neighbours. My journeys were hazardous and made in secret, and Crimthain accompanied me. We've remained firm friends ever since.'

Anroth looked up at the moon and yawned. 'The last quarter of the night has yet to run its course,' he said. 'There's more than enough sleep-time left for me before today's uncertain morrow. I'll sleep here, my bed would be too comfortable.'

He drew his legs up in front of him, rested his head on his folded arms and fell into a deep sleep. His last thoughts before his mind slipped into slumber were of death. It was a night for dreaming.

Anroth found himself walking along a dusty road with a young man beside him, who admired Cernunnos's gift, the golden wand. Anroth gave it to him. 'Well, Jesus, any thoughts for tomorrow?' he asked.

The young man smiled and handed back the wand. 'Your wand may prove useful,' he said. 'Use it to create the druid's mist. It might save your life.'

Anroth thanked him, for he'd completely forgotten how useful the druid's mist could be. The young man turned, as if to go, but then Anroth felt a reassuring hand on his shoulder. He opened his eyes, expecting to see Nuada, but he was alone and at peace, left to find solace in the company of his real or imaginary friend.

***

As the first faint light before the dawn filtered through his window, she moved lightly across the floor. Lifting his cloak, she slipped in beside him and lay quite still. In his troubled slumbers, his arm moved out and around her, unaware she was there.

Nothing moved, everything suspended in that frozen moment, as if laid out in a grave. Luchtain opened his eyes and felt the warmth of her body, her fast-beating heart. Sirona spoke.

'I have dreamt the darkest, most malevolent of imaginings, too real to be a dream,' she said. 'There was the smell of burning, the sound of tumult, the clash of arms. Crimthain was lifting the queen onto a pony. She was wounded and blood ran down her leg. Crimthain's eyes were blazing, his lips snarling, his leather jerkin slashed, torn, and covered in gore. He bore no wounds. Taking the pony's bridle, he led the queen away, loping along like a wolf beside her.

'Anroth was on his pony and he called out to us, "Mount up. Ride for the Eden valley and Rheged, tell them what's happened here. Stay there till I send for you." As I turned to look behind me, he shouted, "Don't look back. Goodbye!"

'We rode the forest trail. We stopped, I looked at you…'

Luchtain, interrupted.

'We dreamt the same dream, and Anroth didn't say "goodbye", he said "farewell". I fear we'll meet him no more. Sirona, we share the same ominous prophecy, darker by far than the dreams of dawning.' She put her arms around him.

'Anroth always says to cherish the moment; to cherish the day.'

Luchtain, turned towards her.

The Fifth Day Of Lunasa

26 The Druid's Mist

It was the fifth day of the festival of Lunasa. Luchtain rode north and Sirona rode south, searching for any sign of the Saxons.

As Anroth and Nuada departed the watchtower, they saw Crimthain standing on the headland. Cliona came down to join them. She had spent much of the night sitting beside Ida, taking turns with Aine to sleep. Ida may not have been one of their own, but he was some mother's son. Cliona warned them he had suffered grievously through the night, delirious, his body in a state of crisis.

Anroth and Nuada went to see him. The festering wound in his thigh showed some improvement and his leg was less swollen, but the serpents still raged within. The conflict was coming to its climax. His body was consumed by fire, locked in a battle of life or death. Unless the fever broke soon, it was a battle he would lose.

Anroth had seen it all too often. However, when it dawned on Nuada that Ida was close to death he was visibly distraught. Worried by Nuada's reaction, Crimthain pulled Anroth aside.

'I've never seen him like this before a battle. He's normally so calm and spoiling for the fight.'

Anroth nodded. 'I talked to him last night and warned him of the importance of keeping a level head,' he said. 'Part of his problem is he fears the arrival of the Saxons will threaten Ida's chance of survival. His desire to heal people clouds his warrior mind. His behaviour is becoming confused and contradictory. Over the years, you and I have seen so much; it's easy for us to know when to let our hearts grow cold. He lacks our familiarity with death.'

'Do you want me to speak to him?' asked Crimthain.

'Yes.'

Crimthain talked to Nuada just as Midar would. 'Listen to me,' he said. 'And in the heat of battle, remember my words. Your job is to do what damage you can, inspire the men and get out alive to fight another day. If you lose your head, you may well lose the battle for all of us.'

Nuada nodded, but said nothing.

Sirona returned to report that four Saxon ships were sailing in from the south, with more behind them.

Crimthain was pleased. Four ships landing ahead of the others would give them a tactical advantage, provided they succeeded in drawing the Saxons into a fight. If they could inflict a heavy defeat on the advance party, the rest might take their dead and leave.

Cliona and Aine went to the great hall and, using all the armour and weaponry that hung from its walls, they kitted out the servants and non-combatants.

Nuada positioned them up on the causeway, behind the dunes. He gambled that, from a distance, the Saxons would not be able to distinguish them from warriors. He mounted some of them on the few remaining ponies and partly hid them among the trees, hoping to convey the impression they were Celtic cavalry. If the battle went in the Saxons' favour, these servants and non-combatants were to shed their armour and flee through the forest, taking no part in the hand- to- hand fighting to follow.

The tide was high. Crimthain hid all his warriors in the dunes, as close as he dared to the beach. Where they needed, they dug shallow slip trenches.

The leading Saxon ship beached, but the others held back and bobbed at anchor some distance out. The phantom army on the causeway gave them a rousing welcome, beating swords on their shields, then chanting together and insulting the Saxons with lewd gestures.

Standing in the bow of the lead boat was a powerfully built, flaxen-haired warrior, who resembled Ida. Nuada went down to the beach with some of his warriors and challenged the Saxon to single combat. Ida's elder brother ignored him and stood unmoved as he carefully studied everything around him. He wondered where the rest of the Celt's warriors were. With so many warriors soon to join him, he was in no hurry to do battle.

Their plan, to provoke those on the first four ships into a fight, wasn't working. Crimthain sent down some spearmen and those with slingshots to join Nuada. But, despite suffering a few direct hits, the Saxons remained well-disciplined and impassive. They continued to wait.

Sirona returned with news that a further two Saxon ships had landed in South Bay and those warriors were disembarking and cutting off Nuada's line of retreat back to the stronghold. They were running out of time.

Crimthain looked at Anroth. Over the years, on their numerous hazardous journeys, Anroth had always seemed to have a trick up his sleeve. The more dangerous Anroth's predicament, the more he appeared to treat life as a game. A cold smile played on Crimthain's lips as he wondered how the old druid could possibly provoke the Saxons.

'Well?' he said. Anroth sighed, and spoke.

'This dirty trick you haven't seen, I fear I may offend the queen. Time for me to intervene.'

The old, cold warrior of the mind stood up and leapt out from behind the rocks. Like a wild thing, he danced and spun around, resembling something not quite sound. In one hand he held Ida's sword, in the other the pig's heart that Ollathir had left him. He stuck the heart in his mouth and pretended to eat it raw.

He had the full attention of the Saxons. Recognising Ida's sword, they assumed the heart must also be Ida's.

Anroth let fly with some blood-curdling gibberish that was quite innocuous: nothing more than his usual incantation for toothache. But, to the Saxons, the wails and screams, were spine-chilling, otherworldly sounds of doom and despair.

Cliona looked at Crimthain. Anroth was horrifying her, never mind the Saxons.

'He's tiring,' she said, shaking her head. 'He may have overplayed his hand.'

There were signs of anger and dismay in the lead Saxon boat, but they steadfastly refused to alight and fight.

Bringing his macabre ceremony of inspired invention to a crescendo, Anroth skewered the heart on Ida's sword and threw them both down on the sand. To add insult to injury, he proceeded to urinate on them. Everybody cheered wildly, as if this contrived brilliance was a ceremony, he performed every Lunasa. It produced the desired result.

The flaxen-haired warrior bellowed a battle cry, pointed his axe at Anroth and jumped ashore, closely followed by many more. First, though, they had to get past Nuada and his men, who closed ranks.

As only one boat of warriors had landed, they were evenly balanced. However, the other three boats were now heading for the beach.

Sirona and Luchtain stood up, and fired off a lethal hail of arrows that stopped several warriors in their tracks. They knew that, if the Saxons got past Nuada and his men, Anroth would be finished. He'd never make it back up the beach.

Crimthain stood up and drew his sword.

'Wait,' commanded Cliona.

Crimthain thought he had seen all the old druid's magic, but he was mistaken.

Taking out Cernunnos's golden wand, Anroth raised it above his head and drew a circle around himself. The fabled druid's mist descended and enveloped him. A herring gull flew from the mist. When the haze cleared, the wily wizard had disappeared.

The Saxons hesitated, two more dropped dead, transfixed by Sirona and Luchtain's arrows. The gull landed beside Crimthain and the queen. They turned towards it, only to see Anroth preening himself. He was panting and somewhat ruffled. 'Did I miss anything?' he asked innocently.

'Even by your standards, that was spectacular,' said Crimthain with admiration.

'Indeed, it was,' said Cliona. 'But I confess I found your lewd parting shot uncouth. A druid should save his silver serpent for special occasions.'

'That was a special occasion,' said Anroth. 'I couldn't hold it in any longer.'

None of them had noticed Aine standing close by.

She had smartened herself up. Her hair was plaited into two long tresses and was agreeably festooned with flowers of the meadowsweet, mixed in with buttercups and dandelions. She'd rammed a helmet on top of her head. And, to complete her assemblage, she'd buckled herself into a large breastplate that wasn't quite large enough.

With so much to think about, she'd forgotten to drink her infusion of Sulis Jove's Wort. Far from being fearful of the Saxons, she started shouting abuse when she saw them circling around Nuada and his men.

Many times, she'd sat across the kitchen table from Nuada, enthralled as he described the clash of arms he'd lately returned from. She loved his stories and had never worried about his safety, but as she witnessed what actually happened on a real battlefield, her maternal instincts and selfless courage took over. They would prove ill-considered, and unfortunately, unstoppable.

Fearing Nuada was about to be killed, she was unable to contain herself. She ran forward, yelling a wild, old Gaelic war cry. Cliona looked on, admiring her courage but fearing for her safety. She shook her head.

'I do hope those ruffians don't think that's me,' she said.

'I didn't realise women could become possessed by the warp spasm of battle,' said Crimthain.

'I don't think that's the problem,' said Cliona. 'This is the wrong time of the moon for Aine when she becomes prone to periods of petulance. Indeed, I once saw her throw a plate. Now, she's driven by her love of Nuada and she feels compelled to intervene. I feel her pain, he's my son, However, I'm the queen.'

For one so large, Aine had a remarkable turn of speed. She ran straight past Nuada and his men. As she approached the Saxon chieftain, his bodyguards laughed at her. It was a fatal mistake. They'd failed to notice the large club hanging down from her right hand. In one swift movement, she swung it over her shoulder and brought it crashing down on the young chieftain's head, crushing his skull and killing him instantly.

Horrified Anroth shook his head.

'That definitely wasn't part of the plan,' he said.

With the death of Ida's elder brother, the prospects of avoiding a full-blown battle were over. Aine had as good as signed her own death warrant. Nuada and his flashing blades moved like lightning to save her, as if all three brothers fought as one.

When he was a child, Nuada had been protected by the god Tethra. Not once in all the battles he'd fought, had he ever suffered an injury from a Pictish warrior. He wasn't to know, that, Tethra was unable to protect him from Saxons. Not that it would have made any difference. Nuada had been taken by the warp spasm, caution and common sense deserted him. As more Saxons piled out of their boats, Nuada fought on, glorying in the carnage he'd created with no thought as to how he'd safely retreat. He, too, was a marked man.

Crimthain waited until all the Saxons were out of their boats and begun to slowly wade ashore before leading his warriors into the fray.

Just as he'd expected, the Saxons were stiff after their long, cramped voyage. Catching them by surprise, before they had a chance to loosen up or fight in formation, the Celts cut them down as they struggled out of the sea.

Then came word that more Saxons from the south were closing in on the stronghold. More ships sailed into the bay, including one that contained their high chieftain.

Shocked to see so many of his men dead or dying, his battle horn bellowed, sounding the retreat.

Nuada and Crimthain led their warriors back to the stronghold while Cliona, Anroth and the others withdrew to the woods. The Saxons retrieved their dead prince and rowed him out to the high chieftain's vessel. He knelt down beside his son.

Nuada looked down from the stronghold. The Saxons had taken heavy losses. Perhaps he'd done enough? But then the high chieftain went to the bow of his boat and stretched out his arms, an axe in one hand, a sword in the other. All his warriors stood in like manner. As a prelude to his intent, he threw back his head and howled the Saxon war cry. The sound echoed out over the waters and washed up over the lands of the Brigantes.

27 The Battle For Balores

It was that uncertain hour before the dawn on the fifth day of the festival of Lunasa. Balor's sentries paced the northern banks of the river as a dense sea fret rolled up from the estuary and billowed around them. Mist cloaked the southern banks.

Hidden in his transient robes, Tethra, the god of fog, harbinger of storm and flood, surveyed the scene. His grey and gloomy face, shrouded in mist.

The sentries heard the eerie sound of a crying baby – the warning lament of the mystical blue hare. A low, rolling sound followed. It rose and fell like a storm-tossed sea, seeming to come from beyond the brow of the hill. Crouching low, they waited anxiously. As the sun burnt away the mists, they saw what looked like a wave break over the southern hills. The white cattle had fanned out and now stretched as far as the eye could see.

Danu sat upon Chillingo and looked down into the valley. The mist covered the low ground like a lake, obscuring most of Balores. To the soldiers, looking up through the mist, the hill had been transformed into a foam-crested wave. It hovered above and threatened to engulf them. At its centre, something golden sparkled. They sent for Balor's champion.

The brave young warrior stepped out from the doors of the fortress and ordered his men to position themselves along the riverbank. His presence calmed them. He was assured, still youthful; his shoulders broad, his waist still slim, not yet lost to too many banquets.

Proudly he held Bres's sword and wore his war bonnet, for he was a worthy successor to the valiant champion they'd not long lost. He cupped his eyes, to better see what held the monster wave in sway.

'It's a woman on a white bull,' he said, turning to his men. 'Why's the weakling warrior Midar hiding behind one so fair?'

The mist began to dissipate and Chillingo moved forward into the sunlight. Danu's shield dazzled the warriors below, and the white wave began to cascade over the hill.

Balor's warriors called out in consternation. A shower of spears, stones and arrows flew across the river, but all fell short of Danu and the magical cattle. Further showers followed but, however hard they tried, nothing touched the great white herd.

By now, Balor's men had lost much of their weaponry. It lay spent and wasted across the river. The men murmured with alarm, wondering whether it would be prudent to pull back.

'Hold fast men, hold fast,' called out the champion. 'We'll have them all once they try to cross the river. Hear me well. Loose no more weapons. Stand ready to repel.'

Danu looked down on the warriors and the fortress below. Where were Dancer and Goibniu? Her eyes searched the mighty throng on the other side of the river, waiting for her and the great white herd. Where was Birog?

Buckling on his belt, Balor came out from the doors of the fortress. His dishevelled hair hung down below his shoulders and a single putrid tooth projected down from his upper jaw. Seeing the merciless warrior, his men cheered loudly. With Balor to lead them they were invincible.

****

Down at the mouth of the estuary, waves lapped around the hulls of the Pictish ships moored by the bank. In the faint, first light of the morning, the onboard night watch looked down the estuary and could scarcely believe their eyes. All along the shore, they saw forty pigs with piglets, maybe more. A little man sat on a magnificent beast, oh, what a feast! It looked as though the little man was trying to lead his pigs away from their ships.

The prospect of taking on a large supply of fresh pork, which could be slaughtered as and when they needed it, proved impossible to resist, the watchmen expected they'd soon be putting out to sea. They roused their pirate crewmen and, in no time at all, they had deserted their ships in droves, running towards the pigs, leaving just a few men behind.

The moment Ollathir saw the Picts in pursuit, he charged off with his herd. When they had gone some distance, he and Bebhionn disappeared into the dunes while the rest of the pigs continued to run down the beach. Dian and his warriors, who were stretched out all along the dunes, remained hidden. He and his commander had positioned themselves at the mouth of the estuary with a clear view up the river and down along the beach.

'I hope that little chap knows what he's doing,' he said. 'If those rogues catch him, he's finished.' Much to his relief, Dian suddenly saw Ollathir trotting towards them through the dunes. A moment later, he jumped down beside Dian.

'Well done, Olly, you frightened the life out of me, leave the rest to us.'

As Dian spoke, he noticed a ship moored in the middle of the estuary.

'I didn't know the Picts had female pirates,' said the commander.

Dian looked out across the water and saw a tall woman with flaming-red hair stood in the stern of the boat beside the pirate captain. A young man who'd pulled up the anchor at the bow was unfurling the sail. The woman shouted at a sailor who stood on the edge of the ship, readying himself to swim ashore and grab a piglet for himself. When he refused to come back on deck, she called to the young man, who drew his sword and slashed the deserter's throat, then pushed his body into the estuary. Dian was worried. Why hadn't it occurred to him that Birog might seek refuge with the pirates before the battle?

"There's something very wrong,' said Dian to his commander. 'If that woman's who I think she is, we're in big trouble.'

The pirate captain protested at the murder of his crewman. But the flame-haired woman drew what, at first sight, looked like a dagger. It had a large two-handed grip with a long spike on the end. Mounted between the handle and spike, two short spikes stuck out from either side.

With the point of her poniard at the captain's throat, the woman forced him to take the tiller. As the sail unfurled, a gust of wind caught it and the ship slowly rolled over sideways, corrected itself, then gathered speed and started to make headway out towards the open sea.

The captain struggled and tried to grab her weapon, but he stabbed his hands on the sharp prongs at the side. The woman held the handle of her weapon with both hands and drove the sharp point through the captain's throat and up into his brain.

From his vantage point in the dunes, Dian could hear her sadistic, triumphant laughter. Blood spurted into the air and some landed on her cloak, she didn't seem to care. The captain squirmed like a maggot on a hook; his body jerked around but gradually became weaker. Forcing him to the edge of the deck, she wrenched out her gruesome weapon and watched as he fell overboard. Then, taking the tiller, she found the safety of the open sea and sailed north.

'Only one creature could be that depraved,' said Dian.

'But, if that's Birog, why's she sailing away?' asked the commander.

'I doubt she'll be away long,' said Dian. 'She can shape-shift, pick her time, then swoop in to attack Danu whenever she pleases.'

''Time for the second part of my plan,' said Ollathir.

Before they could stop him, he remounted Bebhionn and trotted back towards the pirate ships.

******

Danu breathed a sigh of relief as she saw Goibniu and Dancer clamber onto the roof of the fortress. Goibniu lifted Ominnios's carcass up onto Dancer's shoulders, then he left and swung down into a window to search for Anroth's cauldron. Danu raised her shield high in the air and tapped Chillingo lightly with the butt of her spear.

The great white bull bellowed and charged towards the river. The whole herd bellowed in unison then followed.

'Hold your positions,' roared Balor above the din.

All his warriors were tightly packed along the riverbank, their eyes riveted on the charging herd.

Dancer looked down and searched for Birog. As Danu and the herd reached the bank, they dived into the river as one. In a moment, they were gone.

Danu had spotted a large bunch of bulrushes on the north bank, just below where Dancer stood. She surfaced behind them and crouched low, then looked up through the rushes to the fortress roof. She waited for him to make his move.

Deep in the dark, golden waters, the magical white cattle began to transform. Their haunches thinned and shortened, and their legs changed to flippers. As they lost their long horns and ears, their heads became streamlined with large, dark eyes and well-whiskered snouts, their mouths full of vicious teeth. Joyfully, as they swam in the cool and welcoming waters, they flicked their tails in unison.

A great wave rose up, rolling across the river, towering above the Picts. Terror spread among them. The wave crashed down, drenching their bodies, sapping their spirit. They packed even tighter together. It was to prove their undoing.

There followed, an ominous calm, the surface of the river stilled. Deep below, welcoming their return to the underwater world, half of the seals, patiently wait for their unsuspecting meals, as they watched the shimmering faces of the warriors above. The rest swam down to the mouth of the river.

******

Those remaining on the pirate ships were surprised when Ollathir reappeared. Trotting dangerously close to the boats, he dismounted and threw back the hood of his cloak to reveal Balor's prized raven war bonnet on his head. He jumped up and down, and the raven's wings flapped provocatively.

Whoever captured the swineherd and recovered Balor's helmet would be richly rewarded. So, all the remaining Picts jumped overboard to chase Ollathir, who immediately remounted Bebhionn, intending to make his escape. But, tired out by her excessive exertions, the magnificent sow could only manage a dignified saunter. Dian and his warriors were too far away to help.

Ollathir turned to see his pursuers closing in. It wasn't quite as easy being a warrior as he'd expected. He'd heard Balor took particular pleasure in mutilating his enemies, and would often insert red-hot irons into all sorts of sensitive orifices. He hoped that wouldn't include his little nose.

Chillingo – now in the form of a seal – surfaced at the mouth of the river. In the distance, he saw the pirates still chasing the pigs down the beach. And, close by, he saw the others racing after Ollathir. Bebhionn, who was hot and tired from the exertions of the day, and unaware of the grave danger they were in, had decided to go for a dip.

If Bebhionn had a fault it was her fastidious nature. She'd noticed that her master was actually quite smelly and thought a bath in the estuary would do them both the world of good. The last thing on Ollathir's mind was cleanliness, but Bebhionn was a lady with a mind of her own. As she cheerfully trotted out into the water, the seals surfaced and flew over the swineherd's head.

'All praise to Moccus the pig god!' squealed Ollathir.

As he landed on the sand, Chillingo shook himself down to bullhood. Then, leading his transformed herd, they charged at the pirates who pursued Ollathir.

Further along the beach, more seals came ashore. Changing back into white cattle, they attacked the rest of the pirate band. Many Picts perished on their horns that day. Some tried to escape by running up into the sand dunes, where Dian and his men dispatched them. Others, unaware that many more of the mighty white herd still lurked in the water, ran into the sea. The foam atop the waves became red and white from all the slaughter.

Dian and his men came down from the dunes to find Ollathir sitting on the sand with his arm round his rusty-red lady friend.

'Are you alright, Olly?' asked Dian. 'You're a great hero and, like your father, a warrior. He'd have been so proud of you for saving so many lives.'

'I'm a little damp, but otherwise fine,' replied Ollathir.

Dian raised his arms to his men and cheering broke out as they all celebrated the swineherd and his bravery.

'We'll light a fire in your honour, so you may dry yourself,' said Dian as he and his men set the Pictish fleet ablaze.

Ollathir basked in the warmth all around him.

******

Perched high on the rooftop of the fortress, Dancer had no way of knowing how Ollathir and Dian were getting on. He was unable to see what was happening downriver, which was fortunate.

Dian had mistakenly assumed that the sadistic, flame-haired woman he'd seen on the pirate ship was Birog, but she was actually Balor's daughter Eithne who, along with her brother, had been sent by Balor to one of his pirate ships, for her own safety.

Dancer looked down from the roof at the seething mass of soldiery. Where was Birog?

From nowhere Snibo swooped in, gripped the shoulder of Balor's handsome young champion and caused consternation among the Picts as he pecked at his face. The champion let out an unearthly scream. Snibo took flight.

Dancer lifted the lifeless body of Ominnios high above his head and tossed it down. As the dead hound hit the ground, it transformed back into Cu Roi's pathetic, skinny corpse.

The champion bent forward and touched the body, and immediately the handsome, young warrior changed into the figure of Birog. Above her, Dancer gave a long, loud growl, but there was no submission in the sound.

The black druidess's face contorted with fury as another growl taunted her. She raised her hands to the heavens, intent on destroying Dancer, for how could a man who must have been madly in love with her, have betrayed her all those years ago? How could any man have walked out on someone as beautiful as she, even if her plans at the time, included consuming him for supper?

Dancer looked down on all that was evil. In her wicked life, the oft unnoticed crow was one creature Birog would magically shape shift into. But she had never noticed, the crows, within whose bodies she loved to dwell, had marked her well, imprinting their feet around her cold and sunken eyes. Like a nest of vipers, her once rich, red hair had become tangled and twisted, greasy and grey, and her nose long thin and beaklike.

Quivering with anger, Birog let out another ear-splitting screech and called down a death curse upon Dancer.

Goibniu stepped out from the doors of Balores's great hall. Seeking to distract her, he slapped his sides and roared with laughter. 'Birog or is it Strebo?' he said. 'When you came to visit us, my father promised he'd return your idiot son to you if he proved unsuitable. We like to keep our promises.'

Before Birog could react, Goibniu stepped smartly back into the hall and closed the doors.

Leaping like a salmon, Danu rose from the river and flew above the bulrushes, borne upon the golden shield. It shone in the sunlight and hovering in the air, her spear flashed brightly as it flew from her hand.

'Ibar!' she cried.

Birog failed to feel the spear as it pierced her spine, and the spearhead came out of her chest. Impaled upon it, still beating were her three hearts. The spear passed right through her and fell to the ground.

Though she was still standing, Birog knew she was dead. Exposed to the air, the three hearts began to disintegrate. From two of the hearts a serpent slithered. As the sunlight touched them, they withered and died in the dust.

Birog began to cough uncontrollably and desperately sucked air into her open chest. She gulped and pleaded for help from the terrified onlookers, then she made a desperate grab for a young soldier's arm and, for the briefest of moments, she managed to hang on to him. He screamed in agony as her sharp fingernails tore open his skin. Forcing her finger deep within him, she implanted her remaining foul serpent.

Birog's lungs deflated, and she staggered backwards, tripping over something. It would have been of some comfort to Cu Roi to know that his mother's last dying thoughts were of him. As she departed this world, she realised she'd stumbled over the body of her dead son.

'Poisonous little whelk,' she said, with a dying hiss. And, true to her malign nature, her final act was to grab Cu Roi's scraggy little leg as she fell into the river and drag his body down beneath the water with her.

'Athibar!' commanded Danu, and the sacred spear of Assal flew back into her hand.

Losing their champion in such a shocking manner struck panic into the hearts of Balor's warriors. All discipline and strength of purpose deserted them. The river foamed crimson, as they watched the milk-white seals tear Birog and Cu Roi's bodies limb from limb.

Sweeping in from the west, Midar and his warriors had launched their attack at the moment when Danu had risen from the river. Lugh and his warriors charged in from the north, and trapped the Picts between the river and Midar's forces. Pressed tightly together, they were unable to wield their weapons. Forced backwards, they fell into the river, where the white seals tore them to shreds. The conflict was speedily concluded.

Leaning on his sword, Midar looked down the blood-red river, before he burnt Balores to the ground. He stepped over the threshold and into the great hall where Balor was waiting, his baleful staring eyes seeking to dominate Midar.

Midar paid no heed, for he believed that, in matters of mortal combat, the death of your enemy should be achieved as quickly as possible.

The two chieftains circled each other and began to fight. They cut, thrusted, parried, clashed their swords in the air, crossed swords on the floor, then Midar raised his sword and slashed it down towards Balor's shoulder. The Pictish chieftain parried, but Midar spun around in a circle and caught Balor from behind, slicing through the back of his neck. As he fell beside the door, his head rolled across the floor.

Goibniu stepped out from the shadows and sheathed his half-drawn sword.

'The cauldron, Goibniu,' said Midar. 'We need the cauldron!'

Goibniu held it up. It had been hacked into little pieces.

'And Balor's children, where are they?' asked Midar.

'They're not here,' said Goibniu. 'They've escaped.'

Midar picked up Balor's head and, braiding his long hair, he hung it from his belt. It was a trophy devoid of satisfaction. For though he understood Balor and his need to protect his kingdom, he failed to comprehend why Birog had dragged down so many of her own to join her in death. Goibniu read his mind.

'You can never quite bring yourself to believe in pure evil, can you, father?' he said. 'But you saw for yourself her rotting, rancid hearts and the serpents within.'

So Balores burned, Balor and Birog were dead. Part of Anroth's prophecy had been fulfilled.

Midar had not forgotten how the prophecy ended.

28 The Howl Of The Wolf

It's often said, that it takes far longer to clear up after a battle than the time it takes to fight it, which was not true on this occasion. The injuries inflicted on Midar's men were mercifully few. As soon they were rested, they would embark on an orderly retreat. Midar was concerned that Balor's northern allies might arrive at any moment.

He wished to put the dismal day behind him. His warriors were welcome to the victor's spoils. There was nothing in Balores he coveted, he'd fought so many battles and wearied of the wasteful necessity of war. He rested under a tree by the river, with Lugh, his two sons, Danu and Dancer.

He asked his sons if there was anything they wanted.

'We've pilfered from this place before and all it brought was war,' said Goibniu.

Midar asked Lugh the same question.

'Yes,' said Lugh. 'The long lost Eagle of the Ninth Roman Legion. The one that Strebo – I mean Birog, brought down to bargain with. It'll be good for morale. The men have discovered much gold coinage, which I plan to share among them.'

Midar nodded. 'It's theirs,' he said. 'But don't spend too much time distributing it.'

He looked at Danu and Dancer.

Danu shook her head. 'We got what we came for,' she said. 'Birog destroyed what was left of my beautiful childhood, she deserved to lose her life.'

Midar looked over his shoulder. There were voices at the river crossing. The sight of Crimthain approaching filled them with foreboding. His torn leather jacket was covered in dried blood, his cheeks were hollow and his face was drawn. His exhausted pony staggered to a halt in front of them.

Crimthain was hunched forwards, bent low in the saddle, and he struggled to raise his head. 'My lord, I bring you the gravest news,' he said. 'You must leave this place. Your kingdom may be lost.'

Dancer went in search of food and drink for his friend while Midar lifted Crimthain from his saddle and propped him up against the tree. The pony, released from its rider, went down to the river to drink.

Displaying no emotion, Midar spoke and gave instructions to post more lookouts to the north. There was a calm, distant intonation in his voice as he turned towards Crimthain.

'Take your time, my old friend,' he said. 'Bad news is never improved by telling it any the sooner.'

Danu soaked part of her cloak in the river, and washed the blood from Crimthain's face and hair. He gratefully accepted a mug of beer from Dancer and drained it. Dancer refilled it. Close to tears, Crimthain looked into Midar's eyes.

'Nuada is dead, the queen is wounded, and the stronghold, our barns and dwellings have all been burnt to the ground,' he said. 'We've withdrawn to the Valley of the High Waters.'

Anticipation of grim tidings is no preparation for their arrival, cold fear gripped Midar.

'The queen,' he said. 'What of Cliona?'

'Anroth has remedied the wound,' said Crimthain. 'It was a trivial flesh wound to the thigh, he assured me. There was more blood than damage done.'

'Dian, get down there now,' said Midar.

Calling to his commander and men to follow, Dian mounted his pony and made for the ford in the river.

'Where's Aine?' asked Midar. 'Why isn't she attending to her mistress?'

'She's dead.'

Crimthain could no longer contain his emotions and gulped in air he didn't need. Dancer took him by the shoulders and fixed Crimthain's anguished eyes with his own, absorbing the waves of emotional turmoil rolling out of a man who'd spent a lifetime hiding his feelings.

'I failed you, Midar,' Crimthain said finally.

'No, Wolf, you must have saved the lives of many,' said the chieftain. 'Look at you, you're still bloodied by the battle. No man's more deserving of my trust than you. Rest yourself awhile.'

Crimthain slumped back against the tree and closed his eyelids, using them as curtains to cover his feelings while he tried to collect his thoughts. Dancer removed the exhausted pony's saddle, tore out some rushes from the bank and began to wash away the sweat that had lathered on its flanks. Then, in a disciplined, methodical manner, Crimthain began to describe the catastrophic circumstances of the Saxon attack.

'The day before the battle,' he said. 'Anroth, with Nuada's help, had saved the life of a Saxon prince, who had been brought to the point of death by a festering wound. Pre-warned of the Saxons' arrival, we used all the armour and weaponry that hung from the walls of the great hall to kit out the non-combatants, gambling that, from a distance, the Saxons might mistake them for warriors.'

Midar interrupted. 'I've no doubt you and Nuada would have fought the battle just as I would have done,' he said as he took Crimthain's shaking hand and sat down beside him. 'But spare me the details about how the battle began. Take me to its climax. Tell me about its bitter end.'

'We'd inflicted heavy casualties on the Saxons before we were forced to retreat to the great hall,' said Crimthain. 'Cliona, Anroth and the others hid out in the woods, ready to warn us if our situation became hopeless and we needed to break out and escape.'

He paused. Wishing to spare Midar the ghastly details, Crimthain tried to delay telling him.'

'My lord, we must leave this baleful place,' he said. 'Make haste to Cliona. There is little more I wish to tell and none of it will be to your liking.'

'Crimthain, Dian and his men are more than capable of repulsing any attack at the waterfall, and Goibniu has lookouts posted north of here,' said Midar. 'We'll have warning enough of any enemies approaching. Our warriors and ponies need time to recover, for time spent resting before our next battle is time well spent. Pray continue. Tell me to the fateful end.'

With a heavy heart, Crimthain carried on. ''The best we could hope for was to inflict as much damage as possible,' he said. ''The more men the Saxons lost in the battle, the less likely it'd be they'd realise the main body of our warriors were no longer in Northumbria. That way, we could retain the element of surprise when you counter-attacked.

'But this was no ordinary raiding party, Midar. It was an invasion force that was heading for Deira, intent on settling there. Now they think they have Northumbria; they'll fight rather than be forced back.'

Midar nodded.

'The battle, when it came, was brief and the bloodletting remorseless,' continued Crimthain. 'We made them pay heavily for the privilege of the prize they sought. We did so with no great loss, when compared with the desperate slaughter they endured, but in the process, we sacrificed a prince beyond price. It was not Nuada's fighting skills that were in question, but his judgement in the heat of battle.

'Lost in the warp spasm he was lethal. But even great warriors need time to rest before rejoining the fray lest their stamina fail them. Nuada possessed great skill, but not his brothers' strength. He promised me that, when he heard the Carnyx sound the retreat, he would flee the stronghold.

'We'd barricaded the doors and windows, knowing this would only give brief respite. And, indeed, they set fire to the walls and the doors of the great hall. But we knew that, if they believed there was a chance their young Prince Ida still lived, they wouldn't stand idly by and wait for the building to burn down around us. So, we deliberately left some high windows loosely shuttered to encourage them in.

When they came through, we made them welcome with a sea of spearheads. Our advantage couldn't last, eventually bloody, hand-to-hand combat raged across the hall. As the building burnt around us, a battering ram crashed into the great doors.

'When we'd first entered the stronghold, no one had noticed Aine slipping in behind us, determined not to be separated from Nuada. Without warning, the heavy kitchen door opened and there she stood.

"I told you to stay close to my mother," Nuada shouted across to her.

"I'm as good as any man," she shouted back defiantly. "I won't leave without you."

'The Saxons assumed she was the queen and advanced upon her. She was like a she bear with a cub – I swear she growled –she hurled anything heavy that came to hand at them, then she slammed the kitchen door shut, and bolted it. The Saxons tried to break it down.

Nuada waded in and set about them with a new-found ferocity, raining blows down upon them and lunging forward with his two swords. But, just then, the doors of the great hall shattered and those outside broke in.

'Watching from the safety of the woods, Cliona decided it was time to abandon the stronghold and she sounded the battle horn. I fought my way to Nuada and insisted he fall back.

"I'm right behind you," he called.

'We were separated as I fought my way to the doors and, when I turned, I saw that Nuada had stayed behind to try to save Aine. His back was to the kitchen door and he was surrounded by Saxons. He was tiring and taking blows.' Crimthain paused as he recalled those final moments. The listeners waited. Eventually he said.

'I watched in horror as an axe fell and split Nuada's skull in two.'

Midar put his head in his hands and convulsed. Tears ran down his face.

'Aine must have been watching through the hole in the door, for it opened and she dragged him in,' said Crimthain. 'She tried to close it but the Saxons forced it open. As we stood outside, there was uproar. The bellow of the mighty carnyx rang out once more and was answered by echoes of war horns sounding all around.

'I heard the bark of the dogs of war, the rhythmic beat of sword on shield, the muffled drum beat of ponies' hooves as the battle cry of the Brigantes rose up from many a warrior's throat. Believing reinforcements had arrived, the Saxons began to panic. They ran from the stronghold and retreated to the south. Sirona, Luchtain and the queen ran towards us from the woods.

'"Midar has returned!" I cried.

'The queen shook her head. '

"There's nobody here but the old men and us," she said. "Anroth has created this delusion by using the mystical power in Cernunnos's wand. But his strength of mind drains from him. He cannot sustain the illusion for much longer."

'I called to Luchtain. "Get everybody out," I said. "Set up your rear-guard action, fill our remaining boats and have them sail. Evacuate the rest north along the trail."

'"Where's Nuada?" asked Cliona.

'I shook my head.

'My lord Midar,' said Crimthain. 'I've told you most of what I know, the men are ready now to go. The ponies snort and paw the dust. If we don't leave, we'll not reach the waterfall by dusk.'

'Wolf,' said Midar. 'You're nearly there. It's no kindness to leave the ending in the air.'

'Cliona bade me take her to Nuada,' said Crimthain reluctantly. 'We crossed the great hall, which was littered with the dead. And, in the kitchen, we found two Saxons gloating, each holding a gruesome trophy high in the air. Shocked by the sight of it, Cliona seemed to trip and stumble beside one of the warriors then twisted her body and ran her sword in, under his raised arm, and into his heart. She watched him die.

The other Saxon looked on, Sirona slipped in behind him, and with her spear stabbed him in the back. He staggered and fell; she twisted her spear transfixing him to the floor. His arms and legs thrashed around, then moved no more. Cliona looked at Aine holding Nuada.

' She lay in a pool of blood, slumped back against the wall. She'll sing no more, they slit her throat. Nuada lay between her legs. She was holding his head, which she'd cradled on her stomach.

''The Saxons had hacked off Nuada's hands and forearms. These were the trophies they'd been holding aloft when Cliona and Sirona killed them. Seeing her son and the only woman she loved dead, Cliona swore vengeance. By now the sounds of battle had subsided. Anroth's magical spell had drained him of everything.'

'What happened to Nuada's arms?' asked Midar.

''The queen has taken them,' said Crimthain. His voice had intensified, the pace of his words had quickened. He was determined to reach the end of his anguished tale.

'I heard the door creak behind me,' he said. 'I looked around and, leaning against the door frame, I saw a ghost with empty eyes. The wraith floated right past me; unaware I was even there. I barricaded the door behind it with a chair. It fell to its knees in front of Aine.

'In all the confusion, we'd forgotten Prince Ida. His crisis had passed, but now he was confronted with another. His head fell on Aine's fulsome breasts, his flaxen hair washed in her blood. As if in disbelief, his splinted arms tried to hold what was left of Nuada's arms. Not long before, pure magic had flowed through Nuada's fingers and refashioned Ida's shattered wrists.

'Ida's body was spent. With what little strength he had left, he raised his head and howled to the heavens an anguished lament. As he swore, he beat the floor, and cursed Woden, cursed Thor and every gruesome god of war. Soon we heard Saxon voices, banging on the door.

'Ida staggered to his feet. He slid open the bolt on the outer door, which led to the courtyard where he'd first encountered Aine, and motioned us out. He slid the bolt shut behind us. As we went widdershins around the building, we heard him crash backwards. Whether he's alive or dead, we know not. So, Ida saved all our lives. Aine's love for Nuada cost him his life and she forfeited her own.'

'One question, Crimthain, then we leave,' said Midar. 'When that first Saxon boat arrived and beached, where did the vessel end up?'

'It was firmly embedded in the sand, my lord,' said Crimthain. 'The tide was fast receding.'

A grim smile played on Midar's lips. He had a plan.

'Mount up,' he commanded.

'We ride for the Valley of the High Waters.'

Goibniu stayed behind, to give Midar time to put some distance between himself and Balores. He wondered what weakness his father had thought he'd discovered in the Saxon attack, hidden among Crimthain's appalling revelations.

He had time enough to work it out as they rode south. One battle won, another just begun.

29 Midar's Last Journey

Midar felt responsible. He should never have left Nuada behind. Goibniu or even Dian would have handled things better. At least Cliona was alive with Anroth by her side. Balor and Birog were dead, the inevitable battle for Balores had been a triumph. However, he reflected that, when two kingdoms were always at each other's throats, even the death of a high chieftain like Balor rarely brought long-term respite. There would always be others eager to provoke further conflict, seeking to profit from the chaos left behind.

He was confident he would defeat the Saxons. It would involve establishing the distribution of all the Saxon troops, and wiping out the smaller groups first. Then with the tide out, his cavalry would attack the beaches, capturing and burning some of the Saxon ships, that were held fast in the sand. These were very valuable assets; the Saxons could not afford to lose.

The Saxons' main force would be camped out in the woods. To save the rest, of their fleet, the Saxons would be forced to leave the safety of the trees, fighting on the open beaches where Midar's cavalry held the advantage. Midar wondered when best to break the news about the loss of Bamburgh to his men. He decided tomorrow would be soon enough, but he was wrong.

He knew he could lift his men's spirits by holding Balor's head aloft then tossing it down, so they could kick it around in the dust. But such displays did not commend themselves to Midar, and he left the raising of the men's morale to Lugh.

Instead of hanging Balor's head from his belt, he would have been well advised to dispose of it there and then. He should have remembered Anroth's warning, because his long-standing conflict with the Pictish chieftain had one final, bitter twist to it. Before Midar reached the Valley of the High Waters, Balor would have his revenge.

Snibo circled the sky above, Dancer and Danu scouted ahead as Midar moved slowly south with Crimthain by his side and nine warrior bodyguards surrounding them. But the real enemy was already within, hanging from Midar's belt. Balor's apparently dead head waited for the moment when it could take its repulsive revenge.

Lugh held back until the cavalry were on the move and readied the foot soldiers to fall in behind. To raise their spirits, he uncovered the legendary Eagle of the Ninth Roman Legion. It had lain hidden since its mysterious disappearance centuries earlier. In spite of this, the lustrous gold of the standard still burned brightly in the weak afternoon sun. There wasn't a man there who hadn't heard of the fabled eagle, for the mystery surrounding it, was the stuff of legends.

In the second century of the Roman occupation, the whole of the Ninth Roman legion – upwards of five thousand legionnaires with their baggage train, cooks, camp followers, servants, slaves and loose women – had marched out from their headquarters in York to wage war on the rebellious Picts. The Roman soldiers were eager for action. Those merciless men couldn't wait to indulge in the barbarity they were infamous for.

But that was the last anyone ever heard of them. Not one soul was seen again. They disappeared without trace.

The Romans sent their spies into the lands of the Picts many times, hoping to learn what had happened. Some returned, but none had any news.

When such a major disaster befalls an army, the details of how it happened tend to emerge eventually. But not one word, not one snatched snippet of drunken conversation in the borderland oppidas and vici, ever hinted at what had befallen the legion and their fabled talisman, the Eagle of the Ninth.

Holding the standard high on its wooden shaft, Lugh galloped up and down in front of his warriors, stirring up clouds of dust as he skidded his pony to an abrupt halt. The warriors cheered. The eagle retained its power to inspire, just as it had once inspired – but not protected – the doomed Ninth Legion. Lugh arranged outriders on either side of the column to protect the flanks and the men marched off, tired but proud to be part of the victorious cavalcade.

But all was not well with Lugh, compared to previous battles, he had hardly exerted himself. He'd run a few Picts through with his sword and beheaded the occasional warrior with his axe, just to encourage the men. He'd suffered no wounds but, as he rode off, he felt nauseated. He started to sweat and had crippling pains in his back. This was no time to show weakness, he gripped his thigh, forced his shoulders back and rode on.

They left behind a strangely deserted battlefield. Most of Balor's warriors had ended up in the river during the first attack and, after the battle, the dead and dying had been tossed in to join them.

Any passing stranger who chanced upon Balores and saw its smouldering ruins would barely have been able to imagine the carnage the place had so recently borne witness to. That which time usually takes years to return to some semblance of normality was cleansed and washed away by the river in a day.

As the army travelled south, they encountered the remnants of Balor's forces and when they saw Midar, they scattered into the woods. Then Danu and Dancer returned, warning of a large force of Picts that blocked the trail ahead. Midar and his men picked up pace. When the Picts realised the size of the force bearing down on them, they made as if to disperse. But then they saw Balor's head, bouncing up and down on Midar's naked thigh.

Balor's eyes were wide-open. To the startled Picts, he seemed to be staring right through them, as he'd so often done in life. Just as a tree washed away by a river takes on a new existence, Balor's head, devoid of its body, had taken on a new life. Who knew how much consciousness in a tree washed up as driftwood may still remain? Who could say how much awareness Balor's brain might yet retain?'

As Balor's jaw opened and closed as it bounced up and down, he seemed to be speaking to the Picts and calling them to stand and fight. Though their chieftain was dead and all that was left was his head, to a man they remained loyal, standing their ground, deciding to fight, duty-bound.

Midar and his men brought their ponies to a gallop and charged forward. Balor's head bounced high and low, and spun around, fast and slow. Midar hardly noticed as the head bounced against him. He felt nothing as Balor's putrid tooth sank itself deep into his thigh.

In the dark recesses of Balor's evil brain, serpents slithered and squirmed. They passed through the putrid fang and wriggled their way into Midar's leg. The tooth broke off and buried itself deep in Midar's flesh, Balor's lethal parting gift.

The skirmish was brief, decisive and futile. Those brave Picts who died, left their lives without knowing they'd helped inflict more damage on the tribe of the Brigantes than Birog and Balor had managed in the many years they'd sought to destroy Midar.

Midar was well over halfway to the Valley of the High Waters before he noticed anything was wrong. His thigh felt as though cold water trickled down inside it and, when he looked down, he saw it was bloated and stiff. He could no longer lift it.

Lugh noticed Midar's skin had lost its high, weather-beaten colour, and now looked yellow. He thought little of it, for by this time, their way was lit by moonlight, which often plays tricks on weary minds. But Crimthain noticed all wasn't well for a different reason. With his highly developed senses, he could smell mouldering decay, - he was riding beside a dead man.

When they reached the waterfall, Crimthain sought out Anroth, and found him with Dian and Cliona. Returning to Midar, they discovered that the high chieftain was unable to dismount.

Goibniu arrived from the back of the column, and Dian took him and Lugh to one side before they went over to their father. The princes lifted him from his pony and carried him to a tent. As they and Anroth set Midar down in the semi-darkness, Balor's head rolled on the ground behind him. On the ride down, Balor's hair had worked its way around the back of Midar's belt.

There was a large circular area on the outside of Midar's thigh where the skin was black and as hard as leather. Dian took one look then went outside to stick the blade of his dagger in the red-hot embers of the fire.

Dancer came in with Danu, carrying a tallow torch. Anroth bent forwards and felt the thigh. As he moved his fingers outwards, he experienced a strange, crepitus, crinkling feeling.

Gangrenous gases bubbled beneath the skin.

'How many days ago did this start?' asked the druid.

'I was fine when I mounted my pony in Balores,' said Midar. 'The leg was normal then.'

'Were there any skirmishes on the way down?' asked Anroth. 'Any wounds? Any poisoned arrows?'

'One small skirmish, no injuries,' said Midar.

Dancer brought the torch nearer and Anroth looked more closely at the thigh. 'There's a small puncture wound here,' he said.

As the contagion spread throughout his body, Midar's stomach began to swell. Goibniu loosened his father's belt and, finding the hair wrapped around it, he gave it a yank. Balor's head flew forwards into the light. The queen picked it up. 'So that's what he looked like,' she said.

She handed the head to Anroth, who inspected it carefully. He opened the mouth and looked inside. 'Where's his tooth?' he asked.

'It was there when I strung his head on my belt,' said Midar. 'It must have fallen out on the way down. My old friend, the final part of your prophecy is turning out to be true. I'm about to die, but I don't understand why.'

Dian returned. 'Father will feel better if you can relieve the pressure,' he said to Anroth as he handed him the knife he'd taken from the fire.

'Well, let's find out, shall we?' said Anroth.

Using the point of the red-hot blade, Anroth probed down into the puncture wound until he felt something gritty and solid deep within the muscle. Midar had endured wounds in the past. Like all warriors it was a matter of pride, showing an example to his men, never to react to pain.

In one movement, Anroth sliced down the thigh and the blackened skin split open. There was a hiss of gas and the sickly-sweet smell of rotting flowers on a warm, still summer's evening swirled all around them. It was a unique, nauseating odour that, once smelt, was never forgotten. The smell seduced the senses with its sweetness and invited those who experienced it to savour more. Then came revulsion. The odour repulsing them all with its cloying, all-pervasive, sickly intensity.

The edges of the wound stretched outwards under pressure until brown, frothy fluid foamed in the exposed flesh. Then bubbles of gas popped and released their gangrenous humours into the air. The dead muscles had changed in colour to a bloodless salmon-pink. The gas and gangrene had spread throughout the leg.

Anroth probed deeper. He could feel the tooth on the point of the blade. Manoeuvring the tip behind the tooth, he carefully manipulated it out of the wound. For something so lethal, it looked insignificant. Apart from some oozing from what remained of Midar's healthy skin, there was no bleeding.

Midar sighed. 'That feels a lot more comfortable,' he said.

His body was failing him. His cold hand stretched out to Lugh and his voice became little more than a whisper. 'From the moment I made you my champion, not one day has passed when you haven't ridden out beside me,' he said. 'Without you, I'd never have succeeded.'

Lugh lent forward in order to hear more clearly. 'To become a worthy champion, you must first find an inspiring leader,' he said. 'Fortune favoured me. I found you.'

Midar groaned. 'They say this isn't a bad way to die,' he said. 'But it's not the way of a warrior.'

'Come now,' said Lugh, shaking his head. 'You've lived your life as a hero and the manner of your death doesn't change that. Show me a braver man than you!'

'I'm looking at him, Lugh,' said Midar.

The noble warriors laughed. Just two men talking, reaffirming their love and making their last farewell.

'We'll go now,' said Anroth. He and the others departed, leaving just Cliona and the princes with Midar.

'Do you want us to leave, father?' asked Dian, 'so the two of you can be together?'

'No, don't leave me,' said Midar. 'We're all as one. If I've forgotten to tell you both before, please remember you'll never know how much I've loved the three sons your mother gave me or how complete I felt, to know I was your father.'

Midar hung on grimly as he turned to Cliona. At last, he was alone with those he loved – save for one. 'Where's Nuada, where's my son, when's he coming?' he asked, his memory mercifully playing tricks.

'Soon, you'll see him soon,' Cliona reassured him.

'Are you alright?' asked Midar. 'I was told the Saxons wounded you.'

'Just a glancing blow,' she said. 'Anroth has remedied it.'

'Cliona, my life didn't begin till I first saw you,' he said. 'The rest of my life was just a part of loving you. I hope I made you happy. I felt my love for you more than I ever showed it. My mistress was my kingdom, but she proved a fickle lover. Leaving life doesn't grieve me. It has served me long and well. I leave behind the best part of me.'

Tears streamed down Cliona's face. 'You made me happy, you gave me a kingdom, respect and dignity,' she said. 'You made me a queen. Did I feel your love? Oh yes, it was in everything you did. It wasn't just the love of a man, but a man so much more than any other. Don't grieve about leaving me, for nothing can touch the love we shared. Had you been born a bonded man and I a slave, I'd have still been a queen.'

Cliona held Midar's ice-cold fingers to her cheek. He motioned weakly with his other hand. 'Come closer,' he said.

They huddled round him – as did Death. Midar ignored the impatient stranger.

'How will we fight the Saxons?' asked Dian with urgency in his voice. 'Where is their weakness?'

'Well, Goibniu, you're in command now,' said Midar. 'How will you defeat the Saxons?'

'They're careless with their ships, that's their weakness,' he said. 'When the tide goes out, they're left high, dry, stuck in the sand and vulnerable. We'll swoop in without warning, and attack and burn their boats.

The Saxons will be forced to leave the safety of the woods to save the rest of their fleet. We'll wait for them on the beaches, where we hold the advantage fighting from horseback.' Midar gave a faint smile.

'When you've defeated them, bury me on the headland, below the ruins of my great hall,' he said, his voice growing weaker. 'Stand me tall and upright, so I can look out to sea.'

His throat rattled, but he managed to continue. 'One other thought, Goibniu, try to kill their high chieftain. If anything ensures their departure, that will. I'll be fighting beside you. Take care of your mother.'

'We'll go now,' said Goibniu. 'You need your time together.'

Midar closed his eyes. 'Cliona, how is Anroth?' he asked. 'I fear he carries a heavy burden.'

'The battle with the Saxons drained him,' she replied. 'Without his sorcery, they'd have slaughtered us. He's taken Nuada's death so very hard. He loved him like a son.'

Midar opened his eyes wide, holding the moment, looking into hers.

'I know,' he said slowly.

****

The princes found Anroth and the others sitting by the fire.

'Snout, you can do anything. Danu, I've seen your immense power with my own eyes,' said Goibniu, his eyes pleading more eloquently than his words.

'There must be something you can do to save our father.'

'I wish we could, Goibniu, but there is no remedy for gas gangrene,' said Anroth.

'I'll never find friendship such as his again. He was the pillar around which all of us built our lives and reasserted the pride of the Brigantes.'

Danu rested her hand upon the druid's shoulder. 'But we can try, Snout,' she said. 'For Cliona and the boys.'

'Danu, all that remains is his heart and mind,' said Anroth. 'And soon they, too, will depart him.'

Danu persisted. 'We can still try, Snout,' she said. 'Love's many faces can always find something more to give.'

Anroth sighed.

Crimthain came over with his eyes burning fiercely. He stared at Anroth.

'Please do it for me,' he said. 'For all the journeys you and I have travelled together. Please!'

Anroth looked at Crimthain and nodded. 'Yes, Wolf, we can at least try to save him,' he said. 'Let my son, Dancer, come too, for he's a druid in all but name. We must add the intertwined loves we share to the love between Cliona and Midar.'

Anroth motioned for the others to join them. When they re-entered the tent, they saw the chieftain's head had fallen on Cliona's shoulder. He appeared to be sleeping. The queen smiled when she saw them; reassured by their loving company.

Anroth, Dancer and Danu sat cross-legged and joined hands in a circle at the failing warrior's feet. The power of three very different forms of love flowed between them, indivisible in what it wished to give. Different interrelated loves resonated between the others present.

What began as a prayer of supplication to heal Midar became a loving last rite of passage. Lugh, Crimthain and the two princes stood respectfully behind them. As Midar lay dying, all of them knew how much they'd loved him, but wondered if they'd ever really known him.

Cliona took Midar's hand from her cheek and let it come to rest on his chest. The noble chieftain was no more. He had found a peace in death that had always eluded him in life.

Cliona would find that her faithfulness to Midar would be stronger in death than it had ever been during his life.

30 The Gathering Storm

The Saxons had no idea that Midar's battle-hardened warriors were close at hand and an attack was imminent. Their high chieftain had intended to invade Deira, but Ida's unsanctioned landing and subsequent capture in Northumbria, which had been partly due to the unseasonal winds, partly because of the boy's poor judgement, changed his plans.

When news reached the warlord that his son had been taken prisoner, the attack on Deira was already well-advanced. His warriors had made major incursions inland. He abandoned the attack, and sailed north with as many men as he could muster, leaving orders for the rest to withdraw and follow.

None of the celts, had anticipated the size of his invasion force. The Saxon warlord had overwhelmed Nuada and the garrison with less than half of his army. Having paid for the land in blood, abandoning it did not enter into his thinking. When the rest of the Saxons forces arrived, they moored their vessels in the bay to the south of the stronghold.

Goibniu had sent scouts ahead, hoping to discover roughly how many Saxons remained. Finding the woodlands full of warriors, his scouts failed to reach the bay to the south. All they saw on the northern beaches were a dozen Saxon ships. Things looked much the same as they had done when Anroth and the others had fled.

So, when the scouts reported back to Goibniu, they told him the situation was unchanged.

When Ollathir returned, Goibniu welcomed the hero of Balores.

'Good to see you, we wondered where you were. Where are your children?'

'When I saw fires burning in the south, I bid them a sad farewell,' said Ollathir. 'The acorns will soon be falling. There'll be plenty for them to forage in the forests. I fancy you've more important things for me to do.'

Goibniu nodded. 'While we were busy in Balores, the Saxons attacked and destroyed Bamburgh,' he said. 'Now they're camped out in the woods. You know the terrain better than anyone, so your advice and experience would be welcome. Midar, our brother Nuada and the beloved Aine are dead.'

Ollathir bowed his head.

'Allow me to leave the grieving till later,' he said. Goibniu turned to Anroth.

'Any ideas?' he asked.

'Yes, I strongly suggest a night attack,' said the druid. 'We will kill as many as we can and keep the rest awake all night, sapping their spirit.'

Crimthain nodded. 'Just my kind of fight,' he said. 'But, before we discuss things in detail, we should make sure we know what we're up against. Don't forget they could still have ships and men in South Bay. It would make a lot of sense to destroy them early on.'

'And while we are at it, we should burn the boats below the stronghold,' added Dian. 'Knowing they've lost some of their fleet may persuade them to come out of the woods sooner to protect those that remain.'

'How might we find their high chieftain?' asked Danu. 'Midar believed it would shorten the battle if we killed him, and it'd be even better if we did it before the main battle began.'

'Well,' said Anroth. 'It's possible he's camped out in the open, proclaiming his ownership, but our scouts report no large concentration of men or campfires on the beach.

The most likely place to find him would be up in the woods, where he's got a good view of the beach. He'll be surrounded by his bodyguards and his greatest concentration of men will be at his back, deeper in the woods.'

'At least the Saxons should be in a fairly relaxed mood, still congratulating themselves on their victory,' he continued. 'You should be able to move around without being seen. We could try to soften them up by giving them the impression the woods are full of evil spirits.'

'Take Dian's cavalry,' said Goibniu, turning to Lugh. 'Give the Saxons a wide berth, get behind them and move down to South Bay. Wipe the Saxons out and burn any boats you find. When you return, hold your position beside what's left of the settlement and await further orders. The rest of us will work in small groups and take out as many Saxons as we can. Anroth, do you feel up to a little archery?'

The druid nodded.

'Crimthain, you work with Dancer,' continued Goibniu. 'Danu, you'll be fighting between Dian and me, where Nuada used to stand.'

The power of the Mindglow still clouded Danu's judgement. She shook her head.

'No, I'm fighting with Dancer,' she said.

Dian was quick to recognise the danger.

'Danu, I'd have thought the death of my brother and Aine would be a brutal enough demonstration of the consequences of mixing emotions with warfare,' he said. 'It's one thing too many to have think to about. It takes the edge off your fighting prowess.'

'Well, you fight with your brothers,' she said defensively.

'That's different,' said Dian. 'We've trained and fought together since childhood.'

'Danu, remember the warning I gave you on the beach,' said Anroth. 'Too much love can be a source of weakness. Show Dian respect. He's trying to protect you.'

'But Dancer needs someone to look after him,' pleaded Danu. 'He can't hear.'

Exasperated by the frustrations of leadership and jealous of Dancer, Goibniu snapped at her.

'You already nearly got yourself killed by Cu Roi. Dancer managed well enough on his own before you started getting in the way. I don't have time to waste arguing. Have it your own way, Danu.'

Danu looked across at Dancer and stretched out her hand. He walked towards her. Goibniu looked around for someone else to replace Nuada. Dian intervened.

'Olly, we're one short in the front row. Why don't you take Nuada's place? You fight with us now. If that doesn't confuse the Saxons, I don't know what will. I'm sure you can bring many a Saxon to his knees with that club of yours.'

He looked down at the little hero.

'I hope you're reasonably accurate with that club,' he continued. 'You know how prone you are to fits of exuberance when excited. I hate to imagine the damage you might do with your backswing. Please be careful with our kneecaps?'

'Fear not my little brothers!' said Ollathir. 'May I point out that, as a man who's had more opportunity than most to observe kneecaps, I've long held the view that both you and your brother have the finest-looking kneecaps to be found the length and breadth of the kingdom. I've no intention of doing anything that might, in any way, change that state of affairs. I'll adjust my backswing so that it swings upwards rather than backwards.'

'That could be even worse, Olly,' pointed out Goibniu. 'Just make sure you're standing well in front of us before you start swinging.'

Dian noticed Cliona. 'Mother's got that certain look in her eye,' he whispered to Goibniu. 'Give her something to do before she decides on it herself.'

Goibniu nodded and turned to Cliona. 'In the morning, can you lead my cavalry down onto the beach from the north, and attack and burn their boats?' he asked.

Cliona nodded.

Anroth approved. 'That may well provoke the Saxons to come out of the woods,' he said. 'They don't have female warriors and they certainly won't want to be shown up in battle by a woman. But, once you've led the charge, Cliona, please withdraw to the dunes. Direct the rest of the battle from there.'

'Your signal to start will be when you see the smoke rising from Lugh's attack on South Bay,' said Goibniu. 'If the Saxons do leave the woods, we'll attack them from the rear, cut and run, and keep them moving.'

Seeing the meeting was nearing its end, Anroth stood up. 'We're forgetting one other warrior, even smaller than Ollathir, and well-suited to striking terror into the

Saxons,' he said. 'We've never unleashed him in battle before.'

The druid made a clicking sound with his tongue, and Snibo flew down and landed on his arm. Anroth stroked the side of his beak with the back of his finger, and the raven began to chunter and chat.

'Bid welcome to one whose presence on any battlefield no enemy welcomes,' said Anroth. ''The winged necromancer of evil portent, the harbinger of Saxon misfortune, he who turns dreams to nightmares.'

Dedicating themselves to Midar, Nuada and Aine, the company parted. Lugh left with his cavalry for South Bay, the warrior queen Cliona took her cavalry north, and Goibniu and the others infiltrated the woods.

The Sixth Day Of Lunasa

31 The Raven's Eye

It was the early hours of the sixth and last day of Lunasa. Goibniu, Dian and Ollathir advanced through the northern end of the wildwood; Crimthain, encountering large numbers of Saxons, worked his way to the southern end of their encampments, whilst Danu and Dancer moved through the centre. As Anroth had anticipated, they found the high chieftain's large camp, set back from the beach in the trees.

When they saw it, Dancer lifted Snibo off his shoulder onto his wrist and, as he raised his arm, the bird flew off and perched on the awning of the chieftain's tent. Dancer cupped his hands and blew the Call of the Owl, a series of soft, haunting sounds that invited the owls of the forest to join them.

The tent flap flew open, Dancer pulled Danu down beside him. Out stepped an impressive, well-built man. Snibo, perched on the awning above him, remained motionless, but cocked his head to one side and studied him with his beady cycs.

Clearly the worse for wear, the Saxon staggered around the campfire. One of the bodyguards lay on his back, his mouth wide open, snoring loudly. The drunkard stood astride the open-mouthed warrior, intent on relieving himself and giving the bodyguard a wake-up call, and an unwelcome drink.

The bodyguard stirred, drew his knife and thrust it above him. The Saxon from the tent, thought better of his plan, and moved away, cursing and kicking some smouldering log ends into the burning embers. Directing his aim at the edge of the fire, he started to empty his bloated bladder.

Dancer and Danu were not alone, behind them Anroth looked on. The sight of the Saxon struggling to pass urine, reminded him of the infamous curse of the Druid Figol. Why hadn't he thought of it before? It was just what they needed to shorten the odds.

In the long-lost days of myth and legend, the Master Druid Figol had invoked the curse when the Tuatha de Danann were doing battle with the Fomorians, a race of one-eyed giants. Figol's curse had made it impossible for the Fomorians to pass water. Throughout the battle, their bladders had gradually filled to bursting until they were forced to stagger from the battlefield in agony.

Anroth had never attempted the curse before. Now casting it with some trepidation, he laid down the ancient incantation on the Saxons. To sanctify the oath, he opened his robe and, with due ceremony, urinated silently against a venerable oak, beseeching the tree's forgiveness. He earnestly implored the venerable Druid Figol not to allow the misfortune to rebound on him - the strength of his own stream was by no means what it had once been.

Dancer cupped his hands again and called for the owls to reclaim their forest. Mixed in with his call, he added the harsh croak and chatter of the raven, which stirred Snibo into direct action. The high chieftain was about to discover that nowhere was safe in the lands of the Brigantes, even when you were surrounded with bodyguards.

Snibo struck at the warrior stood by the fire urinating, his hands fully occupied. The bird swooped down, gripped the man's neck with his sharp claws and, with his vicious, curved beak, made a lightning-quick jab and plucked out one of the man's eyes, throwing it on the fire where it sizzled and popped. The Saxon bellowed in agony, tripped over and fell backwards over the fire.

Snibo let out a loud squawk and flew down to him, opening his wings wide so they completely covered his victim's head. Then he plunged his beak into the other socket and ripped out the remaining eye.

The bodyguards staggered to their feet, believing themselves to be part of a horrific shared nightmare, they cried out in terror.

Snibo flew back to the tent awning, holding his bloodied trophy in his beak, and flapped his wings in triumph. The bodyguards helped the blinded, badly burnt warrior to his feet. His bellows and screams, the opening act of a night of Celtic sorcery, reverberated through the woods. Save for those about to die, the Saxons would sleep no more that night.

Danu looked on in amazement. When Snibo was good, he was very good. When he was bad, he was horrific.

Another warrior stepped out of the tent. He needed no fine armour to proclaim his status, for his bearing marked him out as the high chieftain. He looked at Snibo, who still held the eye in his beak, then he looked at his tormented, mutilated champion as the blood that ran down from his empty eye sockets.

Realising he'd been spared a gruesome fate, he drew his sword to slash at Snibo, but the bird flew off, still grasping his grisly trophy.

Dancer looked at Danu, and signalled to her they'd got the wrong man. She nodded. At least they now knew what the high chieftain looked like.

Anroth wasn't the only person watching Dancer and Danu. As they retreated, a shadowy figure followed, a creature of the darkness, the Saxon high chieftain's assassin. He was lithe and, lightly armed, carrying a dagger in his belt and a garrotte in his hand.

Danu should have heeded the warning not to mix emotion with warfare, for she paid far too much attention to what Dancer was doing and gave little thought to her own safety. Less sure-footed than her lover as they walked in the moonlight, she fell some distance behind him. Without a sound, the shadow drew closer.

As he raised his arms to encircle Danu's neck with his garrotte, an arrow pierced his throat. Departing this world with a death croak, he lurched forward and stumbled into Danu. She watched him fall as he frantically clutched at the arrow.

Anroth stepped from the shadows, raised his hand then slipped back out of sight. Realising what had happened, Dancer returned to Danu and took her hand to guide her through the wood. Soon, they were accompanied by a mighty gathering of owls, swooping low, making no sound.

In the daytime, the majestic goshawk – the phantom of the forest – and its little brother, the sparrowhawk, fly fast and slip between the dense branches of the wildwood. Now, in the darkness, the owls flitted around the Saxon campsites like a multitude of monstrous bats.

They were hinted at rather than seen, the wind from their wings feeling like the breath of an invisible, ghostly fiend.

Fear spread among the Saxons, who were uncertain what haunted that melancholy place. Already woken by the bellows of their champion, they soon heard the news he'd been blinded and they started to desert their numerous campsites. Desperate to escape the wildwood, they headed for the beach, where they were easy prey for Crimthain and the others.

All warriors grow fearful, on the night before a battle, looking for omens that might hint at its outcome. the Saxons were as superstitious as anyone else. On that particular night, it seemed the harbinger of death was among them. An evil eye in the beak of a raven is a fearful portent.

Flying to each Saxon camp in turn, Snibo would land on a branch where he could be clearly seen by the warriors, and simply rest there, not attempting to attack or draw attention to himself. Eventually, the warriors would notice the eye in his beak, shining in the moonlight, and then they'd see the raven himself, head cocked to one side, staring at them his wings outstretched. Alarmed and distracted, they would fall to Danu's spear or Dancer's sword.

Unsettled by the sound of so much carnage, more and more warriors fell back and, in the confusion, sometimes fought among themselves.

Goibniu, Dian and Ollathir, coming up from the rear, scythed their way forward. In the darkness, few Saxons actually noticed Ollathir before he set about their legs and feet, bringing them to their knees, to be beheaded by Goibniu's sword or Dian's axe.

Anroth added to the cacophony of doom and despair, with high-pitched incantations and banshee-like wails; welcoming those about to die.

'He's off again,' said Dian. Goibniu nodded.

'Back in demented druid mode,' he said.

'It works for me,' said a voice from below.

Goibniu was delighted with their success, but he'd also realised there were far more Saxons than he'd expected. He harboured no illusions about the magnitude of their task in the morning, - the more they could kill under cover of darkness, the better.

Then Ollathir decided being part of a team, wasn't quite challenging enough.

'I bet I could dispatch the next bunch of Saxons we meet, without any help from you two,' he boasted, sticking out his little chest.

The princes agreed to let him try, provided there weren't too many of the enemy.

The next camp they came to was all but deserted. Just two warriors remained. Ollathir dispatched the first, who was sitting by the fire, with a blow to the back of the head. Then, swinging his club around, he aimed for the other warrior's legs. The Saxon fell to the ground and rolled around, groaning.

Ollathir bent over his victim, grunting and giggling, before leaving to check the other warrior was dead. The Saxon, whose legs were bruised rather than broken, managed to escape, crawling through the undergrowth. Fearful the weird little creature that had attacked him would follow, he staggered to his feet and ran as best he could until he found the high chieftain.

'My lord, these woods are enchanted,' he told him. 'I've just been attacked and nearly killed by a troll. They're fighting your warriors all over the woods.'

"Nonsense man!' said the chieftain. 'You should know better than to believe the fairytales of the forest. Everyone knows there are no trolls here. These uncivilised Celts hunted them to extinction centuries ago. Trolls should be respected and protected, as they are in our own lands.'

'It was a troll, my lord, I swear,' said the warrior. 'I saw it with my own eyes. Look at what it did to my legs.'

The chieftain looked at the legs.

'I've never seen injuries like those before, send for Bea Odo,' he commanded.

Hannibal terrified his enemies with his elephants, the Saxon chieftain achieved the same effect with Bea Odo. Set back from his tent was a smaller, but far taller tent from which emerged a veritable giant, a man mountain.

As Odo lumbered over to the chieftain, the ground beneath him trembled. Odo's mother had proudly named him after Odoacer, the first king of Italy following the fall of the Roman Empire, who had been of Saxon blood.

'Ah Odo,' said the chieftain. ''There's unrest in the forest. This man claims he was attacked by a troll, but there are no trolls up here.'

'A troll?' said Odo. 'You mean a big troll like me?'

'How many times do I have to tell you?' asked the exasperated chieftain. 'You're not a troll, just an overgrown man. Go and find out what's going on, but take your mighty hammer. You might need it. And don't bring any more firewood back. We've more than enough tree trunks to last us through the winter.'

As the three heroes continued to fight their way forward, they noticed an overpowering, sweaty stench wafting towards them. Something was heading their way, crashing through the trees. It saw them at the same time they saw it.

'What in the name of Galata is that?' said Dian. 'It's almost too big to be a giant, and look at the size of it. Look at the massive hammer it's carrying!'

As Bea Odo continued to crash towards them, a voice from below asked, 'How many giants have you seen? This one smells a bit like you on a bad day, Dian.'

'We've never seen a giant before,' whispered Goibniu. 'Will you be quiet, Olly? I'm trying to think. It's too late to run. It's seen us. What are we going to do?'

'How about playing that game we played as children?' said Dian.

'Game? What game?' asked Goibniu.

'The one in which we pretend we're statues.'

'That'll never work.'

'Any better ideas?' asked Dian.

Odo thought he'd seen two warriors in front of him, but, like many giants, his eyesight wasn't very good. His vision was better from distance than it was close-up. The closer he got, the more the warriors looked like statues. He was delighted, for he loved to knock statues' heads off with his hammer. Hitting human heads was much too squelchy for his liking. He continued to crash through the undergrowth, breaking into a lumbering run.

'Goibniu?' said Dian.

'Yes.'

'When are we going to stop playing the statue game?'

'Quite soon.'

'Fear not, brothers,' said the voice from below. 'If what you see coming towards you is attached to the tree trunk-like legs that are coming towards me, then they're about to be kneecapitated.'

Before the giant had a chance to put his plan into action, Ollathir swung his club, shattering his kneecaps. Odo was confused, for it took some time for the agonising pain to reach his brain, and as he looked down, he just had time to see Ollathir frantically trying to get out of the way, like a woodsman who has felled an enormous tree.

Odo's knees disintegrated, his massive frame shuddered and he crashed to the ground at the princes' feet, howling and growling. They wasted no time in dispatching him. Satisfied with their night's work, the three withdrew to await Lugh's dawn attack.

Any normal warrior would have died from the many wounds the princes had inflicted, but Bea Odo was no ordinary warrior. Somehow, he survived and succeeded in dragging himself back to the high chieftain's camp.

When the warlord saw the corpse in waiting, he groaned. He was not having a good night: his troops had deserted him, his champion had been blinded and now his giant, Bea Odo, was mortally wounded.

'Odo, who did this to you?' he asked.

'I was in the woods and this little creature came up at me out of the ground and smashed my knees,' said Odo.

'Did you get a chance to see it?' asked the chieftain. 'What was it?'

'You were right, my lord, it wasn't a troll.'

'Well, what was it?'

'It was a hobgoblin, my lord,' said Odo. 'Just a little hobgoblin. Nothing for you to worry about.'

And, so saying, Bea Odo expired.

The chieftain buried his head in his hands. Deira hadn't been like this, he thought. Here, he was fighting an enemy he couldn't see and another precious asset had been squandered. Daylight couldn't come too soon. The seasoned campaigner was astute enough to realise, though, that whatever was going on was designed to draw him and his men from the woods. He was well aware of the formidable reputation of the Celtic cavalry. He had no intention of fighting out in the open.

32 The Flight Of The Sea Eagle

Lugh lay on his chest and looked down into South Bay. He was sweating, his head pounding. The evening before, his fingers had turned a dusky blue and now they were going into bouts of uncontrollable spasm. If the pain in his hands persisted, he doubted he would be able to hold or swing his axe.

Instead of the couple of Saxon ships he'd expected to see, he could make out nine in the early morning light. Even worse, he could smell, rather than see, a huge Saxon encampment in the sand dunes just below him. He was heavily outnumbered. This changed everything.

Goibniu had fallen into the trap of dividing his army before he knew the strength and locations of the enemy. Had he first mounted a surprise attack with all his warriors and wiped out those on the beach below then his chances of defeating the rest of the Saxon army would have been high. But now, it was left to Lugh. Unless he could kill all these Saxons, preventing them from joining up with the rest of their army, Northumbria would be lost.

As he stood up, every blow he'd ever taken in battle came back to haunt him. His back muscles went into agonising spasm. Then it dawned on him, he had been fatally poisoned by the Lama's slippery embrace.

Washing away the behemoth's slime and skin in the sea had failed to protect him. Just as Balor had killed

Midar from beyond the grave, so Birog was slowly killing him. Venom, in any form, once created, has a life of its own, persisting long after its creator's demise.

This was the final day of Lunasa, the day of the warrior, and a golden time for a last great battle. But the deaths of Midar and Bres seemed as though they'd deny him the prize, he was alone.

Then enlightenment dawned, the trial of strength he was about to embark on that summer morning was no more than the end of a battle that had started with the princes' cattle raid on Gododdin. The death of Bres and later Midar, and everything that had followed, all flowed from that first skirmish. As the festival drew to its close, one continuous, inter-connected conflict would come to its blood-spattered conclusion.

The powerful god Lugh had inaugurated the festival of Lunasa to honour the goddess who had cared for him. Lugh had been born on the first day of the festival and had been named in honour of the god.

The festival was a propitious omen because it was a celebration of the life of a warrior Celt. His life had been a testament to it. The last day of Lunasa, in the late summer of his life, was a glorious day to bid farewell.

Lugh returned to his warriors and warned them they were heavily outnumbered. He pointed out that, unless they could destroy the Saxons, Goibniu would be overwhelmed and the kingdom lost.

His men had fashioned brushwood torches to burn the boats and the Saxon camp and, as the flame passed from one torch to another, they began to move forward on their ponies until they had climbed to the plateau above the camp. Lugh waited as everyone lined up. Then, in the dawn light, he turned to his men.

'When all the Saxons are dead, we ride to join Goibniu,' he said. 'We meet tonight in celebration or in paradise.'

Lugh felt light-headed. Dazzled by the sun, he shaded his eyes and looked around. His lifelong friends and comrades in arms had come to join him. Midar rode on his right and, beyond him, he could see Bres.

Their bodies were youthful, their backs straight, their heads held high. For one, precious moment, the vanity, vigour and vitality of youth flowed in Lugh's veins. He rose high in his saddle, his solid golden torque blazed in the sunshine, and he swung his battleaxe around his head and sliced it down over one side of his pony's flanks then the other.

Throwing his head back, he bellowed the battle cry of the Brigantes with all his remaining strength. The carnyx burst forth and filled the air with its deep-throated roar. Lugh was carried forward on the battle cries of his men and the heroes charged from the plateau towards the Saxon camp. Bres the Prince of Laughter, Midar the Noble Tyrant and Lugh the Shining One rode together three as one, into their final battle.

Much to their surprise, Lugh's men found that most of the Saxon warriors were standing behind their tents, trying to urinate. Like floodwaters, Lugh and his men swept through the camp, cut down the guards, sliced through tent ropes and tossed burning torches inside. Some of Lugh's men rode out to the beached boats, threw torches inside, setting them on fire.

Saxons swarmed towards them like angry bees, but, unlike those insects, the acrid smoke did nothing to assuage their anger. Men roused to battle in such a manner are intemperate in their movements, prone to extravagant, inaccurate slashes with sword and axe, and vulnerable to a well-timed Celtic counter-thrust.

Lugh fought as in those olden and golden days, when chance favoured the brave. Like most of the Celtic warrior class, his men relied on the skilful use of their agile ponies. They did not fight as a cavalry in the Roman sense. Though they were happy enough to fight from horseback, they preferred close-quarter combat on foot.

They used their mounts to swoop in to where the enemy were at their weakest and launch a hail of spears, before they dismounted and engaged in hand-to-hand combat. When each skirmish was won, they would collect their spears, remount their ponies and engage the enemy elsewhere.

This fluid style of combat was difficult to defend against, the prelude to confusion, retreat and defeat, it worked well on the open beach. But Lugh's men were starting to tire.

Lugh's military mind began to worry that his losses were unsustainable. Normally, he'd have made a tactical retreat, regrouped and launched a further attack. But now his only option was to press on, hope the Saxon resistance would crumble, and that they'd turn and run.

When Lugh and his men had charged down from the plateau, many Celtic women, some with children, had left the safety of the woods and pressed forward to the plateau edge. The wives, daughters, mothers and sisters of Lugh's warriors chanted and wailed as they watched the battle rage below, out in the bay, the fast-flowing tide swept in from the sea.

Situated back from the beach, deep within the sand dunes, the Saxons had created an inner defensive enclave, protected by a hastily dug ditch with sand banked up behind. The battle finally began to swing in the Celts' favour, when they discovered this inner encampment. To their surprise, there were no warriors in this part of the camp, just blacksmiths, cooks and camp followers, along with large quantities of supplies for a winter campaign. Lugh realised there weren't as many fighting men as he'd first thought.

Encountering scant resistance in the enclave, his men slaughtered those they found before returning to the main battle. But, by then, the remaining Saxons had already begun to retreat north, towards their chieftain and the main army in the woods. The mounted Celtic warriors charged after them cutting them down mercilessly, before they had a chance to get off the beach.

Then, almost without warning, it was over. Against the odds, Lugh and his men had annihilated the Saxons. An eerie silence followed as what remained of the Celtic cavalry regrouped and moved out, ready to join up with Goibniu. Behind them, the hulks of the Saxon ships burned. Bodies littered the dunes and the beach.

Some of the women climbed down from the plateau to the sands below. One woman and her daughter stood alone, looking down from the edge. Whatever was left of that girl's childhood died that day, as she watched dead bodies and the wounded being carried away. The wailing and chanting resumed. It rose and fell, increasing in intensity, a joyless dirge for the dead and dying.

Midar's champion lay dead on the wet sand; his pony waiting patiently beside him. Lugh The Shining One, the last of the three great heroes, had gone to join his comrades. The waves swept in, swirled around him and sucked him out to sea.

The wailers returned to the woods and there was silence. Only the mother and her daughter – Lugh's wife and child – remained.

Suddenly, there was a splash. A majestic sea eagle with a forked, white tail rose from the waters. In its talons was Lugh's golden torque. The mother and daughter watched as the raptor flew higher and higher towards the sun. Lugh, immortal before he was even born, rejoiced as he journeyed to join Bres and Midar in the Otherworld, there to remain until the cycle and the circle of their lives spun around once more. Lugh's wife put her arm around her daughter. She'd said farewell to her husband so many times before. 'Lunasa, it was a good time for us to say our last goodbye,' she said.

33 Warrior Queen

Cliona saw the smoke rising in the south. It was time for her cavalry to move in from the north. She planned to burn more ships, but spare some in the hope the Saxons would eventually take flight and sail away. Goibniu had sent word that large numbers of Saxons remained in the woods. It was essential she killed as many as possible by luring them out onto the beach.

Behind the northern headland, she and her commander crouched down in the dunes. One solitary sentry stood in their way. He paced up and down the beach, guarding the northern approaches.

'A couple of my men can work their way through the rocks and deal with him,' suggested the commander.

Cliona shook her head.

'No, he's in full view of the Saxons on the other side of the headland,' she said. 'If we give them a warning, we'll lose the element of surprise. Leave this to me.'

She unbuckled her breastplate and sword, hiding her long, thin dagger in the folds of her gown. She was about to use the gift the goddess Cliona had given her – that of being able to create the magical sound of songbirds singing. In the past, she'd always used it to help heal the sick, but now she'd use it to lethal effect, to delight and beguile the mind of a young man, before killing him in cold blood.

The Saxon sentry leant on his spear, grateful to welcome the dawn. He'd only had the occasional visit from the watch commander since sundown and the screams he'd heard coming from the woods during that long, lonely night had unnerved him. Then he heard the beautiful, magical sound of skylarks, welcoming in the day.

Entranced, he turned to see Cliona, casually walking towards him. She smiled and waved, beckoned him to come to her. The irresistible purity of the birdsong filled his head. Captivated, oblivious to any danger, delighted to spend some time, with anyone, even with a stranger, he walked towards her, until he was hidden behind the northern headland, and no longer visible to the other sentries.

When he drew close, she was smiling, and she pointed upwards into to the sky. He looked above, searching for the imaginary skylarks. Cliona slipped her outstretched arm, still pointing skywards, around his neck, bringing him closer. Then, with her free hand, she ran the sharp point of her long, thin dagger upwards into the top of his belly, behind his breastbone and into his heart. He scarce felt a thing.

Confused but feeling no pain, he looked at her again. She smiled once more, and like a mother kissed him softly, holding him close, waiting for him to pass away. His empty eyes still searched for skylarks, his body slowly sinking down, his precious blood had stained her gown.

On the fourth day of Lunasa, she had fought with Anroth and the others to save the life of a young Saxon and spent half the night tending to him. On the sixth day of Lunasa, she had slaughtered one. Her brow furrowed; she looked down at the body of the young sentry.

Cliona's commander and men came out from the dunes.

Remorse came to call, the Saxon was some mother's son, but it didn't stay long, she had an important mission to complete, persuading the Saxons out of the woods.

'Cut his head off and mount it on my spear,' she said.

She took a carnyx from one of her warriors, tied it to her saddle, mounted her pony. The commander handed her the spear with the head impaled upon it, mounting his pony to ride beside her. Their bodyguard closed around them with the cavalry lined up behind.

By now, reports had filtered through to the Saxon high chieftain that his men in South Bay had been massacred and all his vessels set ablaze. Realising he needed to protect what was left of his fleet, he ordered some of his warriors to defend the remaining boats. Most of his men, remained in the woods.

First blooded in the battle to defend the stronghold, Cliona was ready for more. Turning to her men and raising the sentry's head on the spear for all to see, she shouted.

'We dedicate our lives to the memory of Aine, Midar and Nuada and to victory!'

To a man, they all cheered her adoringly. Filled with pride that their queen was leading them into battle,

As she cantered around the promontory at the head of her warriors, Cliona tasted for the first time what she'd yearned for all her life, the thrill of riding into battle. Her childhood fantasy of living the life of a warrior queen had been transformed into reality.

Spotting Saxons on the beach, some of the horsemen broke away and rode them down. Cliona lined up the rest of her troops to face the woods. Ordering her bodyguard to hold back, she rode forward, brandishing the sentry's head. The splashes and stains of his blood where it had soaked her clothes, could clearly be seen. This sight, and the screams of the Saxons her men were attacking and slaughtering behind her, proved a potent provocation.

The Saxon chieftain was well-acquainted with the legend of the merciless Celtic warrior queen Boudicca: she who'd first grievously mutilated then slaughtered all the Roman women she captured. His heart sank. The legend of Boudicca lived on in Cliona.

A sea of Saxon warriors rose up, from the woods. They started to run towards her. With great difficulty, the chieftain managed to hold them back. As Cliona stuck her spear, with the mounted head upright in the sand her bodyguard moved forward. She threw back her head, laughing, pointing at the severed head.

One soldier, who recognised the head on the spear as that of his friend, ignoring orders, ran towards Cliona. Before her bodyguard could cut him down, he hurled his spear. Seeing it flying towards her, Cliona turned, and the spear glanced off the carnyx. This took most of the force out of it before it came to rest in her flesh. The Saxons cheered, beating swords on their shields.

Cliona thought of Aine and Nuada, and she felt no pain or fear. Cold anger welled in her heart. She calmly yanked the spear out of her thigh, throwing it defiantly back at the Saxons. Her warriors bellowed and cheered her on. She rode forward, taunting the Saxons with her authority and proud beauty. She might have been a mere woman, but she had already slaughtered one of their own. Now she goaded them to attack her.

She put the carnyx to her lips, blowing a long, guttural note, which bellowed out along the beach. Then she laughed out loud and pointed towards the Saxons. Her warriors roared out their approval. Scornfully, she turned and rode back to her cheering warriors, seemingly oblivious to the hail of spears and the seething, cursing crowd in the woods behind her.

Her warriors jeered at the Saxons. Provoked beyond endurance, they charged forward in defiance of the chieftain's orders, desperate to kill the queen rather than save their remaining ships.

As the two sides fought, the victorious remains of Lugh's cavalry rode in from the south and charged straight into the fray. After doing what she'd set out to do, Cliona withdrew to have her wound attended to. Meanwhile, the Saxons' ill-disciplined excursion cost them dear. The Celtic cavalry wiped out those who Cliona had so successfully lured from the woods.

Though the Saxon troops were now significantly depleted, they remained a formidable force. It was impossible to tell who now held the advantage. Goibniu's foot soldiers had been trained as spearmen and they'd be no match for Saxon warriors if it came to hand-to-hand fighting.

If, as Goibniu had hoped, it had been merely a matter of harassing the retreating Saxons back to their boats, all would have been well. But he suspected his forces were still outnumbered. Whatever he chose to do was fraught with danger. Reluctantly, he decided to commit everything in a fight to the death. He couldn't risk delaying his attack any longer.

He sent messengers to his mother and Lugh's men, instructing them to ride into the woods and attack the Saxons on either flank; and he ordered his men, Dancer, Danu and the others forward.

The Saxons had been distracted by what was happening on the beaches and, when the Celts came up from behind and caught them by surprise, they initially did well, but, soon, bitter hand-to-hand fighting broke out all over the woods. The combat raged like a forest fire: its flames burnt fiercely, died back and smouldered, then burst out elsewhere with mounting ferocity, leaving the dead and dying in its wake.

When Danu and Dancer encountered Saxon warriors, Snibo would swoop down in front of the enemy to flap his wings in their faces and distract them, so Dancer and Danu could move in for the kill. But with each new skirmish, they became increasingly separated from the others.

The Saxon high chieftain was a man well-versed in the ways of war. He knew he was the one man the Celts would love to kill, so he dressed like any other warrior and wore no trappings of high status. In the chaos of the conflict, he moved among his fighting men unnoticed. He was unaware Danu and Dancer already knew what he looked like.

As they fought their way along a forest trail, Danu spotted the high chieftain, ahead of them, frantically trying to pass urine, surrounded by bodyguards. She launched the spear of Assal, screaming, 'Ibar!

'The spear flew true, hitting the chieftain between the eyes and splitting his skull. His bodyguards ran towards Danu and Dancer as more Saxons came up the trail behind and cut off their retreat. Hemmed in by the trees and dense undergrowth, Danu could see no way of escape.

Dancer knew the area well though. At their backs was a copse of willows with only a narrow gap between two of the trees. Behind these was a deep bog. He knew they'd be safe enough on the other side, provided they stuck close to the tree roots and skirted around the marsh.

He planned to guide Danu around the side then lure the Saxons in. As they ran, straight through the gap in the trees, they would end up in the bog, where with their heavy weapons, they would struggle and sink in the mire. Any Saxons who managed to avoid being sucked down would inevitably try to save their comrades, whilst Danu and Dancer made good their escape.

Dancer brandished his sword defiantly to encourage the Saxons towards him and the narrow gap between the trees. Danu stood behind him as they came closer. She didn't realise he had an escape plan and believed he intended to make a heroic last stand to give her a chance to get away. But she'd lived a long life, while Dancer's had been tragic and brief. One of them had to live, to keep alive, the love they shared inside, the Mindglow.

Her mortal life had more meaning than the thousands of years she'd lived as goddess. It was all she had left to give Dancer. She held the butt of her sword high above his head and brought it crashing down. He fell, senseless into the undergrowth. She loosened her cloak and, as it fell, it covered her lover.

Standing over him and raising her arm, Danu called out, 'Athibar!' But her magical spear was firmly fixed in the Saxon chieftain's skull and unable to return to her hand.

Finding herself attacked from both sides, she tried to rise up into the air, high above those merciless Saxon swords and axes, but, imbued by the Mindglow and her love of Dancer, her body refused to be parted from his.

She fought on until a deluge of Saxons blows overwhelmed her and she fell over Dancer's body, bathing him in the blood that gushed from her wounds.

Without the Saxon chieftain the day was lost, and hearing their battle horn sounding the retreat, the warriors left, sparing Danu's body the indignity of further mutilation.

With the battle over, Anroth's spell was lifted, and, much relieved, the Saxons started to urinate. All over the battlefield, willy nilly, the floodgates opened before the tattered remnants of the invasion force took flight.

In the relentless, unforgiving hand-to-hand fighting, Goibniu had been grievously wounded. Dian had taken command and, when he saw the Saxons making for their boats, he ordered his troops to pull back. He was desperate not to lose any more men.

Wet and weary, the surviving Saxon warriors, many still relieving their bloated bladders, set sail for home, frantically bailing their boats, less they sank in the chaos, overburdened with all the urine sloshing around them.

On their forlorn voyage, the survivors swore never to reveal how their chieftain and Ida's brother had died, unable to admit their leaders had departed this world at the hands of two Celtic women.

34 The Day That Lovers Dream Alone

Dancer regained consciousness late in the afternoon. Licking his lips, he tasted blood. It was congealed in his hair, and had run down into his ears and mouth. He thought he must have bled heavily from a head wound but, apart from a big bump, he found no other injuries. All he could see was something dark-crimson fluttering in front of him and wondered if the blow to the head had blinded him. He raised his arm, and Danu's cloak slipped from his face, revealing dense foliage and, above it, the sky.

He rolled over and something soft slid down beside him.

Danu lay there, silent and still, as if asleep. He stroked her raven-black hair from her face. She was dead. A groan welled up from deep within him and tears ran down his bloodstained face.

'Oh no,' he thought. 'Not now we've found each other.'

As she'd lain there dying, Danu's blood had washed over Dancer's ears and mouth. It had been her sanctifying gift of love. In death she bore no blemish. Her sister goddesses had come to minister to her, healing over her mortal wounds.

Dancer heard a dejected croak. He saw Snibo crouched down in the bracken, one wing broken and outstretched. And, above him, he heard a couple of goldcrests singing. The forest fire of battle had burnt itself out, and save for Snibo and the dead, he was alone.

He was glad he didn't have to share his grief. Desolate, he embraced Danu's cold body and buried his face in her hair, and still the tears flowed. He was overcome with a compulsion to take her from that loathsome place, to find somewhere beautiful where they might rest in peace.

Reaching down, he stroked Snibo and swung him up onto his shoulder. Then gently he picked up Danu, - for one so tall, she was as light as a feather. He held her limp body close and kissed her softly, before they departed for the dark waters.

Snibo grasped Dancer's ear with his beak to steady himself. There wasn't a breath of wind, the air hung heavy, waiting for the thunder, begging for a breeze.

Dancer heard the occasional branch break underfoot, gulls crying somewhere in the distance and the sound of his own voice.

'I scarcely knew you,' he said. 'You'll never know how much I loved you. Why did you die? Why you? Why not I?'

It was only then it dawned on him he could hear himself speak.

He could hear!

He could speak!

But Danu was dead.

Who was there to listen to?

To talk to?

The conversations he'd shared with Danu were some of the most fulfilling and beautiful moments of his life. He realised her dying wish must have been to restore his hearing and free his tongue, washing his ears and mouth in her blood. But she would never hear him now. All he wanted was to be beside her. In his wounded anger, he cursed the gift she'd so lovingly bestowed.

It seemed to take no time at all to reach the dark waters. For a while he held back, watching and listening. They were alone. Carefully, he laid her down on a mossy bed and placed her cloak beside her. There she rested at peace.

Dancer waded out into the lake, his body sticky with sweat and blood. Removing his clothes, he washed them and tossed them onto the alder bushes at the water's edge. He rinsed Danu's blood from his hair and ears, and washed it from his neck and lips. He felt the large bump on his head, Danu's last, defiant act of love.

He prayed the lump would never leave him. But the lump did depart and he grieved for it, for it was the last precious reminder of her loving touch. And though he eventually grew old and grey, he'd forever run his fingers through his hair to feel the lump that wasn't there.

Dancer swam out into the lake. Though the day had been hot and humid, the waters were ice-cold.

Memories flitted in and out of his mind. It seemed so long ago that Keeva had swam here in the moonlight, in those waters of love and despair.

Dancer swam back to the bank, and from nowhere a breeze blew up and lifted Danu's cloak, wrapping around his shoulders. Set in the rock behind her was the statue of Bridget, weathered and old before her time. Looking down, she seemed to say, 'Join me, grandmother; adoration is better by far than love.'

He held Danu's hand and kissed it, then stroked her wrist. How could one so strong in life have such small and delicate wrists? He lay beside her, and twilight turned to moonlight.

Later, Dancer went to the cave and took Danu's coracle, carrying down to the water. A mist rose up from its surface, slim, beckoning fingers swirled up and down, somewhere far away, Aine was singing.

He lifted Danu into the coracle and waded out with it into the Dark Waters, then he removed the golden torque she had given him and returned it to her neck. Flooding the coracle with his love, he took one last, grief-laden look at her. She seemed so serene, as if she'd been cast in marble. Why, he thought, did the dead look so beautiful in the moonlight?

Dancer let go of the coracle and it drifted into the mist. Danu had come to them from far out at sea, all had beheld her. Now she was leaving him, all alone, in that secluded place.

He returned to his mossy bed and propped himself up so he had a good view of the lake. A moonlit world made all things possible and he hoped that, if he looked for long enough, he'd see her rise from the water and walk towards him, smiling. But the mist, rose and fell, and spilt out onto the banks. The more he tried to penetrate it, the more it seemed to suck him in.

'Where are you, my love?' he pleaded.

He turned his eyes back to the banks and tried to retain a grip on reality. But, as he drifted off into a fitful slumber, his eyes half-opened and he saw her walking towards him. Then he'd look again, but not find her there. She'd run through the woods, laugh, hide behind the trees, peep out at him. But when he searched for her, he'd find himself standing in the lake, looking down into an empty coracle. He was left wondering if he'd lain awake or dreamed the night away.

In the morning, he rose with the sun to a bright, new day. Shielding his eyes, he looked out from the bank and scanned the dark waters. The coracle and Danu were nowhere to be seen.

He stroked the dried-out, springy moss beside him. It was responsive and soft to the touch, and retained the resilience of a simple life. He knew it could be anything from bone-dry to heavy and swollen when the rains came.

Snibo seemed somewhat improved and the raven chattered away to him as Dancer stroked the side of his head. He removed the feathers where his wing was broken and, after some token objections from the bird, who made as if to stab at him with his beak, Snibo sat quietly on his knee.

Dancer repositioned the broken wing with the aid of a splint and secured it with leather sinews for support. Leaving Snibo by the mouth of the cave, he promised to return with something for him to eat.

To make quite certain Danu and the coracle had vanished, he decided to walk right around the lake. He looked in every inlet, every densely wooded bay, but found nothing. He hoped Danu's sisters and brothers, the goddesses and the gods, had seen fit to welcome her back to the Otherworld. This was something he fervently wished for, rather than believed.

In his travels, he'd encountered the bodies of Celts and Saxons, many high-status warriors had died beside those dark waters. Now all were as one. Common soldier and the well-attired warrior shared the same shroud of death.

He collected what he could of their weapons and jewellery – the richly encrusted bracelets and belt buckles of the Saxons, the torques and cloak pins of the Celts and hid them inside a hollow tree. One day, the tribe of the Brigantes might need such treasure and weaponry.

Taking some throwing spears, a circular, engraved bronze shield and a fine Saxon axe with him, Dancer walked to the upper end of the lake. A fragile sense of normality was returning. He was starving and tried to remember when he'd last eaten.

It had been a dry summer. The water level was low. He sat on the edge of the bank, his legs dangling down. Below him was stony shingle, with the edge of the water some distance out. At the top end of the lake, the stream had been reduced to a trickle though over the years, it had cut a deep channel through the rich silt, and, beside this, was a water meadow made up of lush pasture and reed beds.

From his secluded vantage point, Dancer could see a fawn with its mother and another hind grazing in the water meadow, seeking out the most succulent young stems. He reflected on how little deer moved when undisturbed, and cropping pasture.

Further away, but nearer the bank, he saw a young stag on his own. The animal was restless and held his head high to look about him and watch the other deer. Further back, where the water meadow ended and the tree line began, more deer moved out from the wildwood. Once they reached the water meadow, they stood like statues until they were satisfied it was safe before they moved forward to graze.

Dancer needed to test himself against the harsh realities of the world. A gentle warm westerly blew towards him from the direction of the deer, and, keeping out of sight, he moved closer. When he reached the lower borders of the water meadow, he climbed down to the riverbed where the stream cut through the silt. He rested beside the lake before moving forward for the kill.

Two otter cubs dived and splashed about nearby. They swam over to investigate him, in no great hurry to leave until their mother called to them from the far bank. Dancer moved forward, over the dried mud and stones, invisible to the deer. He raised his head and watched them through the stems of the swaying reeds.

Not knowing which of the two hinds was mother to the fawn, he passed them by and moved up the bed of the stream until he was below the stag. He raised his head until he could just see the tips of its antlers. It turned its head away from him to watch the deer coming from the wood and Dancer waited until it went back to cropping the grass.

Then, as it raised its head again, in one continuous movement, Dancer rose up and launched his spear. It caught the deer below the shoulder blade, ran through its ribs and into its heart. The stag stood up on its hind legs as if untouched, about to take flight, then it collapsed.

Dancer stood still. The hinds and the fawn looked up then, in no great haste, they turned and walked away, and melted back into the wildwood with the other deer.

He climbed out of the riverbed. It had been a clean kill. The young stag's life had been more of a promise than something fulfilled. Dancer looked at the magnificent creature and sighed.

'Yes, I know, Danu, I could have taught you to kill a deer without your magical spear,' he said to. 'You'd have been really excited about that.'

He bent down and looked into the animal's beautiful, empty eyes, then thanked the stag, for the gift of its life. He hoped he hadn't caused the beast too much pain. Slinging it over his shoulder, he crossed the stream.

Beside the cave was a sheltered inlet with plentiful brushwood. After lighting a fire, he carried the stag down to the lake and gutted it. He felt Danu standing behind him, watching over his shoulder and smiling, but when he turned to look at her there was no one there.

'Yes, my love, I know,' he said. 'I could have taught you how clean and butcher a deer.'

He had known her no time at all but, in death, she would not leave him. He watched as the stag's entrails drifted away. The lake teemed with small, brown trout, but the peaty waters gave them scant sustenance. The fish would feed well on what he'd left them.

Dancer cut himself a couple of steaks from one of the stag's hind legs, then sliced up some more meat to feed Snibo, who had hopped over to join him. He cooked the steaks on the bronze Saxon shield and they proved to be delicious.

He heard voices. Crimthain entered the clearing with some warriors, closely followed by Cliona, Anroth and Dian. Dancer cut more steaks and fed them, and they supplemented their meal with the meagre provisions they had brought. Midar's body had remained behind in the Valley of the High Waters.

As they awaited its arrival, groups of Celts large and small, warriors and common soldiery, those that worked the land, their families and many more, joined them at the dark waters.

Anroth sat with his son beside the lake. The previous few days had drained him, but when he discovered Dancer could speak and hear, he was ecstatic and tears filled his eyes. When Anroth embraced him, he noticed Dancer's limp body, his slumped shoulders. Fear gripped the old man.

'Danu? Where's Danu?' he asked.

Dancer swallowed and slowly shook his head. He looked at his father with anguished eyes, the torment within was impossible to disguise.

Anroth blamed himself for her death.

'I failed Keeva,' he said. 'I failed Danu and, in doing so, I failed you.'

Dancer shook his head.

'No, it was I who failed you,' he said. 'All those years ago, when I set out in search of Fintan, the wise salmon, in my quest for wisdom, you warned me against myself. But I paid you no heed. I paid a heavy price. Now, new consequences have followed my old failings, and we have all paid dearly.

' They sat in silence. Dancer put his arm around the old man, the better to share their pain.

'You know there were so many things I wanted to tell her,'He said.

'In no time at all, we fell in love. How could love leave no room for doubt when I never heard her voice nor she mine?'

'Sometimes, the less we know about people, the easier it is to fall in love with them,' said Anroth. 'You're easy to love and Danu never conformed to the reverential idea we have of a goddess. When it first dawned on me who she was, I was more than happy to do what I could to help her. I never expected to love her. She was adorable from the moment we met.'

Dancer nodded. 'Unlike others, she ignored my deafness and talked to me as if I could hear,' he said. 'I tried to imagine I was talking to her, but even a goddess can't hear a dumb man thinking aloud. I hoped she realised, that somewhere within me, there dwelt a kind and loving mind. Maybe gods and goddesses are nicer than we imagine.'

'No, she was special,' said Anroth. 'Most gods and goddesses are full of anger, and they're bad-tempered and jealous of others. They have all the vices of those with not enough to do, too much power and too high an opinion of themselves. She was different. She spoke to you with her eyes. Her voice was like laughter, like a blackbird singing, like a mountain stream, a magical, refreshing, babbling brook of words.'

'It's tragic about Nuada,' said Dancer, changing the subject.

'There's something I need to tell you about Nuada,' said Anroth.

'I already know,' said Dancer. 'He was my brother.'

'How long have you known?'

'I've always known, from the night he was born when we met in the clearing,' said Dancer. 'He was my little brother, a part of you, a part of me. Now he's dead and he never knew I was there for him. I could have done more to protect him and shown him the way warriors like me stay alive.'

Feelings of guilt and desolation tormented Anroth, but talking and listening to the son he'd never stopped loving brought him some consolation. One day that anguish would change into something more merciful. Between them they'd lost a son, a brother and Danu, a daughter and a lover. She who'd found something in human love, many would never discover.

35 The Sentinel

The pallbearers laid Midar's body down on Dancer's mossy bed. Cliona asked Anroth to speak. Recalling the chieftain's heroic life, he talked of a man who had lived with honour, courage and compassion. One who had loved and served those he ruled. Above all, he was a man whose love for Cliona had transcended everything. His life and kingdom were the precious gifts he'd bestowed on her.

Cliona had been his wife, but his mistress had been Northumbria. Only a druid could properly portray that irresistibly beautiful kingdom as the living, breathing creature Midar had created. He had devoted his life to protecting her people, her pastures, her swaying fields, her cattle, sheep and swine. The Northumbria that Midar had made his dominion would live on forever, a sacred place.

Danu, the goddess of rivers and fertile fields, had lost her life fighting to protect his kingdom. Now Northumbria was one of her daughters, sanctified by her blood.

Anroth pointed out that, while Midar had the constant reassurance of Cliona's love, his mistress Northumbria had always been fickle. He'd never been able to tell from one season to the next how she'd reward him or when her crops might fail and famine stalk her land. He did not describe Midar as the powerful warlord they all recognised, but instead, chose to remember him as the servant of the people, of nature, and everything it animated, and those they worshipped.

He mourned the deaths of Nuada, Aine and many more – Ollathir was still missing, presumed dead. He paid tribute to Goibniu and informed the assembled company that with so many grievous wounds, Goibniu would never be able to rule. He had relinquished his claim to the kingdom, passing it to his surviving brother.

Anroth then formally bestowed the high chieftainship on Dian, reminding him of his duties and responsibilities. Cliona and all those assembled swore their allegiance to him by the battered, weathered statue of the goddess Bridget. Dian stepped forward to embrace his mother, Anroth and Dancer, before addressing the company.

'We'll bury my father as he ordered,' he said. 'Beneath the floor of the great hall, proudly standing upright, looking out to sea. He'll be a sentinel and a warning to unwelcome strangers who approach our shores. I accept the high chieftainship as a duty, but with regret. Were it not for Goibniu's injuries and Nuada's tragic death, I would not be standing here.'

'Not only was my noble brother Nuada, a heroic warrior, he was also a healer, possessed of magic in his hands. With my own eyes, I saw him heal the Saxon prince's broken arms. I laughed at him when he said it gave him more happiness than killing a man in battle. Now he's dead and Northumbria drenched in blood, I begin to understand.'

The queen handed Nuada's arms to Dian and he raised them above his head. 'Forgive me, brother,' he said. 'There were so many others these healing hands, so cruelly hacked off, could have cured.'

Caught in the sunlight, Nuada's clenched fists slowly began to open, his fingers started to separate, then the two hands came together conferring a blessing as the Brigantes bent low in homage. Dian returned the arms to his mother.

Lost for words, he looked down at the ground and noticed Balor's head, wrapped in rags. He picked it up, threw the rags on the fire and walked down to the lake. Holding the head by its long tresses, he swung it as if it were a slingshot and tossed it far out into the dark waters.

Against all nature, it refused to sink, and floated defiantly, bobbing up and down. Finally, it slipped beneath the surface and sank to the darkest depths and serpents slithered from the sockets of Balor's eyes.

Turning back to the assembled company, Dian concluded.

'We've memories to honour, a kingdom to reclaim and we'll do it together.'

Everyone applauded, and when the noise died down, Dian noticed Crimthain looking up to a spot above Anroth's cave. Standing motionless at the top of the cliff was a visitor from the Otherworld, Midar's magnificent hunting hound Oengus – an emissary sent by the great god Cernunnos to honour the noble tyrant. His thick, grey hair had turned pure silvery-white.

The cortege moved off. Dancer whistled and Oengus reappeared at the foot of the cliff and walked beside him.

Later that afternoon, they reached the blackened ruins of the great hall, where foxes, gulls and crows scavenged among the dead. Some of the men set out for South Bay to salvage what they could of the Saxon supplies and weapons. The remainder stayed to bury their fallen comrades.

They stripped the corpses of the fallen Saxons and took what booty and weapons they could find, then tossed the bodies over the cliffs, back into the sea from whence they came.

As they dragged away the burnt wooden rafters and walls of the great hall, they discovered Nuada and Aine. Their charred remains were curled up together, in a final embrace. Not wishing to disturb what pure love and the fire had created, they buried the bodies as one, beneath a young hazel tree.

Dian ordered his men to clear the floor area nearest to the rocky headland. They scraped away the ash and dug through the thick, pounded clay floor of the hall to create a deep, narrow pit. Dian climbed in and the men passed Midar's body down to him. He positioned Midar upright, leaning forward, looking east and out to the sea.

As the men pulled Dian from the pit, Oengus jumped down behind his master. Rearing up on his hind legs and resting his front paws on Midar's broad shoulders, he opened his mouth wide and let out an anguished growl that trailed away to emptiness. As he did so, his features froze. He had turned to stone.

Lightning flashed across the horizon and thunder rolled around the sky. Howling in sorrow with the grief of the Brigantes, the east winds blew, and their tears fell as rain and splattering the muddy ground. It ran in rivulets down the walls of the pit.

Dian picked up Goibniu's gift, the golden shield, and laid it over the mouth of the grave. They piled the clay on top and smoothed it over, leaving no marker.

By the time the work was completed, no one could rightly tell where the grave had been dug, as clay, ash and sand all mixed as one. Though halls and castles might rise and fall above them, Oengus and Midar would remain there undisturbed forever, protected by the golden shield.

It was the time of the high summer tides. The waves, whipped up by the strong easterlies, crashed against the rocks below them. And, further along the bay, breakers pounded up the beach.

Waves swirled around Danu and Anroth's tree-trunk seat, washed away the sand around its base, and uprooted it. Finding its freedom, it rolled up and down the beach in concert with the breakers until, finally, they carried it back to the sea and set it drifting to who knew where.

36 The Vanishing Days Of The Celt

Greyeyes was coming to the end of his tale. The gathering had come closer, strangers had become friends.

'And what of those brave heroes who shared our fireside tonight?' he said. 'Of Ollathir, Aine, Lugh, Midar, Frii, Crimthain and so many more? Is there no lasting imprint? No shadows falling or echoes calling from our past?

'They're still with us, and those who look may find them. Move slowly, take your time when you walk the golden beaches, or wander the hills and valleys of old Northumbria, where the wildwood once grew.

'Watch the sun rising through the mist. Without the wind, the silver birch is motionless, its leaves without tremble. Warmed by the sun, the mist departs. The surface of those dark, golden waters is mirror-calm. Reflections of the trees hang down from the banks above until they're lost to the breeze.

An Otherworld breeze from the western seas brings with it ripples to caress the stony shore. The trees awaken, leaves begin to tremble and the branches start to softly sway. The wind from the west passes by on a journey without beginning or end, and borne upon it, Aine's song rises, falls and fades away.'

The bonny little girl with the tousled hair ran across to Greyeyes. Her mother called her back.

'Ilona, come here now, come and sit beside me.' Ignoring her mother, she climbed on top of the stone wall surrounding the fire. Turning round, she announced.

'I'm going to go off on my own, to live in the wildwood.' Putting her hands on her hips, she continucd, 'I'm going to meet all Greyeyes's friends.'

Greyeyes sat down on the wall beside her, fearing if she did go off on her own, she might get lost in the wild wood and never be found. Ilona climbed up onto his knee. When she was comfortable, with the storyteller's whisper he warned her.

'When wandering in the wildwood, do not be surprised to find a little person, staying well-disguised,'

Ilona's eyes opened wide.

'You may see the little fellow sitting on a log and, somewhere not so far away, piglets, sows and a hog. Do not try to find him if he disappears from view. He's trying hard to catch you and he hopes that's what you'll do. So do not try to talk to him. Be sure to leave that place. You may hear his laughter but you'll never see his face.'

Greyeyes wagged his finger slowly to emphasise his point.

'Little children, listen and attend to my concern, those who choose to follow him never do return. Remember what I told you. Be suitably deterred. Listen to your mother lest you join his ghostly herd.'

Ilona stretched out her arms. Greyeyes bent forward and she put them round his neck, giving him a kiss on the cheek. Her happy little face had gone all serious.

She whispered in his ear, 'I don't think I will go and live in the wildwood.' Then she ran back to her mother.

Greyeyes continued. 'Walk down to the beach, sit among the dunes. The sound of ponies' hooves on wet sand draws closer, just one more forgotten horseman on an empty beach, silhouetted by the sky. Wish him well, as Lugh the noble warrior rides by.'

'Shade your eyes and search the horizon. Somewhere out there is the Wave Wanderer, beneath that mackerel sky. Hold firm the helm. Farewell bold Frii, your life's one long goodbye. A twig of hazel in his cap, as proof against the storm, he's wearing queen Cliona's cloak to keep him dry and warm. Gusting in his face, the spindrift and the foam. Go trim the sail and set a course for home.

'Climb the high ground and you'll hear the howl of the wolf that welcomes Crimthain back to the pack he ran with as a child. Linger awhile for the full moon and listen as warriors march with measured tread, chanting a joyless dirge for the dead.'

'Midar's ghostly bodyguards crunch through the silver-lined cloud lands, marching along, finding solace in one last song. "Bury me deep, standing proud and tall. Bury me deep, in the ruins of my great hall. One day I'll walk beside the bitter tide. Those who watch may wonder how I died. Bury me deep, looking out to sea. Bury me deep and pray remember me."

'Turn your eyes to the headland. Behold that imposing pile, a fortress built on bygone ramparts and hallowed halls, which stands on top of mean and humble hovels, and, below them, the burnt and naked earth.

Somewhere deep beneath the floor, Midar the warrior wakes once more and passes through the bolted door. He's high above his sombre tomb, a presence in an empty room, something fearful in the gloom, and lingering still a faint perfume.

Sometimes by the castle wall, he's there beside you standing tall. Midar the watcher in the night, his faithful hound all silver-white, and borne upon the restless breeze, swirling round those vaulted towers, sickly sweet, the smell of dying flowers.'

Our story of days gone by is ended now. But remember this. Those with eyes to see will find the past close by. When you meet an old couple walking along the beach, bid them well and walk beside them for a while. Take time to wonder from where they came and where they may be going, your whole life may be walking with you.

37 The Wayfarers

The gathering departed and Greyeyes sat on the low stone wall that encircled his fire. He listened. Something was moving down by the Dark Waters. He thought of the statue of Bridget, weathered beyond recognition, growing old from the moment she'd been set in stone. He remembered the night Keeva had laid his head down to rest on her feet as he'd watched from the shadows. He remembered him diving deep into those Dark Waters, then rising to the surface to emerge changed forever, intent on self-destruction.

Greyeyes sighed. He lamented how men sometimes walked down the road to perdition, believing it was what the deities demanded of them. So much of the malevolence in the confused, world he lived in had been incited by the religious ramblings of bitter, twisted men and the seeds of the evil they had sown.

Recounting the epic tale had drained him. He lay down to rest, but his mind continued to race and skip from one set of thoughts to another, resolving nothing and going around in circles. He became fearful. What would happen when he finally succumbed to inviting slumber?

He always knew that, one night, he would have to tell the tale of Midar's demise. Now the deed was done. There was nothing left to do. Would this be the night he departed the world, passing away in his sleep to be taken to a new dawn? He had dreamed of facing the journey with Danu beside him. Would she be waiting for him on the other side? Unlike Bridget's mouldering statue, Danu had never changed in his mind. She was forever young and happy.

He drifted off. His body was borne away in a coracle and his mind meandered down a tranquil, restful river. As the riverbanks drifted by, he watched his long life play out before him. He rounded a bend in the river and new, exciting vistas opened up from a time long before the barbarity of the Romans had cast its dark shadow. He was travelling back thousands of years, to the birth of Celtic awareness, when differing strands of life intertwined and wove together a vibrant, multicoloured garment – the tribes of Celts. It was a mesmerising vision. If this was the manner an old man might die in his sleep, then it would be no hardship.

The coracle brought Greyeyes to the riverbank. He stepped ashore and walked with his ancestors from thousands of years before. Warfare creates empires, but never nations. It's a cruel and clumsy intrusion, for it destroys what is unique and often good, tribal identity.

It leaves behind serfdom or slavery, and masquerades under many disguises. It wasn't warfare that had created the Celts and bonded so many differing tribes together. It was the Wayfarers, men just like Greyeyes, his father Anroth and Frii.

Each of them had many different skills but one thing in common, the wanderlust. Theirs was a hazardous, unpredictable world, as they searched for just one more lost horizon.

Safety, if you could find it, was in numbers, in closely knitted clans and societies. But there had always been those who had gone before them, preferring to walk the world alone. The Wayfarers ignored the dangers others sought to avoid, for they believed their lives were less important than where life's journey took them.

Greyeyes watched, captivated, as a culture but never a unified nation gradually emerged. Some of them were like the young Greyeyes, not searching for a place but a state of mind. They were the wanderers and the dreamers, the strangers passing by, searching for the next horizon, never knowing why.

Some were craftsmen and artisans, potters capable of turning clay into statues, amulets, pots for cooking and vases for storage. Then there were those who worked with stone from the quarry to create buildings or statues; those possessed of the magic to create different metals; craftsmen capable of producing beakers, magnificent cauldrons, exquisite jewellery, knives, swords and other accoutrements of war.

Then there were the soldiers of fortune; the master mariners and merchants that crossed the unpredictable and unforgiving seas. Among them were the seers, the singers, the storytellers, the holy men, the mystics, healers and wise men. These represented the primitive beginnings of druidic belief. Walking together or alone, the Wayfarers built bridges between the separate societies they encountered.

Greyeyes watched it all with awe and admiration. He saw flickering cave paintings, cup-and-saucer carvings, chevrons, complex swirling circles, mysterious triplicate symbolism and spirals, tripartite gods, mystical tales, the lost meaning of the number three, sky, earth and the Otherworld below. All things were revealed in the old man's dreaming reverie.

Theirs was a culture that would never have come to pass were it not for the Wayfarers. Their motives were mixed and many. Some had decided to settle down and teach new skills to those who had offered them a home. Others would search forever, wondering what was over the next horizon.

Some had returned to where they'd come from. Most had died on the journey. As individuals, none of them had earned a place in history or lived on in the Celts' many myths. But taken together, over thousands of years, they were the vital sinews that had held together seemingly disparate societies, and created shared traditions and a common heritage.

Rejoicing, Greyeyes walked back down to the banks of the river. His coracle floated in towards him and he climbed on board. The river lapped against the stretched leather sides as it moved back out into the current.

He came to another bend in the river, which took him to a place he did not wish to be. He found himself looking into the future. It looked into his uncertain future, when Saxon culture would eventually supplant all that was Celtic.

As he drifted past the riverbanks, he realised the end of the Celts' days was not dissimilar from how it had all begun. In Northumbria, as elsewhere, those whose origins were Saxon remained in the minority.

The bulk of the population were Celtic by blood, but those who wished to rise found it convenient to forget their past. And, slowly, Saxon traditions replaced the Celtic ones. The dawning of Celtic awareness had taken thousands of years. But, in comparison, the loss of that awareness could be measured in centuries.

Greyeyes passed a promontory that projected out into the river. A naked man stood tall, proud and alone, looking towards the horizon. Greyeyes wondered where he came from and where he might be going. Was he from the pre-Celtic past, the days of Celtic culture or from a time when Celtic awareness had already been lost?

Greyeyes tossed and turned, and woke from his slumbers with the dawn. The naked man turned and walked away. Half-dreaming, Greyeyes heard himself say, 'Does it matter who he really is? What matters is what he's allowed to become.'

Epilogue

Greyeyes rubbed his eyes, his dreams already half-forgotten, contented the gathering had gone well. Shared identities triumphed over lost ones. He had worried his story might have left some feeling melancholy, but having rediscovered lost heroes, they'd left with a sense of dignity. They'd laughed, cried, sighed and pondered in equal measure.

What a gift it was to gather people together, and enhance their sense of wellbeing, then watch as something quite magical happened. They departed, taking with them, more love than they'd brought with them.

He stood in the sunshine and ran his fingers through his hair, feeling for the lump that wasn't there. Leaning against the smooth rock at the entrance to his cave and refreshed by its cool contours, he bathed in the afterglow of giving something back to life.

He heard gentle snoring. Not the full-blown reverberations of a wide-mouthed male, but the soft, sonorous sound only a lady of refinement would make. He found the old lady slumped over his woodpile. She opened her eyes and blinked in the sunshine.

'I hope I didn't wake you,' she said, apologising.

'No, you didn't disturb me,' said Greyeyes. 'You can't have been very comfortable resting there.'

He lifted her from the logs.

'I wanted to thank you for making my flower bracelet and being with me,' she said. 'It reminded me of days gone by.'

She tried to straighten up, but was clearly in some discomfort.

'Are you in pain?' asked Greyeyes.

'Just old wounds.'

'Have you far to go?'

'I travelled far to find you,' she said. 'Now my journey has ended.'

He looked at her again. She was different in the daylight, strangely familiar. They ate and drank, then ambled down to the lake.

'Last night when I told my tale, others hung on every word, not knowing where my tale might take them, but you sat there smiling, sometimes nodding,' said Greyeyes. 'I felt you'd been with me, as if you knew what was coming next.'

'I did,' she said. 'It all came back to me at the start of your story. You described a coracle that beached below the stronghold at Bamburgh. You said,

"None had seen one so fair, with golden torque and raven hair. That's when I knew."

She laughed and her eyes sparkled. She undid her brooch and her shawl slipped down over her shoulders. Around her neck, she wore a golden torque.

Though their bodies were decrepit beyond all imagining, the Mindglow flowed back between them as if they'd achieved it only yesterday. Time stood still. They stood there, looked at each other and tried to comprehend the magic of the moment, before Dancer – as Greyeyes had been known in his youth – kissed her softly on the cheek and smiled.

'I have something for you, Danu,' he said.

He stumbled off into the cave, re-emerging with her folded cloak. He shook the garment out and, as he did so, it slipped from his grasp and floated in the air until it came to rest upon her shoulders. It was as pristine and lustrous as on the day she'd first stepped ashore on the beaches of Bamburgh.

Danu laughed rediscovering the love they'd once shared.

'I've wanted to give this to you for over fifty years,' said Dancer. 'My love, where have you been?'

Danu smiled a toothless smile and kissed him on the lips. Her hands, now gnarled and twisted, reached out just as they'd done so long ago. He pressed them to his face and closed his eyes, feeding off the magic of her touch. Old age could not disguise the beauty he found in her. Young lovers imagine how beautiful love will be, but aged lovers are sustained by the remembrance of how it had once been.

'You have a beautiful voice, Danu, everything about you is beautiful,' said Dancer. 'Have you any idea how happy just being beside you makes me? Why didn't you tell me last night?'

'By the time you'd finished, you were exhausted,' she said. 'You needed your sleep. You always needed your sleep, Dancer. I just wanted to be alone, to walk down to the lake, to remember those precious days. Then I came and sat here to dream and think of Snout, of Cliona, of all those many things I'd forgotten. I drifted off to sleep in sweet contentment.'

'How did farewell become just goodbye?' asked Dancer

'Do you remember that, after the battle, you carried my body back here?'

'Yes.'

'On the journey, I awoke,' she said. 'I could see you and I could feel you, but I couldn't move. Later, you carried me to the coracle. You floated it out and stood there in the water. Your eyes filled with loneliness and love as you looked down on me. I felt the coracle fill to the brim and overflow with your love. You kissed me goodbye. It was then I knew I wasn't destined to die.'

'When we made love at the waterfall, you made me feel like a goddess. You restored my immortality, so I took you to the edge of existence, knowing that, when your mind returned to your body, you too would be immortal. I had no means of telling you, even though I wanted to.

'We may both be immortal but, because we live in this world, we cannot help but grow old. As we grow older, nature allows us to live out our days in many different ways. Soon I will show you, or we can always go to the Otherworld if you prefer.'

Dancer shook his head.

'That night, as I floated out on the lake, I slept a deep and peaceful sleep,' said Danu. 'When I awoke, I'd lost my memory. I finally settled far away. I knew I must have had a past, but I didn't know what it was. Sometimes I saw you in fleeting dreams, but I knew not who you were. Almost by chance, I decided to make the journey here, to celebrate Lunasa. I'd heard tell of Greyeyes the mystical storyteller and seer, the magical weaver of words. But last night, when first we met, it never occurred to me you were part of my past.' She paused.

'Then you kissed me,' she said, and paused.

'You awakened forgotten dreams.'

Dancer held her close. 'Do you like my fireside, my humble cave, Danu?' he said. 'They've been patiently waiting for you.'

She hugged him. 'Dancer?'

'Yes?' She laughed.

'Have you got any pots?'

'I've got pots a plenty, Danu,' he said.

'I never knew I was immortal, so I expected every harsh winter to be my last. And there was me not knowing you'd ever existed,' she said. 'I wonder what's worse – longing for what you've lost, or losing your memory and never knowing there was someone you loved?'

'I fancy you carried the heavier burden,' said Dancer. 'For I could feed off the magical memories you left me.'

Danu sat beside him and patted the back of his hand. Her happiness overflowed all over again, all over Dancer.

'When we were at the waterfall, I asked you if we could see Lindisfarne one day,' she said. 'I'd love to go back to the beach.'

'We can do that, Danu. We can do anything you want.'

Effortlessly, they rediscovered the happiness of that brief time they'd spent together long ago, for love renewed is never love grown old. Danu taught Dancer how to allow his body to become at one with nature. They found they could slip quite naturally between one of nature's realities and another. Afterwards, they returned to their aging bodies, refreshed.

Dancer might sit on the riverbank with his feet dangling in the water. Then, if Danu decided to be the river, Dancer would become a willow tree and let his branches caress her undulating surface, and suck up her waters with his deep roots, rejuvenated by her.

At other times, they'd be in the clearing in front of the cave, and Dancer would lean back against the rock as Danu sat by the fire. Dancer's body would merge into the stone as Danu became a flame, and her heat glowed brightly within him. In those mellow twilight days, new colours of love flooded into their lives. It wasn't the vibrancy of youth, but the restful, subtle shades of age.

Then there were those special days when they'd rise up above the wildwood onto the windswept moor. Dancer would lie on the high pasture and change into a meadow, carpeted in grasses and fresh flowers. The woodwose of the wildwood would dance amid his blooms, blowing in the breeze. Danu would become the legendary lost white hind of the storytellers.

As the rippling waves of bent grass flowed over Dancer, she would feed from his succulent shoots and drink in the fragrances of the flowers. Danu would be rejuvenated by him. Replete, she would lie down to rest upon Dancer and her contented contours would merge with his living landscape. Day by day, nature drew them closer.

When they wished to travel, Danu became the breeze and blew Dancer before her as swirling leaves, sometimes all the way down to the sea. Then they'd walk together through the many ages of man, passing people who barely noticed them. Who can say? You may have passed them by one day.

One summer's afternoon, as they walked towards the island of Lindisfarne, Danu recalled Anroth.

'This reminds me of a beautiful, happy time I spent here with your father,' she said. 'He promised to take me to Lindisfarne, but that day was never to be. Did you enjoy me blowing you down to the beach, Dancer?'

'I loved it!' he said. 'But spinning around has left me a confusion of imperfections.'

Danu paused. There was silence.

'What did you just say?'

'I said I was a confusion of imperfections,' he said. 'That's what my father used to say when I exasperated him.'

'That sly old wizard, he tricked me!' said Danu.

'Who?'

'Your father, that's who!'

'How so?'

'All those years ago, when Snout and I walked this way, I asked him what love was,' said Danu. 'He told me it was a confusion of imperfections. I told him to stop talking in riddles, but he explained to me that, one day, on my travels, I might meet a man who made me laugh, made me happy. If I found him strangely attractive and wondered if I was in love, I'd be able to tell that I truly was.

'He promised me that, if the man was a confusion of imperfections, then I'd definitely be in love with him. He knew we'd meet. He knew what you were like. He knew I'd think you were a confusion of imperfections. That wily wizard tricked me into loving you!'

'Well, with the benefit of hindsight, did you or didn't you love me?' asked Dancer.

'I was already in love with you, but that's not the point,' said Danu. 'It wasn't fair.'

'If it wasn't fair, why are you laughing all these years later?' said Dancer. 'He loved you; he loved me. He was only trying to help. You know Danu, it never occurred to me how dangerous the Mindglow would prove to be. Perhaps it is best discovered in old age,'

She laughed, 'No one is going to discover it, at our time of life!'

Dancer smiled.

'Exactly, maybe we are just imagining the way it was. He paused, 'love is like that Danu.'

'I like the way it is now Dancer.'

She put her hand through his arm, they walked on. The weak, late-afternoon sun came out from behind a cloud and illuminated the island of Lindisfarne.

'It doesn't seem so far away, Dancer.'

'Magical memories, Danu, and the mystical islands we search for, in our lives, are always further away than they seem.'

Casting a long shadow on the sand, she stopped, holding Dancer beside her, looking at Lindisfarne.

'How long will it take to get there?' she asked.

'Eternity, Danu.'

'Good.'

There we'll leave them, fading into the forever, but never very far away.

The author studied Medicine in the early sixties. When rock climbing in Northumberland he found a raven chick. He hand-reared 'Snibo' to adulthood. All these years later, Snibo takes flight again, as a significant character in Anroth the Druid. All of the other characters in the novel are fictional. In real life, Snibo was a very friendly bird. In 'Anroth the Druid', he is more sinister.
After qualifying the author worked as a ship's doctor, on a rusty old cargo ship, built during the second world war, eventually going right round the world. It stimulated his interest in how, many centuries ago, societies used to cope, without hospitals and healthcare services.
Later, as a consultant gynaecologist he used a high powered operating microscope, operating on infertile women, with damaged Fallopian tubes.
Gynaecologists often fall victim to people making fun of them. Giving a lecture to fellow Gynaecologists, he was once introduced by the chairman, 'Our next speaker is Michael Burke, who is going to tell us how he got 400

Printed in Great Britain
by Amazon

56096796R00249

women pregnant, using his amazing tool, which apparently weighs a third of a ton.'

He thanked the chairman, pointing out, unlike the chairman's little tool, his was insured for £80,000.

After retiring, he ran an Angling Association, in Northumbria, near the Scottish border. The beauty of his surroundings, and isolation, influenced much of the background writing of Anroth the Druid.